Henry James

Essays In London And Elsewhere

Henry James

Essays In London And Elsewhere

ISBN/EAN: 9783743310667

Manufactured in Europe, USA, Canada, Australia, Japa

Cover: Foto ©ninafisch / pixelio.de

Manufactured and distributed by brebook publishing software (www.brebook.com)

Henry James

Essays In London And Elsewhere

Essays in London
and
Elsewhere

BY

HENRY JAMES

NEW YORK
HARPER & BROTHERS PUBLISHERS
1893

Copyright, 1893, by HARPER & BROTHERS.

All rights reserved.

CONTENTS

	PAGE
LONDON	1
JAMES RUSSELL LOWELL	44
FRANCES ANNE KEMBLE	81
GUSTAVE FLAUBERT	121
PIERRE LOTI	151
THE JOURNAL OF THE BROTHERS DE GONCOURT	186
BROWNING IN WESTMINSTER ABBEY	222
HENRIK IBSEN	230
MRS. HUMPHRY WARD	253
CRITICISM	259
AN ANIMATED CONVERSATION	267

LONDON

I

THERE is a certain evening that I count as virtually a first impression—the end of a wet, black Sunday, twenty years ago, about the first of March. There had been an earlier vision, but it had turned gray, like faded ink, and the occasion I speak of was a fresh beginning. No doubt I had a mystic prescience of how fond of the murky modern Babylon I was one day to become; certain it is that as I look back I find every small circumstance of those hours of approach and arrival still as vivid as if the solemnity of an opening era had breathed upon it. The sense of approach was already almost intolerably strong at Liverpool, where, as I remember, the perception of the English character of everything was as acute as a surprise, though it could only be a surprise without a shock. It was expectation exquisitely gratified, superabundantly confirmed. There was a kind of wonder, indeed, that England should be as English as, for my entertainment, she took the trouble to be; but the wonder would have been greater, and all the pleasure absent, if the sensation had not been violent. It seems to sit there again like a visiting presence, as it sat opposite to me at breakfast at a small table in a window of the old coffee-room of the Adelphi Hotel —the unextended (as it then was), the unimproved, the unblushingly local Adelphi. Liverpool is not a romantic city, but that smoky Saturday returns to me as a supreme success, measured by its association with the kind of emotion in the hope of which, for the most part, we betake ourselves to far countries.

It assumed this character at an early hour — or rather, indeed, twenty-four hours before — with the sight, as one looked across the wintry ocean, of the strange, dark, lonely freshness of the coast of Ireland. Better still, before we could come up to the city, were the black steamers knocking about in the yellow Mersey, under a sky so low that they seemed to touch it with their funnels, and in the thickest, windiest light. Spring was already in the air, in the town; there was no rain, but there was still less sun —one wondered what had become, on this side of the world, of the big white splotch in the heavens; and the gray mildness, shading away into black at every pretext, appeared in itself a promise. This was how it hung about me, between the window and the fire, in the coffee-room of the hotel—late in the morning for breakfast, as we had been long disembarking. The other passengers had dispersed, knowingly catching trains for London (we had only been a handful); I had the place to myself, and I felt as if I had an exclusive property in the impression. I prolonged it, I sacrificed to it, and it is perfectly recoverable now, with the very taste of the national muffin, the creak of the waiter's shoes as he came and went (could anything be so English as his intensely professional back? it revealed a country of tradition), and the rustle of the newspaper I was too excited to read.

I continued to sacrifice for the rest of the day; it didn't seem to me a sentient thing, as yet, to inquire into the means of getting away. My curiosity must indeed have languished, for I found myself on the morrow in the slowest of Sunday trains, pottering up to London with an interruptedness which might have been tedious without the conversation of an old gentleman who shared the carriage with me and to whom my alien as well as comparatively youthful character had betrayed itself. He instructed me as to the sights of London, and impressed upon me that nothing was more worthy of my attention than the great cathedral of St. Paul. "Have you seen St. Peter's in Rome? St. Peter's is more highly embellished, you know; but you may depend upon it that St. Paul's is the better building of the two." The impression I began with speaking of was, strictly, that of the drive from Euston, after dark, to Morley's Hotel in Trafalgar Square. It was not lovely — it was in fact rather horrible; but as I move again through dusky, tortuous miles, in the greasy four-wheeler to which my luggage had compelled me to commit myself, I recognize the first step in an initiation of which the subsequent stages were to abound in pleasant things. It is a kind of humiliation in a great city not to know where you are going, and Morley's Hotel was then, to my imagination, only a vague ruddy spot in the general immensity. The immensity was the great fact, and that was a charm; the miles of housetops and viaducts, the complication of junctions and signals through which the train made its way to the station had already given me the scale. The weather had turned to wet, and we went deeper and deeper into the Sunday night. The sheep in the fields, on the way from Liverpool, had shown in their demeanor a certain consciousness of the day; but this momentous cab-drive was an introduction to rigidities of custom. The low black houses were as inanimate as so many rows of coal-scuttles, save where at frequent corners, from a gin-shop, there was a flare of light more brutal still than the darkness. The custom of gin — that was equally rigid, and in this first impression the public-houses counted for much.

Morley's Hotel proved indeed to be a ruddy spot; brilliant, in my recollection, is the coffee-room fire, the hospitable mahogany, the sense that in the stupendous city this, at any rate for the hour, was a shelter and a point of view. My remembrance of the rest of the evening—I was probably very tired—is mainly a remembrance of a vast four-poster. My little bedroom candle, set in its deep basin, caused this monument to project a huge shadow and to make me think, I scarce knew why, of "The Ingoldsby Legends." If at a tolerably early hour the next day I found myself approaching St. Paul's, it was not wholly in obedience to the old gentleman in the railway-carriage: I had an errand in the City, and the City was doubtless prodigious. But what I mainly recall is the romantic consciousness of passing under Temple Bar and the way two lines of "Henry Esmond" repeated themselves in my mind as I drew near the masterpiece of Sir Christopher Wren. "The stout, red-faced woman" whom Esmond had seen tearing after the stag-hounds over the slopes at Windsor was not a bit like the effigy "which turns its stony back upon St. Paul's and faces the coaches struggling up Ludgate Hill." As I looked at Queen Anne over the apron of my hansom—she struck me as very small and dirty, and the vehicle ascended the mild incline without an effort—it was a thrilling thought that the statue had been familiar to the hero of the incomparable novel. All history appeared to live again, and the continuity of things to vibrate through my mind.

To this hour, as I pass along the Strand, I take again the walk I took there that afternoon. I love the place to-day, and that was the commencement of my passion. It appeared to me to present phenomena and to contain objects of every kind, of an inexhaustible interest; in particular it struck me as desirable and even indispensable that I should purchase most of the articles in most of the shops. My eyes rest with a certain tenderness on the places where I resisted and on those where I succumbed. The fragrance of Mr. Rimmel's establishment is again in my nostrils; I see the slim young lady (I hear her pronunciation) who waited upon me there. Sacred to me to-day is the particular aroma of the

hair-wash that I bought of her. I pause before the
granite portico of Exeter Hall (it was unexpectedly
narrow and wedge-like), and it evokes a cloud of
associations which are none the less impressive because they are vague; coming from I don't know
where—from *Punch*, from Thackeray, from old volumes of the *Illustrated London News* turned over
in childhood; seeming connected with Mrs. Beecher
Stowe and "Uncle Tom's Cabin." Memorable is a
rush I made into a glover's at Charing Cross—the
one you pass going eastward, just before you turn
into the station; that, however, now that I think of
it, must have been in the morning, as soon as I
issued from the hotel. Keen within me was a sense
of the importance of deflowering, of despoiling the
shop.

A day or two later, in the afternoon, I found
myself staring at my fire, in a lodging of which I
had taken possession on foreseeing that I should
spend some weeks in London. I had just come in,
and, having attended to the distribution of my luggage, sat down to consider my habitation. It was
on the ground floor, and the fading daylight reached
it in a sadly damaged condition. It struck me as
stuffy and unsocial, with its mouldy smell and its
decoration of lithographs and wax-flowers—an impersonal black hole in the huge general blackness.
The uproar of Piccadilly hummed away at the end
of the street, and the rattle of a heartless hansom
passed close to my ears. A sudden horror of the
whole place came over me, like a tiger-pounce of

homesickness which had been watching its moment. London was hideous, vicious, cruel, and above all overwhelming; whether or no she was "careful of the type," she was as indifferent as Nature herself to the single life. In the course of an hour I should have to go out to my dinner, which was not supplied on the premises, and that effort assumed the form of a desperate and dangerous quest. It appeared to me that I would rather remain dinnerless, would rather even starve, than sally forth into the infernal town, where the natural fate of an obscure stranger would be to be trampled to death in Piccadilly and his carcass thrown into the Thames. I did not starve, however, and I eventually attached myself by a hundred human links to the dreadful, delightful city. That momentary vision of its smeared face and stony heart has remained memorable to me, but I am happy to say that I can easily summon up others.

II

It is, no doubt, not the taste of every one, but for the real London-lover the mere immensity of the place is a large part of its merit. A small London would be an abomination, as it fortunately is an impossibility, for the idea and the name are beyond everything an expression of extent and number. Practically, of course, one lives in a quarter, in a plot; but in imagination and by a constant mental act of reference the sympathizing resident inhabits the whole—and it is only of him that I deem it worth while to speak. He fancies himself, as they say, for being a particle in so unequalled an aggregation; and its immeasurable circumference, even though unvisited and lost in smoke, gives him the sense of a social, an intellectual margin. There is a luxury in the knowledge that he may come and go without being noticed, even when his comings and goings have no nefarious end. I don't mean by this that the tongue of London is not a very active member; the tongue of London would indeed be worthy of a chapter by itself. But the eyes which at least in some measure feed its activity are fortunately for the common advantage solicited at any moment by a thouasnd different objects. If the place is big, everything it contains is certainly not so; but this may at least be said, that if small questions play a part there, they play it without illusions about its importance. There are too many questions, small or great; and each day, as it arrives, leads its children, like a kind of mendicant mother, by the hand. Therefore perhaps the most general characteristic is the absence of insistence. Habits and inclinations flourish and fall, but intensity is never one of them. The spirit of the great city is not analytic, and, as they come up, subjects rarely receive at its hands a treatment offensively earnest or indiscreetly thorough. There are not many—of those of which London disposes with the assurance begotten of its large experience—that wouldn't lend themselves to a tenderer manipulation elsewhere. It takes a very great affair, a turn of the Irish screw or a divorce case lasting many days, to be fully threshed out. The mind of Mayfair, when it aspires to show what it really can do, lives in the hope of a new divorce case, and an indulgent providence — London is positively in certain ways the spoiled child of the world — abundantly recognizes this particular aptitude and humors the whim.

The compensation is that material does arise; that there is great variety, if not morbid subtlety; and that the whole of the procession of events and topics passes across your stage. For the moment I am speaking of the inspiration there may be in the sense of far frontiers; the London-lover loses himself in this swelling consciousness, delights in the idea that the town which encloses him is after all only a paved country, a state by itself. This is his condition of mind quite as much if he be an adoptive as if he be a matter-of-course son. I am by no means sure even that he need be of Anglo-Saxon race and have inherited the birthright of English speech; though, on the other hand, I make no doubt that these advantages minister greatly to closeness of allegiance. The great city spreads her dusky mantle over innumerable races and creeds, and I believe there is scarcely a known form of worship that has not some temple there (have I not attended at the Church of Humanity, in Lamb's Conduit, in company with an American lady, a vague old gentleman, and several seamstresses?), or any communion of men that has not some club or guild. London is indeed an epitome of the round world, and just as it is a commonplace to say that there is nothing one can't "get" there, so it is equally true that there is nothing one can't study at first hand.

One doesn't test these truths every day, but they form part of the air one breathes (and welcome, says the London-hater—for there *is* such a benighted animal—to the pestilent compound). They color the thick, dim distances which in my opinion are the most romantic town-vistas in the world; they mingle with the troubled light to which the straight, ungarnished aperture in one's dull, undistinctive housefront affords a passage and which makes an interior of friendly corners, mysterious tones, and unbetrayed ingenuities, as well as with the low, magnificent medium of the sky, where the smoke and the fog and the weather in general, the strangely undefined hour of the day and season of the year, the emanations of industries and the reflection of furnaces, the red gleams and blurs that may or may not be of sunset—as you never see any *source* of radiance you can't in the least tell — all hang together in a confusion, a complication, a shifting but irremovable canopy. They form the undertone of the deep, perpetual voice of the place. One remembers them when one's loyalty is on the defensive; when it is a question of introducing as many striking features as possible into the list of fine reasons one has sometimes to draw up, that eloquent catalogue with which one confronts the hostile indictment—the array of *other* reasons which may easily be as long as one's arm. According to these other reasons, it plausibly and conclusively stands that, as a place to be happy in, London will never do. I don't say it is necessary to meet so absurd an allegation except for one's personal complacency. If indifference, in so gorged an organism, is still livelier than curiosity, you may avail yourself of your own share in it simply to feel that since such and such a person doesn't care for real greatness, so much the worse for such and such a person. But once in a while the best believer recognizes the impulse to set his religion in order, to sweep the temple of his thoughts and trim the sacred lamp. It is at such hours as this that he reflects with elation that the British capital is the particular spot in the world which communicates the greatest sense of life.

III

The reader will perceive that I do not shrink even from the extreme concession of speaking of our capital as British, and this in a shameless connection with the question of loyalty on the part of an adoptive son. For I hasten to explain that if half the source of one's interest in it comes from feeling that it is the property and even the home of the human race—Hawthorne, that best of Americans, says so somewhere, and places it in this sense side by side with Rome—one's appreciation of it is really a large sympathy, a comprehensive love of humanity. For the sake of such a charity as this one may stretch one's allegiance; and the most alien of the cockneyfied, though he may bristle with every protest at the intimation that England has set its stamp upon him, is free to admit with conscious pride that he has submitted to Londonization. It is a real stroke of luck for a particular country that the capital of the human race happens to be British. Surely every other people would have it theirs if they could. Whether the English deserve to hold it any longer might be an interesting field of inquiry; but as they have not yet let it slip, the writer of these lines professes without scruple that the arrangement is to his personal taste. For, after all, if the sense of life is greatest there, it is a sense of the life of people of our incomparable English speech. It is the headquarters of that strangely elastic tongue; and I make this remark with a full sense of the terrible way in which the idiom is misused by the populace in general, than whom it has been given to few races to impart to conversation less of the charm of tone. For a man of letters who endeavors to cultivate, however modestly, the medium of Shakespeare and Milton, of Hawthorne and Emerson, who cherishes the notion of what it has achieved and what it may even yet achieve, London must ever have a great illustrative and suggestive value, and indeed a kind of sanctity. It is the single place in which most readers, most possible lovers, are gathered together; it is the most inclusive public and the largest social incarnation of the language, of the tradition. Such a personage may well let it go for this, and leave the German and the Greek to speak for themselves, to express the grounds of *their* predilection, presumably very different.

When a social product is so vast and various it may be approached on a thousand different sides, and liked and disliked for a thousand different reasons. The reasons of Piccadilly are not those of Camden Town, nor are the curiosities and discouragements of Kilburn the same as those of Westminster and Lambeth. The reasons of Piccadilly—I mean the friendly ones—are those of which, as a general thing, the rooted visitor remains most conscious; but it must be confessed that even these, for the most part, do not lie upon the surface. The absence of style, or rather of the intention of style, is certainly the most general characteristic of the face of London. To cross to Paris under this impression is to find one's self surrounded with far other standards. There everything reminds you that the idea of beautiful and stately arrangement has never been out of fashion, that the art of composition has always been at work or at play. Avenues and squares, gardens and quays, have been distributed for effect, and to-day the splendid city reaps the accumulation of all this ingenuity. The result is not in every quarter interesting, and there is a tiresome monotony of the "fine" and the symmetrical, above all, of the deathly passion for making things "to match." On the other hand, the whole air of the place is architectural. On the banks of the Thames it is a tremendous chapter of accidents—the London-lover has to confess to the existence of miles upon miles of the dreariest, stodgiest commonness. Thousands of acres are covered by low black houses of the cheapest construction, without ornament, without grace, without character, or even identity. In fact, there are many, even in the best quarters, in all the region of Mayfair and Belgravia, of so paltry and inconvenient, and above all of so diminutive a type (those that are let in lodgings—such poor lodgings as they make—may serve as an example), that you wonder what peculiarly limited domestic need they were constructed to meet. The great misfortune of London, to the eye (it is true that this remark applies much less to the City), is the want of elevation. There is no architectural impression without a certain degree of height, and the London street-vista has none of that sort of pride.

All the same, if there be not the intention, there is at least the accident, of style, which, if one looks at it in a friendly way, appears to proceed from three sources. One of these is simply the general greatness, and the manner in which that makes a difference for the better in any particular spot; so that, though you may often perceive yourself to be in a shabby corner, it never occurs to you that this is the end of it. Another is the atmosphere, with its magnificent mystifications, which flatters and superfuses, makes everything brown, rich, dim, vague, magnifies distances and minimizes details, confirms the inference of vastness by suggesting that, as the great city makes everything, it makes its own system of weather and its own optical laws. The last is the congregation of the parks, which constitute an ornament not elsewhere to be matched, and give the place a superiority that none of its uglinesses overcome. They spread themselves with such a luxury of space in the centre of the town that they form a part of the impression of any walk, of almost any view, and, with an audacity altogether their own, make a pastoral landscape under the smoky sky. There is no mood of the rich London climate that is not becoming to them—I have seen them look delightfully romantic, like parks in novels, in the wettest winter—and there is scarcely a mood of the appreciative resident to which they have not something to say. The high things of London, which here and there peep over them, only make the spaces vaster by reminding you that you are, after all, not in Kent or Yorkshire; and these things, whatever they be—rows of "eligible" dwellings, towers of churches, domes of institutions —take such an effective gray-blue tint that a clever water-colorist would seem to have put them in for pictorial reasons.

The view from the bridge over the Serpentine has an extraordinary nobleness, and it has often seemed to me that the Londoner twitted with his low standard may point to it with every confidence. In all the town-scenery of Europe there can be few things so fine; the only reproach it is open to is that it begs the question by seeming—in spite of its being the pride of five millions of people—not to belong to a town at all. The towers of Notre Dame, as they rise, in Paris, from the island that divides the Seine, present themselves no more impressively than those of Westminster as you see them looking doubly far beyond the shining stretch of Hyde Park water. Equally admirable is the large, river-like manner in which the Serpentine opens away between its wooded shores. Just after you have crossed the bridge (whose very banisters, old and ornamental, of yellowish-brown stone, I am particularly fond of), you enjoy on your left, through the gate of Kensington Gardens as you go towards Bayswater, an altogether enchanting vista—a foot-path over the grass, which loses itself beneath the scattered oaks and elms exactly as if the place were a "chase." There could be nothing less like London in general than this particular morsel, and yet it takes London, of all cities, to give you such an impression of the country.

IV

It takes London to put you in the way of a purely rustic walk from Notting Hill to Whitehall. You may traverse this immense distance—a most comprehensive diagonal—altogether on soft, fine turf, amid the song of birds, the bleat of lambs, the ripple of ponds, the rustle of admirable trees. Frequently have I wished that, for the sake of such a daily luxury and of exercise made romantic, I were a government-clerk living, in snug domestic conditions, in a Pembridge villa—let me suppose—and having my matutinal desk in Westminster. I should turn into Kensington Gardens at their northwest limit, and I should have my choice of a hundred pleasant paths to the gates of Hyde Park. In Hyde Park I should follow the water-side, or the Row, or any other fancy of the occasion; liking best, perhaps, after all, the Row in its morning mood, with the mist hanging over the dark-red course, and the scattered early riders taking an identity as the soundless gallop brings them nearer. I am free to admit that in the Season, at the conventional hours, the Row becomes a weariness (save perhaps just for a glimpse, once a year, to remind one's self how much it is like Du Maurier); the preoccupied citizen eschews it, and leaves it for the most part to the gaping barbarian. I speak of it now from the point of view of the pedestrian; but for the rider as well it is at its best when he passes either too early or too late. Then, if he be not bent on comparing it to its disadvantage with the bluer and boskier alleys of the Bois de Boulogne, it will not be spoiled by the fact that, with its surface that looks like tan, its barriers like those of the ring on which the clown stands to hold up the hoop to the young lady, its empty benches and chairs, its occasional orange-peel, its mounted policemen patrolling at intervals like expectant supernumeraries, it offers points of real contact with a circus whose lamps are out. The sky that bends over it is frequently not a bad imitation of the dingy tent of such an establishment. The ghosts of past cavalcades seem to haunt the foggy arena, and somehow they are better company than the mashers and elongated beauties of current seasons. It is not without interest to remember that most of the salient figures of English society during the present century — and English society means, or rather has hitherto meant, in a large degree, English history—have bobbed in the saddle between Apsley House and Queen's Gate. You may call the roll if you care to, and the air will be thick with dumb voices and dead names, like that of some Roman amphitheatre.

It is doubtless a signal proof of being a London-lover *quand même* that one should undertake an apology for so bungled an attempt at a great public place as Hyde Park Corner. It is certain that the improvements and embellishments recently enacted there have only served to call further attention to the poverty of the elements and to the fact that this poverty is terribly illustrative of general conditions. The place is the beating heart of the great West End, yet its main features are a shabby, stuccoed hospital, the low park-gates in their neat but unimposing frame, the drawing-room windows of Apsley House and of the commonplace frontages on the little terrace beside it; to which must be added, of course, the only item in the whole prospect that is in the least monumental — the arch spanning the private road beside the gardens of Buckingham Palace. This structure is now bereaved of the rueful effigy which used to surmount it — the Iron Duke in the guise of a tin soldier — and has not been enriched by the transaction as much as might have been expected.* There is a fine view of Piccadilly and Knightsbridge, and of the noble mansions, as the house-agents call them, of Grosvenor Place, together with a sense of generous space beyond the vulgar little railing of the Green Park; but, except for the impression that there would be room for something better, there is nothing in all this that speaks to the imagination: almost as much as the grimy desert

---

* The monument in the middle of the square, with Sir Edgar Boehm's four fine soldiers, had not been set up when these words were written.

of Trafalgar Square the prospect conveys the idea of an opportunity wasted.

All the same, on a fine day in spring it has an expressiveness of which I shall not pretend to explain the source further than by saying that the flood of life and luxury is immeasurably great there. The edifices are mean, but the social stream itself is monumental, and to an observer not positively stolid there is more excitement and suggestion than I can give a reason for in the long, distributed waves of traffic, with the steady policemen marking their rhythm, which roll together and apart for so many hours. Then the great, dim city becomes bright and kind, the pall of smoke turns into a veil of haze carelessly worn, the air is colored and almost scented by the presence of the biggest society in the world, and most of the things that meet the eye — or perhaps I should say more of them, for the most in London is, no doubt, ever the realm of the dingy—present themselves as "well appointed." Everything shines more or less, from the window-panes to the dog-collars. So it all looks, with its myriad variations and qualifications, to one who surveys it over the apron of a hansom, while that vehicle of vantage, better than any box at the opera, spurts and slackens with the current.

It is not in a hansom, however, that we have figured our punctual young man, whom we must not desert as he fares to the southeast, and who has only to cross Hyde Park Corner to find his way all grassy again. I have a weakness for the convenient, familiar, treeless, or almost treeless, expanse of the Green Park and the friendly part it plays as a kind of encouragement to Piccadilly. I am so fond of Piccadilly that I am grateful to any one or anything that does it a service, and nothing is more worthy of appreciation than the southward look it is permitted to enjoy just after it passes Devonshire House — a sweep of horizon which it would be difficult to match among other haunts of men, and thanks to which, of a summer's day, you may spy, beyond the browsed pastures of the foreground and middle distance, beyond the cold chimneys of Buckingham Palace and the towers of Westminster and the swarming river-side and all the southern parishes, the hard modern twinkle of the roof of the Crystal Palace.

If the Green Park is familiar, there is still less of the exclusive in its pendant, as one may call it—for it literally hangs from the other, down the hill—the remnant of the former garden of the queer, shabby old palace whose black, inelegant face stares up St. James's Street. This popular resort has a great deal of character, but I am free to confess that much of its character comes from its nearness to the Westminster slums. It is a park of intimacy, and perhaps the most democratic corner of London, in spite of its being in the royal and military quarter and close to all kinds of stateliness. There are few hours of the day when a thousand smutty children are not sprawling over it, and the unemployed lie thick on the grass and cover the benches with a brotherhood of greasy corduroys. If the London parks are the drawing-rooms and clubs of the poor—that is, of those poor (I admit it cuts down the number) who live near enough to them to reach them — these particular grass-plots and alleys may be said to constitute the very *salon* of the slums.

I know not why, being such a region of greatness —great towers, great names, great memories; at the foot of the Abbey, the Parliament, the fine fragment of Whitehall, with the quarters of the Guards of the sovereign right and left—but the edge of Westminster evokes as many associations of misery as of empire. The neighborhood has been much purified of late, but it still contains a collection of specimens—though it is far from unique in this — of the low, black element. The air always seems to me heavy and thick, and here more than elsewhere one hears old England —the panting, smoke-stained Titan of Matthew Arnold's fine poem—draw her deep breath with effort. In fact one is nearer to her heroic lungs, if those organs are figured by the great pinnacled and fretted talking-house on the edge of the river. But this same dense and conscious air plays such everlasting tricks to the eye that the Foreign Office, as you see it from the bridge, often looks romantic, and the sheet of water it overhangs poetic—suggests an Indian palace bathing its feet in the Ganges. If our pedestrian achieves such a comparison as this he has nothing left but to go on to his work — which he will find close at hand. He will have come the whole way from the far northwest on the green — which is what was to be demonstrated.

V

I feel as if I were taking a tone almost of boastfulness, and no doubt the best way to consider the matter is simply to say—without going into the treachery of reasons—that, for one's self, one likes this part or the other. Yet this course would not be unattended with danger, inasmuch as at the end of a few such professions we might find ourselves committed to a tolerance of much that is deplorable. London is so clumsy and so brutal, and has gathered together so many of the darkest sides of life, that it is almost ridiculous to talk of her as a lover talks of his mistress, and almost frivolous to appear to ignore her disfigurements and cruelties. She is like a mighty ogress who devours human flesh; but to me it is a mitigating circumstance—though it may not seem so to every one —that the ogress herself is human. It is not in wantonness that she fills her maw, but to keep herself alive and do her tremendous work. She has no time for fine discriminations, but after all she is as good-natured as she is huge, and the more you stand up to her, as the phrase is, the better she takes the joke of it. It is mainly when you fall on your face before her that she gobbles you up. She heeds little what she takes, so long as she has her stint, and the smallest push to the right or the left will divert her wavering bulk from one form of prey to another. It is not to be denied that the heart tends to grow hard in her company; but she is a capital antidote to the morbid, and to live with her successfully is an education of the temper, a consecration of one's private philosophy. She gives one a surface for which in a rough world one can never be too thankful. She may take away reputations, but she forms character. She teaches her victims not to "mind," and the great danger for them is perhaps that they shall learn the lesson too well.

It is sometimes a wonder to ascertain what they do mind, the best-seasoned of her children. Many of them assist, without winking, at the most unfathomable dramas, and the common speech of others denotes a familiarity with the horrible. It is her theory that she both produces and appreciates the exquisite; but if you catch her in flagrant repudiation of both responsibilities and confront her with the shortcoming, she gives you a look, with a shrug of her colossal shoulders, which establishes a private relation with you for evermore. She seems to say: "Do you really take me so seriously as that, you dear, devoted, voluntary dupe, and don't you know what an immeasurable humbug I am?" You reply that you shall know it henceforth; but your tone is good-natured, with a touch of the cynicism that she herself has taught you; for you are aware that if she makes herself out better than she is, she also makes herself out much worse. She is immensely democratic, and that, no doubt, is part of the manner in which she is salutary to the individual; she teaches him his "place" by an incomparable discipline, but deprives him of complaint by letting him see that she has exactly the same lash for every other back. When he has swallowed the lesson he may enjoy the rude but unfailing justice by which, under her eye, reputations and positions elsewhere esteemed great are reduced to the relative. There are so many reputations, so many positions, that supereminence breaks down, and it is difficult to be so rare that London can't match you. It is a part of her good-nature and one of her clumsy coquetries to pretend sometimes that she hasn't your equivalent, as when she takes it into her head to hunt the lion or form a ring round a celebrity. But this artifice is so transparent that the lion must be very candid or the celebrity very obscure to be taken by it. The business is altogether subjective, as the philosophers say, and the great city is primarily looking after herself. Celebrities are convenient—they are one of the things that people can be asked to "meet"—and lion-cutlets, put upon the ice, will nourish a family through periods of dearth.

This is what I mean by calling London democratic. You may be in it, of course, without being of it; but from the moment you *are* of it—and on this point your own sense will soon enough enlighten you—you belong to a body in which a general equality prevails. However exalted, however able, however rich, however renowned you may be, there are too many people at least as much so for your own idiosyncrasies to count. I think it is only by being beautiful that you may really prevail very much; for the loveliness of woman it has long been noticeable that London will go most out of her way. It is when she hunts that particular lion that she becomes most dangerous; then there are really moments when you would believe, for all the world, that she is thinking of what she can give, not of what she can get. Lovely ladies, before this, have paid for believing it, and will continue to pay in days to come. On the whole the people who are least deceived are perhaps those who have permitted themselves to believe, in their own interest, that poverty is not a disgrace. It is certainly not considered so in London, and indeed you can scarcely say where—in virtue of diffusion — it would more naturally be exempt. The possession of money is, of course, immensely an advantage, but that is a very different thing from a disqualification in the lack of it.

Good-natured in so many things in spite of her cynical tongue, and easy-going in spite of her tremendous pace, there is nothing in which the large indulgence of the town is more shown than in the liberal way she looks at obligations of hospitality and the margin she allows in these and cognate matters. She wants above all to be amused; she keeps her books loosely, doesn't stand on small questions of a chop for a chop, and if there be any chance of people's proving a diversion, doesn't know or remember or care whether they have "called." She forgets even if she herself have called. In matters of ceremony she takes and gives a long rope, wasting no time in phrases and circumvallations. It is no doubt incontestable that one result of her inability to stand upon trifles and consider details is that she has been obliged in some ways to lower rather portentously the standard of her manners. She cultivates the abrupt—for even when she asks you to dine a month ahead the invitation goes off like the crack of a pistol—and approaches her ends not exactly *par quatre chemins*. She doesn't pretend to attach importance to the lesson conveyed in Matthew Arnold's poem of "The Sick King in Bokhara," that,

> "Though we snatch what we desire,
> We may not snatch it eagerly."

London snatches it more than eagerly if that be the only way she can get it. Good manners are a succession of details, and I don't mean to say that she doesn't attend to them when she has time. She has it, however, but seldom—*que voulez-vous ?* Perhaps the matter of note-writing is as good an example as another of what certain of the elder traditions inevitably have become in her hands. She lives by notes—they are her very heart-beats; but those that bear her signature are as disjointed as the ravings of delirium, and have nothing but a postage-stamp in common with the epistolary art.

VI

If she doesn't go into particulars it may seem a very presumptuous act to have attempted to do so on her behalf, and the reader will doubtless think I have been punished by having egregiously failed in my enumeration. Indeed nothing could well be more difficult than to add up the items—the column would be altogether too long. One may have dreamed of turning the glow—if glow it be—of one's lantern on each successive facet of the jewel; but, after all, it may be success enough if a confusion of brightness be the result. One has not the alternative of speaking of London as a whole, for the simple reason that there is no such thing as the whole of it. It is immeasurable—embracing arms never meet. Rather it is a collection of many wholes, and of which of them is it most important to speak? Inevitably there must be a choice, and I know of none more scientific than simply to leave out what we may have to apologize for. The uglinesses, the "rookeries," the brutalities, the night-aspect of many of the streets, the gin-shops and the hour when they are cleared out before closing—there are many elements of this kind which have to be counted out before a genial summary can be made.

And yet I should not go so far as to say that it is a condition of such geniality to close one's eyes upon the immense misery; on the contrary, I think it is partly because we are irremediably conscious of that dark gulf that the most general appeal of the great city remains exactly what it is, the largest chapter of human accidents. I have no idea of what the future evolution of the strangely mingled monster may be; whether the poor will improve away the rich, or the rich will expropriate the poor, or they will all continue to dwell together on their present imperfect terms of intercourse. Certain it is, at any rate, that the impression of suffering is a part of the general vibration; it is one of the things that mingle with all the others to make the sound that is supremely dear to the consistent London-lover—the rumble of the tremendous human mill. This is the note which, in all its modulations, haunts and fascinates and inspires him. And whether or no he may succeed in keeping the misery out of the picture, he will freely confess that the latter is not spoiled for him by some of its duskiest shades. We are far from liking London well enough till we like its defects: the dense darkness of much of its winter, the soot on the chimney-pots and everywhere else, the early lamplight, the brown blur of the houses, the splashing of hansoms in Oxford Street or the Strand on December afternoons.

There is still something that recalls to me the enchantments of children—the anticipation of Christmas, the delight of a holiday walk—in the way the shop-fronts shine into the fog. It makes each of them seem a little world of light and warmth, and I can still waste time in looking at them with dirty Bloomsbury on one side and dirtier Soho on the other. There are winter effects, not intrinsically sweet, it would appear, which somehow, in absence, touch the chords of memory and even the fount of tears; as, for instance, the front of the British Museum on a black afternoon, or the portico, when the weather is vile, of one of the big square clubs in Pall Mall. I can give no adequate account of the subtle poetry of such reminiscences; it depends upon associations of which we have often lost the thread. The wide colonnade of the Museum, its symmetrical wings, the high iron fence in its granite setting, the sense of the misty halls within, where all the treasures lie—these things loom patiently through atmospheric layers which instead of making them dreary impart to them something of a cheer of red lights in a storm. I think the romance of a winter afternoon in London arises partly from the fact that, when it is not altogether smothered, the general lamplight takes this hue of hospitality. Such is the color of the interior glow of the clubs in Pall Mall, which I positively like best when the fog loiters upon their monumental staircases.

In saying just now that these retreats may easily be, for the exile, part of the phantasmagoria of homesickness, I by no means alluded simply to their solemn outsides. If they are still more solemn within, that does not make them any less dear in retrospect, at least, to a visitor who is bent upon liking his London to the end. What is the solemnity but a tribute to your nerves, and the stillness but a refined proof of intensity of life? To produce such results as these the balance of many tastes must be struck, and that is only possible in a very high civilization. If I seem to intimate that this last abstract term must be the cheer of him who has lonely possession of a foggy library, without even the excitement of watching for some one to put down the magazine he wants, I am willing to let the supposition pass, for the appreciation of a London club at one of the empty seasons is nothing but the strong expression of a preference for the great city—by no means so unsociable as it may superficially appear—at periods of relative abandonment. The London year is studded with holidays, blessed little islands of comparative leisure—intervals of absence for good society. Then the wonderful English faculty for "going out of town for a little change" comes into illimitable play, and families transport their nurseries and their bath-tubs to those rural scenes which form the real substratum of the national life. Such moments as these are the paradise of the genuine London-lover, for then he finds himself face to face with the object of his passion; he can give himself up to an intercourse which at other times is obstructed by his rivals. Then every one he knows is out of town, and the exhilarating sense of the presence of every one he doesn't know becomes by so much the deeper.

This is why I pronounce his satisfaction not an unsociable, but a positively affectionate emotion. It is the mood in which he most measures the immense humanity of the place, and in which its limits recede furthest into a dimness peopled with possible illustrations. For his acquaintance, however numerous it may be, is finite; whereas the other, the unvisited London, is infinite. It is one of his pleasures to think of the experiments and excursions he may make in it, even when these adventures don't particularly come off. The friendly fog seems to protect and enrich them—to add both to the mystery and security, so that it is most in the winter months that the imagination weaves such delights. They reach their climax, perhaps, during the strictly social desolation of Christmas week, when the country-houses are filled at the expense of the metropolis. Then it is that I am most haunted with the London of Dickens, feel most as if it were still recoverable, still exhaling its queerness in patches perceptible to the appreciative. Then the big fires blaze in the lone twilight of the clubs, and the new books on the tables say, "Now at last you have time to read me," and the afternoon tea and toast, and the torpid old gentleman who wakes up from a doze to order potash-water, appear to make the assurance good. It is not a small matter either, to a man of letters, that this is the best time for writing, and that during the lamplit days the white page he tries to blacken becomes, on his table, in the circle of the lamp, with the screen of the climate folding him in, more vivid and absorbent. Those to whom it is forbidden to sit up to work in the small hours may, between November and March, enjoy a semblance of this luxury in the morning. The weather makes a kind of sedentary midnight and muffles the possible interruptions. It is bad for the eyesight, but excellent for the image.

VII

Of course it is too much to say that all the satisfaction of life in London comes from literally living there, for it is not a paradox that a great deal of it consists in getting away. It is almost easier to leave it than not to, and much of its richness and interest proceeds from its ramifications, the fact that all England is in a suburban relation to it. Such an affair it is in comparison to get away from Paris or to get into it. London melts by wide, ugly zones into the green country, and becomes pretty insidiously, inadvertently — without stopping to change. It is the spoiling, perhaps, of the country, but it is the making of the insatiable town, and if one is a helpless and shameless cockney that is all one is obliged to look at. Anything is excusable which enlarges one's civic consciousness. It ministers immensely to that of the London-lover that, thanks to the tremendous system of coming and going, to the active, hospitable habits of the people, to the elaboration of the railway-service, the frequency and rapidity of trains, and last, though not least, to the fact that much of the loveliest scenery in England lies within a radius of fifty miles—thanks to all this he has the rural picturesque at his door and may cultivate unlimited vagueness as to the line of division between centre and circumference. It is perfectly open to him to consider the remainder of the United Kingdom, or the British empire in general, or even, if he be an American, the total of the English-speaking territories of the globe, as the mere margin, the fitted girdle.

Is it for this reason—because I like to think how great we all are together in the light of heaven and the face of the rest of the world, with the bond of our glorious tongue, in which we labor to write articles and books for each other's candid perusal, how great we all are and how great is the great city which we may unite fraternally to regard as the capital of our race—is it for this that I have a singular kindness for the London railway-stations, that I like them æsthetically, that they interest and fascinate me, and that I view them with complacency even when I wish neither to depart nor to arrive? They remind me of all our reciprocities and activities, our energies and curiosities, and our being all distinguished together from other people by our great common stamp of perpetual motion, our passion for seas and deserts and the other side of the globe, the secret of the impression of strength—I don't say of social roundness and finish—that we produce in any collection of Anglo-Saxon types. If in the beloved foggy season I delight in the spectacle of Paddington, Euston, or Waterloo—I confess I prefer the grave northern stations—I am prepared to defend myself against the charge of puerility; for what I seek and what I find in these vulgar scenes is at bottom simply so much evidence of our larger way of looking at life. The exhibition of variety of type is in general one of the bribes by which London induces you to condone her abominations, and the railway-platform is a kind of compendium of that variety. I think that nowhere so much as in London do people wear—to the eye of observation—definite signs of the sort of people they may be. If you like above all things to know the sort, you hail this fact with joy; you recognize that if the English are immensely distinct from other people, they are also socially—and that brings with it, in England, a train of moral and intellectual consequences — extremely distinct from each other. You may see them all together, with the rich coloring of their differences, in the fine flare of one of Mr. W. H. Smith's bookstalls —a feature not to be omitted in any enumeration of the charms of Paddington and Euston. It is a focus of warmth and light in the vast smoky cavern; it gives the idea that literature is a thing of splendor, of a dazzling essence, of infinite gas-lit red and gold. A glamour hangs over the glittering booth, and a tantalizing air of clever new things. How brilliant must the books all be, how veracious and courteous the fresh, pure journals! Of a Saturday afternoon, as you wait in your corner of the compartment for the starting of the train, the window makes a frame for the glowing picture. I say of a Saturday afternoon, because that is the most characteristic time—it speaks most of the constant circulation and in particular of the quick jump, by express, just before dinner, for the Sunday, into the hall of the country-house and the forms of closer friendliness, the prolonged talks, the familiarizing walks which London excludes.

There is the emptiness of summer as well, when you may have the town to yourself, and I would discourse of it—counting the summer from the first of August—were it not that I fear to seem ungracious in insisting so much on the negative phases. In truth they become positive in another manner, and I have an endearing recollection of certain happy accidents attached to the only period when London life may be said to admit of accident. It is the most luxurious existence in the world, but of that especial luxury—the unexpected, the extemporized—it has in general too little. In a very tight crowd you can't scratch your leg, and in London the social pressure is so great that it is difficult to deflect from the perpendicular or to move otherwise than with the mass. There is too little of the loose change of time; every half-hour has its preappointed use, written down month by month in a little book. As I intimated, however, the pages of this volume exhibit from August to November an attractive blankness; they represent the season during which you may taste of that highest kind of inspiration, the inspiration of the moment.

This is doubtless what a gentleman had in mind who once said to me, in regard to the vast resources of London and its having something for every taste, "Oh, yes; when you are bored or want a little change you can take the boat down to Blackwall." I have never had occasion yet to resort to this particular remedy. Perhaps it's a proof that I have never been bored. Why Blackwall? I indeed asked myself at the time; nor have I yet ascertained what distractions the mysterious name represents. My interlocutor probably used it generically, as a free, comprehensive allusion to the charms of the river at large. Here the London-lover goes with him all the way, and indeed the Thames is altogether such a wonderful affair that he feels he has distributed his picture very clumsily not to have put it in the very forefront. Take it up or take it down, it is equally an adjunct of London life, an expression of London manners.

From Westminster to the sea its uses are commercial, but none the less pictorial for that; while in the other direction—taking it properly a little further up

—they are personal, social, athletic, idyllic. In its recreative character it is absolutely unique. I know of no other classic stream that is so splashed about for the mere fun of it. There is something almost droll and at the same time almost touching in the way that on the smallest pretext of holiday or fine weather the mighty population takes to the boats. They bump each other in the narrow, charming channel; between Oxford and Richmond they make an uninterrupted procession. Nothing is more suggestive of the personal energy of the people and their eagerness to take, in the way of exercise and adventure, whatever they can get. I hasten to add that what they get on the Thames is exquisite, in spite of the smallness of the scale and the contrast between the numbers and the space. In a word, if the river is the busiest suburb of London, it is also by far the prettiest. That term applies to it less of course from the bridges down, but it is only because in this part of its career it deserves a larger praise. To be consistent, I like it best when it is all dyed and disfigured with the town and you look from bridge to bridge—they seem wonderfully big and dim—over the brown, greasy current, the barges and the penny-steamers, the black, sordid, heterogeneous shores. This prospect, of which so many of the elements are ignoble, etches itself to the eye of the lover of "bits" with a power that is worthy perhaps of a better cause.

The way that with her magnificent opportunity London has neglected to achieve a river-front is, of course, the best possible proof that she has rarely, in the past, been in the architectural mood which at present shows somewhat inexpensive signs of settling upon her. Here and there a fine fragment apologizes for the failure which it doesn't remedy. Somerset House stands up higher perhaps than anything else on its granite pedestal, and the palace of Westminster reclines—it can hardly be said to stand—on the big parliamentary bench of its terrace. The Embankment, which is admirable if not particularly interesting, does what it can, and the mannered houses of Chelsea stare across at Battersea Park like eighteenth-century ladies surveying a horrid wilderness. On the other hand, the Charing Cross railway-station, placed where it is, is a national crime; Milbank prison is a worse act of violence than any it was erected to punish, and the water-side generally a shameless renunciation of effect. We acknowledge, however, that its very cynicism is expressive; so that if one were to choose again—short of there being a London Louvre—between the usual English irresponsibility in such matters and some particular flight of conscience, one would perhaps do as well to let the case stand. We know what it is, the stretch from Chelsea to Wapping, but we know not what it might be. It doesn't prevent my being always more or less thrilled, of a summer afternoon, by the journey on a penny-steamer to Greenwich.

VIII

But why do I talk of Greenwich and remind myself of one of the unexecuted vignettes with which it had been my plan that these desultory and, I fear, somewhat incoherent remarks should be studded? They will present to the reader no vignettes but those which the artist who has kindly consented to associate himself with my vagaries may be so good as to bestow upon them. Why should I speak of Hampstead, as the question of summer afternoons just threatened to lead me to do after I should have exhausted the subject of Greenwich, which I may not even touch? Why should I be so arbitrary when I have cheated myself out of the space privately intended for a series of vivid and ingenious sketches of the particular physiognomy of the respective quarters of the town? I had dreamed of doing them all, with their idiosyncrasies and the signs by which you shall know them. It is my pleasure to have learned these signs—a deeply interesting branch of observation—but I must renounce the display of my lore.

I haven't the conscience to talk about Hampstead, and what a pleasant thing it is to ascend the long hill which overhangs, as it were, St. John's Wood and begins at the Swiss Cottage—you must mount from there, it must be confessed, as you can—and pick up a friend at a house of friendship on the top, and stroll with him on the rusty Heath, and skirt the garden-walls of the old square Georgian houses which survive from the time when, near as it is to-day to London, the place was a kind of provincial centre, with Joanna Baillie for its muse, and take the way by the Three Spaniards—I would never miss that—and look down at the smoky city or across at the Scotch firs and the red sunset. It would never do to make a tangent in that direction when I have left Kensington unsung and Bloomsbury unattempted, and have said never a word about the mighty eastward region —the queer corners, the dark secrets, the rich survivals and mementoes of the City. I particularly regret having sacrificed Kensington, the once-delightful, the Thackerayan, with its literary vestiges, its quiet, pompous red palace, its square of Queen Anne, its house of Lady Castlewood, its Greyhound tavern, where Henry Esmond lodged.

But I can reconcile myself to this when I reflect that I have also sacrificed the Season, which doubtless, from an elegant point of view, ought to have been the central *morceau* in the panorama. I have noted that the London-lover loves everything in the place, but I have not cut myself off from saying that his sympathy has degrees, or from remarking that the sentiment of the author of these pages has never gone all the way with the dense movement of the British carnival. That is really the word for the period from Easter to midsummer; it is a fine, decorous, expensive, Protestant carnival, in which the masks are not of velvet or silk, but of wonderful deceptive flesh and blood, the material of the most beautiful complexions in the world. Holding that the great interest of London is the sense the place gives us of multitudinous life, it is doubtless an inconsequence not to care most for the phase of greatest intensity. But there is life and life, and the rush and crush of these weeks of fashion is after all but a tolerably mechanical expression of human forces. No one would deny that it is a more universal, brilliant, spectacular one than can be seen anywhere else, and it is not a defect that these forces often take the form of women extremely beautiful. I risk the declaration that the London season brings together year by year an unequalled collection of handsome persons. I say nothing of the ugly ones; beauty has at the best been allotted to a small minority, and it is never, at the most, anywhere, but a question of the number by which that minority is least insignificant.

There are moments when one can almost forgive the follies of June for the sake of the smile which the sceptical old city puts on for the time, and which, as I noted in an earlier passage of this disquisition, fairly breaks into laughter where she is tickled by the vortex of Hyde Park Corner. Most perhaps does she seem to smile at the end of the summer days, when the light lingers and lingers, though the shadows lengthen and the mists redden and the belated riders, with dinners to dress for, hurry away from the trampled arena of the Park. The population at that hour surges mainly westward and sees the dust of the day's long racket turned into a dull golden haze. There is something that has doubtless often, at this particular moment, touched the fancy even of the bored and the *blasés* in such an emanation of hospitality, of waiting dinners, of the festal idea and the whole spectacle of the West End preparing herself for an evening six parties deep. The scale on which she entertains is stupendous, and her invitations and "reminders" are as thick as the leaves of the forest.

For half an hour, from eight to nine, every pair of wheels presents the portrait of a diner-out. To consider only the rattling hansoms, the white neckties and "dressed" heads which greet you from over the apron in a quick, interminable succession, conveys the overwhelming impression of a complicated world. Who are they all, and where are they all going, and whence have they come, and what smoking kitchens and gaping portals and marshalled flunkies are prepared to receive them, from the southernmost limits of a loosely-interpreted, an almost transpontine Belgravia, to the hyperborean confines of St. John's Wood? There are broughams standing at every door and carpets laid down for the footfall of the issuing if not the entering reveller. The pavements are empty now, in the fading light, in the big sallow squares and the stuccoed streets of gentility, save for the groups of small children holding others that are smaller—Ameliar-Ann intrusted with Sarah Jane— who collect, wherever the strip of carpet lies, to see the fine ladies pass from the carriage or the house. The West End is dotted with these pathetic little gazing groups; it is the party of the poor—*their* Season and way of dining out, and a happy illustration of "the sympathy that prevails between classes." The watchers, I should add, are by no means all children, but the lean mature also, and I am sure these wayside joys are one of the reasons of an inconvenience much deplored—the tendency of the country poor to flock to London. Those who dine only occasionally or never at all have plenty of time to contemplate those with whom the custom has more amplitude.

However, it was not my intention to conclude these remarks in a melancholy strain, and Heaven knows that the diners are a prodigious company. It is as moralistic as I shall venture to be if I drop a very soft sigh on the paper as I affirm that truth. Are they all illuminated spirits and is their conversation the ripest in the world? This is not to be expected, nor should I ever suppose it to be desired that an agreeable society should fail to offer frequent opportunity for intellectual rest. Such a shortcoming is not one of the sins of the London world in general, nor would it be just to complain of that world, on any side, on grounds of deficiency. It is not what London fails to do that strikes the observer, but the general fact that she does everything in excess. Excess is her highest reproach, and it is her incurable misfortune that there is really too much of her. She overwhelms you by quantity and number — she ends by making human life, by making civilization, appear cheap to you. Wherever you go, to parties, exhibitions, concerts, "private views," meetings, solitudes, there are already more people than enough on the field. How it makes you understand the high walls with which so much of English life is surrounded, and the priceless blessing of a park in the country, where there is nothing animated but rabbits and pheasants and, for the worst, the importunate nightingales! And as the monster grows and grows forever, she departs more and more—it must be acknowledged—from the ideal of a convenient society, a society in which intimacy is possible, in which the associated meet often and sound and select and measure and inspire each other, and relations and combinations have time to form themselves. The substitute for this, in London, is the momentary concussion of a million of atoms. It is the difference between seeing a great deal of a few and seeing a little of every one. "When did you come—are you 'going on'?" and it is over; there is no time even for the answer. This may seem a perfidious arraignment, and I should not make it were I not prepared, or rather were I not eager, to add two qualifications. One of these is that, cumbrously vast as the place may be, I would not have had it smaller by a hair's-breadth or have missed one of the fine and fruitful impatiences with which it inspires you and which are at bottom a heartier tribute, I think, than any great city receives. The other is that out of its richness and its inexhaustible good-humor it belies the next hour any generalization you may have been so simple as to make about it.

1888.

JAMES RUSSELL LOWELL

AFTER a man's long work is over and the sound of his voice is still, those in whose regard he has held a high place find his image strangely simplified and summarized. The hand of death, in passing over it, has smoothed the folds, made it more typical and general. The figure retained by the memory is compressed and intensified; accidents have dropped away from it and shades have ceased to count; it stands, sharply, for a few estimated and cherished things, rather than, nebulously, for a swarm of possibilities. We cut the silhouette, in a word, out of the confusion of life, we save and fix the outline, and it is with his eye on this profiled distinction that the critic speaks. It is his function to speak with assurance when once his impression has become final; and it is in noting this circumstance that I perceive how slenderly prompted I am to deliver myself on such an occasion as a critic. It is not that due conviction is absent; it is only that the function is a cold one. It is not that the final impression is dim; it is only that it is made on a softer side of the spirit than the critical sense. The process is more mystical, the deposited image is insistently personal, the generalizing principle is that of loyalty. I can therefore not pretend to write of James

Russell Lowell in the tone of detachment and classification; I can only offer a few anticipatory touches for a portrait that asks for a steadier hand.

It may be professional prejudice, but as the whole color of his life was literary, so it seems to me that we may see in his high and happy fortune the most substantial honor gathered by the practice of letters from a world preoccupied with other things. It was in looking at him as a man of letters that one drew closest to him, and some of his more fanatical friends are not to be deterred from regarding his career as in the last analysis a tribute to the dominion of style. This is the idea that to my sense his name most promptly evokes; and though it was not by any means the only idea he cherished, the unity of his career is surely to be found in it. He carried style—the style of literature—into regions in which we rarely look for it: into politics, of all places in the world, into diplomacy, into stammering civic dinners and ponderous anniversaries, into letters and notes and telegrams, into every turn of the hour—absolutely into conversation, where indeed it freely disguised itself as intensely colloquial wit. Any friendly estimate of him is foredoomed to savor potently of reminiscence, so that I may mention how vividly I recall the occasion on which he first struck me as completely representative.

The association could only grow, but the essence of it was all there on the eve of his going as minister to Spain. It was late in the summer of 1877; he spent a few days in London on his way to Madrid, in the hushed gray August, and I remember dining

with him at a dim little hotel in Park Street, which
I had never entered before and have never entered
since, but which, whenever I pass it, seems to look
at me with the melancholy of those inanimate things
that have participated. That particular evening remained, in my fancy, a kind of bridge between his
old bookish and his new worldly life; which, however,
had much more in common than they had in distinction. He turned the pages of the later experience
with very much the same contemplative reader's sense
with which in his library he had for years smoked
the student's pipe over a thousand volumes: the only
difference was that a good many of the leaves were
still to cut. At any rate, he was enviably gay and
amused, and this preliminary hour struck me literally
as the reward of consistency. It was tinted with the
promise of a singularly interesting future, but the
saturated American time was all behind it, and what
was to come seemed an ideal opportunity for the
nourished mind. That the American years had been
diluted with several visits to Europe was not a flaw
in the harmony, for to recollect certain other foreign
occasions — pleasant Parisian and delightful Italian
strolls — was to remember that, if these had been
months of absence for him, they were for me, on the
wings of his talk, hours of repatriation. This talk
was humorously and racily fond, charged with a
perfect drollery of reference to the *other* country
(there were always two—the one we were in and the
one we weren't), the details of my too sketchy conception of which, admitted for argument, he showed

endless good-nature in filling in. It was a joke, polished by much use, that I was dreadfully at sea about my native land; and it would have been pleasant indeed to know even less than I did, so that I might have learned the whole story from Mr. Lowell's lips.

His America was a country worth hearing about, a magnificent conception, an admirably consistent and lovable object of allegiance. If the sign that in Europe one knew him best by was his intense national consciousness, one felt that this consciousness could not sit lightly on a man in whom it was the strongest form of piety. Fortunately for him and for his friends he was one of the most whimsical, one of the wittiest of human beings, so that he could play with his patriotism and make it various. All the same, one felt in it, in talk, the depth of passion that hums through much of his finest verse — almost the only passion that, to my sense, his poetry contains — the accent of chivalry, of the lover, the knight ready to do battle for his mistress. Above all, it was a particular allegiance to New England — a quarter of the earth in respect to which the hand of long habit, of that affection which is usually half convenience, never let go the prime idea, the standard. New England was heroic to him, for he felt in his pulses the whole history of her *origines;* it was impossible to know him without a sense that he had a rare divination of the hard realities of her past. "The Biglow Papers" show to what a tune he could play with his patriotism — all literature contains, I think, no finer sport; but he is serious enough when he speaks of the

> ... "strange New World, that yit wast never young,
> Whose youth, from thee, by gripin' need was wrung;
> Brown foundlin' of the woods whose baby-bed
> Was prowled round by the Injun's cracklin' tread,
> And who grew'st strong thro' shifts and wants and pains,
> Nussed by stern men with empires in their brains."

He was never at trouble to conceal his respect for such an origin as that, and when he came to Europe in 1877 this sentiment was, in his luggage, one of the articles on which he could most easily put his hand.

One of the others was the extraordinary youthfulness which could make a man considerably younger than himself (so that it was only with the lapse of years that the relation of age settled upon the right note) constantly forget that he had copious antecedents. In the times when the difference counted for more — old Cambridge days that seem far away now — I doubtless thought him more professorial than he felt, but I am sure that in the sequel I never thought him younger. The boy in him was never more clamorous than during the last summer that he spent in England, two years before his death. Since the recollection comes of itself I may mention as my earliest impression of him the charm that certain of his Harvard lectures — on English literature, on Old French — had for a very immature person who was supposed to be pursuing, in one of the schools, a very different branch of knowledge, but who on dusky winter afternoons escaped with irresponsible zeal into the glow of Mr. Lowell's learned lamplight, the particular incidence of which, in the small, still lecture-room, and the illumination of his head and hands, I recall with extreme vividness. He talked communicatively of style, and where else in all the place was any such talk to be heard? It made a romance of the hour — it made even a picture of the scene; it was an unforgetable initiation. If he was American enough in Europe, in America he was abundantly European. He was so steeped in history and literature that to some yearning young persons he made the taste of knowledge almost sweeter than it was ever to be again. He was redolent, intellectually speaking, of Italy and Spain; he had lived in long intimacy with Dante and Cervantes and Calderon; he embodied to envious aspirants the happy intellectual fortune — independent years in a full library, years of acquisition without haste and without rest, a robust love of study which went sociably arm in arm with a robust love of life. This love of life was so strong in him that he could lose himself in little diversions as well as in big books. He was fond of everything human and natural, everything that had color and character, and no gayety, no sense of comedy, was ever more easily kindled by contact. When he was not surrounded by great pleasures he could find his account in small ones, and no situation could be dull for a man in whom all reflection, all reaction, was witty.

I waited some years really to know him, but it was to find at once that he was delightful to walk with.

He spent the winter of 1872-73 in Paris, and if I had not already been fond of the streets of that city his example and companionship would have made me so. We both had the habit of long walks, and he knew his Paris as he knew all his subjects. The history of a thing was always what he first saw in it — he recognized the object as a link in an interminable chain. He led at this season the most home-keeping, book-buying life, and Old French texts made his evenings dear to him. He had dropped (and where he dropped he usually stayed) into an intensely local and extremely savory little hotel in the Faubourg Saint-Germain, unknown to tourists, but patronized by deputies, where the *table d'hôte*, at which the host sat down with the guests and contradiction flourished, was a page of Balzac, full of illustration for the humorist. I used sometimes of a Sunday evening to dine there, and to this day, on rainy winter nights, I never cross the Seine amid the wet flare of the myriad lamps, never note the varnished rush of the river or the way the Louvre grows superb in the darkness, without a recurrent consciousness of the old sociable errand, the sense of dipping into a still denser Paris, with the *Temps* and M. Sarcey in my pocket.

We both spent the following winter — he at least the larger part of it — in Florence, out of manifold memories of which certain hours in his company, certain charmed Italian afternoons in Boboli gardens, on San Miniato terraces, come back to me with a glow of their own. He had indeed memories of earlier Italian times, some of which he has admirably recorded — anecdotes, tormenting to a late-comer, of the superseded, the missed. He himself, in his perpetual freshness, seemed to come so late that it was always a surprise to me that he had started so early. Almost any Italy, however, was good enough for him, and he kept criticism for great occasions, for the wise relapse, the study-chair, and the vanquished hesitation (not timid, but overbrimming, like a vessel dangerous to move) of that large prose pen which was so firm when once set in motion. He liked the Italian people — he liked the people everywhere, and the warm street life and the exquisite idiom; the Tuscan tongue, indeed, so early ripe and yet still so perfectly alive, was one of the comforts of the world to him. He produced that winter a poem so ample and noble that it was worthy to come into being in classic air — the magnificent elegy on the death of Agassiz, which strikes me as a summary of all his vigors and felicities, his most genial achievement, and (after the Harvard "Commemoration Ode") the truest expression of his poetic nature. It is hard to lend to a great old house, in Italy, even when it has become a modern inn, any associations as romantic as those it already wears; but what the high-windowed face of the Florentine Hôtel du Nord speaks to me of to-day, over its chattering cab-stand and across the statued pillar of the little square of the Holy Trinity, is neither its ancient honor nor its actual fall, but the sound, one December evening, by the fire the poet pronounces "starved," of

> "I cannot think he wished so soon to die
>   With all his senses full of eager heat,
> And rosy years that stood expectant by
>   To buckle the winged sandals on their feet,
>   He that was friends with Earth, and all her sweet
> Took with both hands unsparingly."

Of Mr. Lowell's residence in Spain I know nothing but what I gathered from his talk after he took possession, late in the spring of 1879, of the post in London rendered vacant by the retirement of Mr. John Welsh; much of it inevitably referring to the domestic sorrow — the prolonged illness of his admirable wife — which cast over these years a cloud that darkened further during the early part of his English period. I remember getting from him a sense that a diplomatic situation at Madrid was not quite so refreshing a thing as might have been expected, and that for the American representative at least there was not enough business to give a savor to duty. This particular representative's solution of every personal problem, however, was a page of philology in a cloud of tobacco, and as he had seen the picture before through his studies, so now he doubtless saw his studies through the picture. The palace was a part of it, where the ghost of Charles V. still walked and the princesses were what is called in princesses literary. The diplomatic circle was animated—if that be the word—by whist; what his own share of the game was enlivened by may be left to the imagination of those who remember the irrepressibility, on his lips, of the comic idea. It might have been taken for granted that he was well content to be transferred to England; but I have no definite recollection of the degree of his satisfaction beforehand. I think he was mainly conscious of the weight of the new responsibility, so that the unalloyed pleasure was that of his friends and of the most enlightened part of the public in the two countries, to which the appointment appeared to have an unusual felicity. It was made, as it were, for quality, and that continued to be the sign of the function so long as Mr. Lowell exercised it. The difficulty — if I may speak of difficulty — was that all judgment of it was necessarily *a priori*. It was impossible for him to know what a success, in vulgar parlance, he might make of a totally untried character, and, above all, to foresee how this character would adapt itself to his own disposition. During the years of his residence in London on an official footing it constantly struck me that it was the office that inclined at every turn to him, rather than he who inclined to the office.

I may appear to speak too much of this phase of his life as the most memorable part of it—especially considering how short a time it occupied in regard to the whole; but in addition to its being the only long phase of which I can speak at all closely from personal observation, it is just to remember that these were the years in which all the other years were made most evident. " *We* knew him and valued him ages before, and never stinted our appreciation, never waited to care for him till he had become the fashion," his American readers and listeners, his pupils and colleagues, might say; to which the answer is that those who admired him most were just those who might naturally rejoice in the multiplication of his opportunities. He came to London with only a vague notion, evidently, of what these opportunities were to be, and in fact there was no defining them in advance: what they proved to be, on the spot, was anything and everything that he might make them. I remember hearing him say a day or two after his arrival, "Oh, I've lost all my wit—you mustn't look to me for good things *now*." The words were uttered to a gentleman who had found one of his "things" very good, and who, having a political speech to make in a day or two, had thriftily asked his leave to bring it in. There could have been no better example of the experimental nature of his acceptance of the post; for the very foundation of the distinction that he gave it was his great reserve of wit. He had no idea how much he had left till he tried it, and he had never before had so much occasion to try it. This uncertainty might pervade the minds even of such of his friends as had a near view of his start; but those friends would have had singularly little imagination if they had failed to be struck in a general way with the highly civilized character of his mission. There are circumstances in operation (too numerous to recite) which combine to undermine greatly the comfort of the representative of the United States in a foreign country; it is, to speak summarily, in many respects a singularly embarrassing honor. I cannot express more strongly how happy Mr. Lowell's opportunity seemed to be than by saying that he struck people at the moment as enviable. It was an intensification of the impression given by the glimpse of him on his way to Spain. The true reward of an English style was to be sent to England, and if his career in that country was throughout amusing, in the highest sense of the term, this result was, for others at least, a part of their gratified suspense as to the further possibilities of the style.

From the friendly and intimate point of view it was presumable from the first that there would be a kind of drama, a spectacle; and if one had already lived a few years in London one could have an interesting prevision of some of its features. London is a great personage, and with those with whom she establishes a relation she always plays, as it were, her game. This game, throughout Mr. Lowell's residence, but especially during the early part, was exciting; so much so that I remember being positively sorry, as if I were leaving the theatre before the fall of the curtain, when, at that time, more than once I found myself, by visits to the Continent, obliged to turn my back upon it. The sight of his variety was a help to know London better; and it was a question whether *he* could ever know her so well as those who could freely consider the pair together. He offered her from the first a nut to crack, a morsel to roll under her tongue. She is the great consumer of spices and sweets; if I were not afraid of forcing the image I should say that she is too unwieldy to feed herself, and requires, in recurring seasons, as she sits prodigiously at her banquet, to be approached with the consecrated ladle. She placed this implement in Mr. Lowell's hands with a confidence so immediate as to be truly touching—a confidence that speaks for the eventual amalgamation of the Anglo-Saxon race in a way that surely no casual friction can obliterate. She can confer conspicuity, at least for the hour, so well that she is constantly under the temptation to do so; she holds a court for those who speak to her, and she is perpetually trying voices. She recognized Mr. Lowell's from the first, and appointed him really her speaker-in-chief. She has a peculiar need, which when you know her well you understand, of being eased off with herself, and the American minister speedily appeared just the man to ease her. He played into her talk and her speeches, her commemorations and functions, her dinners and discussions, her editorials and anecdotes. She has immense wheels which are always going round, and the ponderous precision of which can be observed only on the spot. They naturally demand something to grind, and the machine holds out great iron hands and draws in reputations and talents, or sometimes only names and phrases.

Mr. Lowell immediately found himself in England, whether to his surprise or no I am unable to say, the first of after-dinner speakers. It was perhaps somewhat to the surprise of his public there, for it was not to have been calculated in advance that he would have become so expert in his own country—a country sparing of feast-days and ceremonies. His practice had been great before he came to London, but his performance there would have been a strain upon any practice. It was a point of honor with him never to refuse a challenge, and this attitude, under the circumstances, was heroic, for he became a convenience that really tended to multiply occasions. It was exactly his high competence in these directions that constituted the practical good effect of his mission, the particular manner in which it made for civilization. It was the *revanche* of letters; that throughout was the particular note of the part he played. There would have been no *revanche* if he had played it inadequately; therefore it was a pleasure to feel that he was accomplished up to the hilt. Those who didn't like him pronounced him too accomplished, too omniscient; but, save in a sense that I will specify, I never saw him commit himself unadvisedly, and much is to be forgiven a love of precise knowledge which keeps a man out of mistakes. He had a horror of them; no one was ever more in love with the idea of being right and of keeping others from being wrong. The famous Puritan conscience, which was a persistent part of his heredity, operated in him perhaps most strongly on the scholarly side. He enjoyed the detail of research and the discussion of differences, and he had an instinct for rectification which was unflinching. All this formed a part of the enviability I have noted—the serenity of that larger reputation which came to him late in life, which had been paid for in advance, and in regard to which his finished discharge of his diplomatic duties acted, if not certainly as a cause, at least as a stimulus. The reputation was not doubtless the happiest thing; the happiest thing was the inward opportunity, the chance to absorb into an intelligence extraordinarily prepared a peculiarly full revelation.

He had studied English history for forty years in the texts, and at last he could study it in the pieces themselves, could handle and verify the relics. For the man who in such a position recognizes his advantages England makes herself a museum of illustration. She is at home in the comfortable dust of her ages, where there is no need of excavation, as she has never been buried, and the explorer finds the ways as open to him as the corridors of an exhibition. It was an exhibition of which Mr. Lowell never grew tired, for it was infinitely various and living; it brought him back repeatedly after his public mission had expired, and it was perpetually suggestive to him while that mission lasted. If he played his part so well here—I allude now more particularly to the social and expressive side of it—it was because he was so open to suggestion. Old England spoke to him so much as a man of letters that it was inevitable he should answer her back. On the firmness and tact with which he acquitted himself of his strictly diplomatic work I shall not presume to touch; his success was promptly appreciated in quarters where the official record may be found, as well as in others less discoverable to-day, columns congruous with their vituperative "headings," where it must be looked for between the lines. These latter responsibilities, begotten mainly of the great Irish complication, were heavy ones, but they were presumably the keenest interest of his term, and I include them essentially in the picture afforded by that term of the supremely symmetrical literary life—the life in which the contrasts have been effectively timed; in which the invading and acclaiming world has entered too late to interfere, to distract, but still in time to fertilize; in which contacts have multiplied and horizons widened gradually; in which, in short, the dessert has come after the dinner, the answer after the question, and the proof after the patience.

I may seem to exaggerate in Mr. Lowell's history the importance of the last dozen years of his life—especially if the reckoning be made of the amount of characteristic production that preceded them. He was the same admirable writer that he appears to-day before he touched diplomacy—he had already given to the world the volumes on which his reputation rests. I cannot attempt in this place and at this hour a critical estimate of his writings; the perspective is too short and our acquaintance too recent. Yet I have been reading him over in fragments, not to judge, but to recall him, and it is as impossible to speak of him without the sense of his high place as it would be with the pretension to be final about it. He looms, in such a renewed impression, very large and ripe and sane, and if he was an admirable man of letters there should be no want of emphasis on the first term of the title. He was indeed in literature a man essentially masculine, upright, downright. Presenting to us survivors that simplified face that I have spoken of, he almost already looks at us as the last accomplished representative of the joy of life. His robust and humorous optimism rounds itself more and more; he has even now something of the air of a classic, and if he really becomes one it will be in virtue of his having placed as fine an irony at the service of hope as certain masters of the other strain have placed at that of despair. Sturdy liberal as he was and contemptuous of all timidities of advance and reservations of faith, one thinks of him to-day, at the point at which we leave him, as the last of the literary conservatives. He took his stand on the ancient cheerful wisdom, many of the ingenious modern emendations of which seemed to him simply droll.

Few things were really so droll as he could make them, and not a great many perhaps are so absolute. The solution of the problem of life lay for him in action, in conduct, in decency; his imagination lighted up to him but scantily the region of analysis and apology. Like all interesting literary figures he is full of tacit as well as of uttered reference to the conditions that engendered him; he really testifies as much as Hawthorne to the New England spirit, though in a totally different tone. The two writers, as witnesses, weigh against each other, and the picture would be imperfect if both had not had a hand in it. If Hawthorne expressed the mysticism and the gloom of the transplanted Puritan, his passive and haunted side, Lowell saw him in the familiar daylight of practice and prosperity and good health. The author of "The Biglow Papers" was surely the healthiest of highly cultivated geniuses, just as he was the least flippant of jesters and the least hysterical of poets. If Hawthorne fairly cherished the idea of evil in man, Lowell's vision of "sin" was operative mainly for a single purpose—that of putting in motion the civic lash. "The Biglow Papers" are mainly an exposure of national injustice and political dishonesty; his satiric ardor was simply the other side of the medal of his patriotism. His poetry is not all satirical, but the highest and most sustained flights of it are patriotic, and in reading it over I am struck with the vivid virtue of this part of it—something strenuous and antique, the watchful citizen smiting the solemn lyre.

The look at life that it embodies is never merely curious, never irresponsible; it is only the author's humor that is whimsical, never his emotion nor his passion. His poetical performance might sometimes, no doubt, be more intensely lyrical, but it is hard to see how it could be more intensely moral—I mean, of course, in the widest sense of the term. His play is as good as a game in the open air; but when he is serious he is as serious as Wordsworth, and much more compact. He is the poet of pluck and purpose and action, of the gayety and liberty of virtue. He commemorates all manly pieties and affections, but rarely conceals his mistrust of overbrimming sensibility. If the ancients and the Elizabethans, he somewhere says, "had not discovered the picturesque, as we understand it, they found surprisingly fine scenery in man and his destiny, and would have seen something ludicrous, it may be suspected, in the spectacle of a grown man running to hide his head in the apron of the Mighty Mother whenever he had an ache in his finger or got a bruise in the tussle for existence." It is visible that the poetic occasion that was most after his own heart was the storm and stress of the Civil War. He vibrated in this long tension more deeply than in any other experience. It was the time that kindled his steadiest fire, prompted his noblest verse, and gave him what he relished most, a ground for high assurance, a sense of being sturdily in the right and having something to stand up for. He never feared and never shirked the obligation to be positive. Firm and liberal critic as he was, and with nothing of party spirit in his utterance save in the sense that his sincerity was his party, his mind had little affinity with superfine estimates and shades and tints of opinion: when he felt at all he felt altogether — was always on the same side as his likings and loyalties. He had no experimental sympathies, and no part of him was traitor to the rest.

This temper drove the principle of subtlety in his intelligence, which is a need for the last refinement, to take refuge in one particular, and I must add very spacious, corner, where indeed it was capable of the widest expansion. The thing he loved most in the world after his country was the English tongue, of which he was an infallible master, and his devotion to which was, in fact, a sort of agent in his patriotism.

The two passions, at any rate, were closely connected, and I will not pretend to have determined whether the Western republic was dear to him because he held that it was a magnificent field for the language, or whether the language was dear to him because it had felt the impact of Massachusetts. He himself was not unhappily responsible for a large part of the latter occurrence. His linguistic sense is perhaps the thing his reputation may best be trusted to rest upon—I mean, of course, in its large outcome of style. There is a high strain of originality in it, for it is difficult to recall a writer of our day in whom the handling of words has been at once such an art and such a science. Mr. Lowell's generous temperament seems here to triumph in one quarter, while his educated patience triumphs in the other. When a man loves words singly he is apt not to care for them in an order, just as a very great painter may be quite indifferent to the chemical composition of his colors. But Mr. Lowell was both chemist and artist; the only wonder was that with so many theories about language he should have had so much lucidity left for practice. He used it both as an antiquarian and as a lover of life, and was a capital instance of the possible harmony between imagination and knowledge — a living proof that the letter does not necessarily kill.

His work represents this reconciled opposition, referable as it is half to the critic and half to the poet. If either half suffers just a little it is perhaps in places his poetry, a part of which is I scarcely know what to say but too literary, more the result of an interest in the general form than of the stirred emotion. One feels at moments that he speaks in verse mainly because he is penetrated with what verse has achieved. But these moments are occasional, and when the stirred emotion does give a hand to the interest in the general form the product is always of the highest order. His poems written during the war all glow with a splendid fusion—one can think of nothing at once more personal and, in the highest sense of the word, more professional. To me, at any rate, there is something fascinating in the way in which, in the Harvard "Commemoration Ode," for instance, the air of the study mingles with the hot breath of passion. The reader who is eternally bribed by form may ask himself whether Mr. Lowell's prose or his poetry has the better chance of a long life—the hesitation being justified by the rare degree in which the prose has the great qualities of style; but in the presence of some of the splendid stanzas inspired by the war-time (and among them I include, of course, the second series of "The Biglow Papers") one feels that, whatever shall become of the essays, the transmission from generation to generation of such things as these may safely be left to the national conscience. They translate with equal exaltation and veracity the highest national mood, and it is in them that all younger Americans, those now and lately reaching manhood, may best feel the great historic throb, the throb unknown to plodding peace. No poet surely has ever placed the concrete idea of his country in a more romantic light than Mr. Lowell; none certainly, speaking as an American to Americans, has found on its behalf accents more eloquently tender, more beguiling to the imagination.

> "Dear land whom triflers now make bold to scorn
> (Thee from whose forehead Earth awaits her morn).
>
> "Oh Beautiful! my Country! ours once more!
>   Smoothing thy gold of war-dishevelled hair
> O'er such sweet brows as never other wore,
>   And letting thy set lips,
>   Freed from wrath's pale eclipse,
> The rosy edges of their smile lay bare!"

Great poetry is made only by a great meaning, and the national bias, I know, never made anything better that was not good in itself; but each time I read over the Harvard "Commemoration Ode" the more full and strong, the more august and pathetic, does it appear. This is only a proof that if the national sentiment preserves it the national sentiment will show excellent taste — which she has been known in some cases not to do.

If I were not afraid of falling into the tone of literary criticism I should speak of several of the impressions—that is, of the charmed absorption—accompanying an attentive reperusal of the four or five volumes of Mr. Lowell's poetry. The word I have already used comes back to me: it is all so masculine, so fine without being thin, so steadied by the temperament of the author. It is intensely literary and yet intensely warm, warm with the contact of friendly and domestic things, loved local sights and sounds, the color and odor of New England, and (here particularly warm without fever) with the sanest, lucidest intellectual life. There is something of seasonable nature in every verse — the freshness of the spirit sociable with earth and sky and stream. In the best things there is the incalculable magic note—all the more effective from the general ground-tone of reason. What could be more strangely sweet than the little poem of "Phœbe," in " Heartsease and Rue "—a reminiscence of the saddest of small bird-notes caught in the dimmest of wakeful dawns? What could be more largely vivid, more in the grand style of friendship and portraiture, than the masterly composition on the death of Agassiz, in which the very tenderness of regret flushes faintly with humor, and ingenuity broadens at every turn into eloquence? Such a poem as this—immensely fortunate in reflecting an extraordinary personality—takes its place with the few great elegies in our language, gives a hand to "Lycidas" and to "Thyrsis."

I may not go into detail, or I should speak of twenty other things, especially of the mellow, witty wisdom of "The Cathedral" and of the infinite, intricate delicacy of "Endymion"—more tremulous, more penetrating than any other of the author's poetic productions, I think, and exceptionally fine in surface. As for "The Biglow Papers," they seem to me, in regard to their author, not so much produced as productive—productive of a clear, delightful image of the temper and nature of the man. One says of them not that they are *by* him, but that they are his very self, so full of his opinions and perceptions, his humor and his wit, his character, his experience, his talk, and his intense consciousness of race. They testify to many things, but most of all to the thing I have last named; and it may seem to those whose observation of the author was most complete during the concluding years of his life that they could testify to nothing more characteristic. If he was inveterately, in England and on the Continent, the American abroad (though jealous, indeed, of the liberty to be at home even there), so the lucubrations of Parson Wilbur and his contributors are an unsurpassably deliberate exhibition of the primitive home-quality. I may seem to be going far when I say that they constitute to my sense the author's most literary production; they exemplify, at any rate, his inexhaustible interest in the question of style and his extraordinary acuteness in dealing with it. They are a wonderful study of style ✓ —by which I mean of organized expression—and nothing could be more significant than the fact that he should have put his finest faculty for linguistics at the service of the Yankee character.

He knew more, I think, about the rustic American speech than all others together who have known anything of it, so much more closely, justly, and sympathetically had he noted it. He honored it with the strongest scientific interest, and indeed he may well have been on terms of reciprocity with a dialect that had enabled him to produce a masterpiece. The only drawback I can imagine to a just complacency in this transaction would have been the sense that the people are few, after all, who can measure the minute perfection of the success—a success not only of swift insight, but of patient observation. Mr. Lowell was as capable of patience in illustrating New England idiosyncrasies as he was capable of impatience. He never forgot, at any rate, that he stood there for all such things—stood for them particularly during the years he spent in England; and his attitude was made up of many curious and complicated and admirable elements. He was so proud—not for himself, but for his country—that he felt the need of a kind of official version of everything at home that in other quarters might be judged anomalous. Theoretically he cared little for the judgment of other quarters, and he was always amused—the good-natured British lion in person could not have been more so—at "well-meaning" compliment or commendation; it required, it must be admitted, more tact than is usually current to incur the visitation of neither the sharper nor the sunnier form of his irony. But, in fact, the national consciousness was too acute in him for slumber at his post, and he paid in a certain restlessness the penalty of his imagination, of the fatal sense of perspective and the terrible faculty of comparison. It would have been intolerable to him, moreover, to be an empirical American, and he had organized his loyalty with a thoroughness of which his admirable wit was an efficient messenger. He never anticipated attack, though it would be a meagre account of his attitude to say it was defensive; but he took appreciation for granted, and eased the way for it with reasons that were cleverer in nothing than in appearing casual. These reasons were innumerable, but they were all the reasons of a lover. It was not simply that he loved his country—he was literally in love with it.

If there be two kinds of patriotism, the latent and the patent, his kind was essentially the latter. Some people for whom the world is various and universal, and who dread nothing so much as seeing it minimized, regard this particular sentiment as a purely practical one, a prescription of duty in a given case, like a knack with the coiled hose when the house is on fire or the plunge of the swimmer when a man is overboard. They grudge it a place in the foreground of the spirit—they consider that it shuts out the view. Others find it constantly comfortable and perpetually fresh—find, as it were, the case always given; for them the immediate view *is* the view and the very atmosphere of the mind, so that it is a question not only of performance, but of contemplation as well. Mr. Lowell's horizon was too wide to be curtained out, and his intellectual curiosity such as to have effectually prevented his shutting himself up in his birth-chamber; but if the local idea never kept his intelligence at home, he solved the difficulty by at least never going forth without it. When he quitted the hearth it was with the household god in his hand, and as he delighted in Europe, it was to Europe that he took it. Never had a household god such a magnificent outing, nor was made free of so many strange rites and climes; never, in short, had any patriotism such a liberal airing. If, however, Mr. Lowell was loath to admit that the American order could have an infirmity, I think it was because it would have cost him so much to acknowledge that it could have communicated one to an object that he cherished as he cherished the English tongue. *That* was the innermost atmosphere of his mind, and he never could have afforded on this general question any policy but a policy of annexation. He was capable of convictions in the light of which it was clear that the language he wrote so admirably had encountered in the United States not corruption, but conservation. Any conviction of his on this subject was a contribution to science, and he was zealous to show that the speech of New England was most largely that of an England older and more vernacular than the England that to-day finds it queer. He was capable of writing perfect American to bring out this archaic element. He kept in general the two tongues apart, save in so far as his English style betrayed a connection by a certain American tact in the art of leaving out. He was perhaps sometimes slightly paradoxical in the contention that the language had incurred no peril in its Western adventures; this is the sense in which I meant just now that he occasionally crossed the line. The difficulty was not that his vision of pure English could not fail in America sometimes to be clouded — the peril was for his vision of pure American. His standard was the highest, and the wish was often no doubt father to the thought. "The Biglow Papers" are delightful, but nothing could be less like "The Biglow Papers" than the style of the American newspaper. He lent his wit to his theories, but one or two of them lived on him like unthrifty sons.

None the less it was impossible to be witness of his general action during his residence in England without feeling that, not only by the particular things he did, but by the general thing he was, he contributed to a large ideal of peace. We certainly owe to him (and by "we" I mean both countries—he made that plural elastic) a mitigation of danger. There is always danger between country and country, and danger in small and shameful forms as well as big and inspiring ones; but the danger is less and the dream of peace more rosy when they have been beguiled into a common admiration. A common aversion even will do—the essential thing is the disposition to share. The poet, the writer, the speaker ministers to this community; he is Orpheus with his lute —the lute that pacifies the great, stupid beasts of international prejudice; so that if a quarrel takes place over the piping form of the loved of Apollo it is as if he were rent again by the Mænads. It was a charm to the observant mind to see how Mr. Lowell kept the Mænads in their place—a work admirably continued by his successor in office, who had, indeed, under his roof an inestimable assistant in the process. Mr. Phelps was not, as I may say, single-handed; which was his predecessor's case even for some time prior to an irreparable bereavement. The prying Furies—at any rate, during these years—were effectually snubbed, and will, it is to be hoped, never again hold their snaky heads very high. The spell that worked upon them was simply the voice of civilization, and Mr. Lowell's advantage was that he happened to find himself in a supremely good place for producing it. He produced it both consciously and unconsciously, both officially and privately, from principle and from instinct, in the hundred spots, on the thousand occasions which it is one of the happiest idiosyncrasies of English life to supply; and since I have spoken so distinctly of his patriotism, I must add that, after all, he exercised the virtue most in this particular way. His new friends liked him because he was at once so fresh and so ripe, and this was predominantly what he understood by being a good American. It was by being one in this sense that he broke the heart of the Furies.

The combination made a quality which pervaded his whole intellectual character; for the quality of his diplomatic action, of his public speeches, of his talk, of his influence, was simply the genius that we had always appreciated in his critical writings. The hours and places with which he had to deal were not equally inspiring; there was inevitably colorless company, there were dull dinners, influences prosaic and functions mechanical; but he was substantially always the messenger of the Muses and of that particular combination of them which had permitted him to include a tenth in their number—the infallible sister to whom humor is dear. I mean that the man and the author, in him, were singularly convertible; it was what made the author so vivid. It was also what made that voice of civilization to whose harmony I have alluded practically the same thing as the voice of literature. Mr. Lowell's style was an indefeasible part of him, as his correspondence, if it be ever published, will copiously show; it was in all relations his natural channel of communication. This is why, at the opening of this paper, I ventured to speak of his happy exercise of a great opportunity as at bottom the revenge of letters. This, at any rate, the literary observer was free to see in it; such an observer made a cross against the day, as an anniversary for form, and an anniversary the more memorable that form, when put to tests that might have been called severe, was so far from being found wanting in substance; met the occasion, in fact, so completely. I do not pretend that, during Mr. Lowell's residence in England, the public which he found constituted there spent most of its time in reading his essays; I only mean that the faculty it relished in him most was the faculty most preserved for us in his volumes of criticism.

It is not an accident that I do not linger over the contents of these volumes—this has not been a part of my undertaking. They will not go out of fashion, they will keep their place and hold their own; for they are full of broad-based judgment and of those stamped sentences of which we are as naturally retentive as of gold and silver coin. Reading them lately over in large portions, I was struck not only with the particular "good things" that abound in them, but with the soundness and fulness of their inspiration. It is intensely the air of letters, but it is like that of some temperate and restorative clime. I judge them, perhaps, with extravagant fondness, for I am attached to the class to which they belong; I like such an atmosphere, I like the aromatic odor of the book-room. In turning over Mr. Lowell's critical pages I seem to hear the door close softly behind me and to find in the shaded lamplight the conditions most in harmony with the sentient soul of man. I see an apartment brown and book-lined, which is the place in the world most convertible into other places. The turning of the leaves, the crackling of the fire, are the only things that break its stillness— the stillness in which mild miracles are wrought. These are the miracles of evocation, of resurrection, of transmission, of insight, of history, of poetry. It may be a little room, but it is a great space; it may be a deep solitude, but it is a mighty concert. In this critical chamber of Mr. Lowell's there is a charm, to my sense, in knowing what is outside of the closed door—it intensifies both the isolation and the experience. The big new Western order is outside, and yet within all seems as immemorial as Persia. It is like a little lighted cabin, full of the ingenuities of home, in the gray of a great ocean. Such ingenuities of home are what represent in Mr. Lowell's case the conservatism of the author. His home was the past that dipped below the verge—it was there that his taste was at ease. From what quarter his disciples in the United States will draw their sustenance it is too soon to say; the question will be better answered when we have the disciples more clearly in our eye.

We seem already, however, to distinguish the quarter from which they will *not* draw it. Few of them as yet appear to have in their hand, or rather in their head, any such treasure of knowledge.

It was when his lifetime was longest that the fruit of culture was finest in him and that his wit was most profuse. In the admirable address on Democracy that he pronounced at Birmingham in 1884, in the beautiful speech on the Harvard anniversary of 1886, things are so supremely well said that we feel ourselves reading some consecrated masterpiece; they represent great literary art in its final phase of great naturalness. There are places where he seems in mystical communication with the richest sources of English prose. "But this imputed and vicarious longevity, though it may be obscurely operative in our lives and fortunes, is no valid offset for the shortness of our days, nor widens by a hair's-breadth the horizon of our memories." He sounds like a younger brother of Bacon and of Milton, either of whom, for instance, could not have uttered a statelier word on the subject of the relinquishment of the required study of Greek than that "Oblivion looks in the face of the Grecian Muse only to forget her errand." On the other hand, in the address delivered in 1884 before the English Wordsworth Society, he sounds like no one but his inveterately felicitous self. In certain cases Wordsworth, like Elias the prophet, "'stands up as fire and his word burns like a lamp.' But too often, when left to his own resources and to the conscientious performance of the duty laid upon him to be a great poet *quand même*, he seems diligently intent on producing fire by the primitive method of rubbing the dry sticks of his blank verse one against the other, while we stand in shivering expectation of the flame that never comes." It would be difficult to express better the curious evening chill of the author of "The Excursion," which is so like the conscious mistake of camping out in autumn.

It was an extreme satisfaction to the very many persons in England who valued Mr. Lowell's society that the termination of his official mission there proved not the termination of the episode. He came back for his friends—he would have done anything for his friends. He also, I surmise, came back somewhat for himself, inasmuch as he entertained an affection for London which he had no reason for concealing. For several successive years he reappeared there with the brightening months, and I am not sure that this irresponsible and less rigorously sociable period did not give him his justest impressions. It surrendered him, at any rate, more completely to his friends and to several close and particularly valued ties. He felt that he had earned the right to a few frank predilections. English life is a big pictured story-book, and he could dip into the volume where he liked. It was altogether delightful to turn some of the pages with him, and especially to pause—for the marginal commentary in finer type, some of it the model of the illuminating foot-note—over the interminable chapter of London.

It is very possible not to feel the charm of London at all; the foreigner who feels it must be tolerably sophisticated. It marks the comparative community of the two big branches of the English race that of all aliens, under this heavy pressure, Americans are the most submissive. They are capable of loving the capital of their race almost with passion, which for the most part is the way it is loved when it is not hated. The sentiment was strong in Mr. Lowell; one of the branches of his tree of knowledge had planted itself and taken root here, and at the end he came back every year to sit in the shade of it. He gave himself English summers, and if some people should say that the gift was scarcely liberal, others who met him on this ground will reply that such seasons drew from him in the circle of friendship a radiance not inherent in their complexion. This association became a feature of the London May and June —it held its own even in the rank confusion of July. It pervaded the quarter he repeatedly inhabited, where a commonplace little house, in the neighborhood of the Paddington station, will long wear in its narrow front, to the inner sense of many passers, a mystical gold-lettered tablet. Here he came and went, during several months, for such and such a succession of years; here one could find him at home in the late afternoon, in his lengthened chair, with his cherished pipe and his table piled high with books. Here he practised little jesting hospitalities, for he was irrepressibly and amusingly hospitable. Whatever he was in his latest time, it was, even in muffled miseries of gout, with a mastery of laughter and forgetfulness. Nothing amused him more than for people to dine with him, and few things certainly amused *them* as much. His youth came back to him not once for all, but twenty times for every occasion. He was certainly the most boyish of learned doctors.

This was always particularly striking during the several weeks of August and September that he had formed the habit of spending at Whitby, on the Yorkshire coast. It was here, I think, that he was most naturally at his ease, most humorously evaded the hard bargain of time. The place is admirable—an old, red-roofed fishing-town in one of the indentations of a high, brave coast, with the ruins of a great abbey just above it, an expanse of purple moor behind, and a convenient extension in the way of an informal little modern watering-place. The mingled breath of the sea and the heather makes a medium that it is a joy to inhale, and all the land is picturesque and noble, a happy hunting-ground for the good walker and the lover of grand lines and fine detail. Mr. Lowell was wonderful in both these characters, and it was in the active exercise of them that I saw him last. He was in such conditions a delightful host and a prime initiator. Two of these happy summer days on the occasion of his last visit to Whitby are marked possessions of my memory; one of them a ramble on the warm, wide moors, after a rough lunch at a little, stony upland inn, in company charming and intimate, the thought of which to-day is a reference to a double loss; the other an excursion, made partly by a longish piece of railway, in his society alone, to

Rievaulx Abbey, most fragmentary, but most graceful, of ruins. The day at Rievaulx was as exquisite as I could have wished it if I had known that it denoted a limit, and in the happy absence of any such revelation altogether given up to adventure and success. I remember the great curving green terrace in Lord Feversham's park — prodigious and surely unique; it hangs over the abbey like a theatrical curtain — and the temples of concord, or whatever they are, at either end of it, and the lovable view, and the dear little dowdy inn-parlor at Helmsley, where there is, moreover, a massive fragment of profaner ruin, a bit of battered old castle, in the grassy *préau* of which (it was a perfect English picture) a company of well-grown young Yorkshire folk of both sexes were making lawn-tennis balls fly in and out of the past. I recall with vividness the very waits and changes of the return and our pleased acceptance of everything. We parted on the morrow, but I met Mr. Lowell a little later in Devonshire—O clustered charms of Ottery!—and spent three days in his company. I travelled back to London with him, and saw him for the last time at Paddington. He was to sail immediately for America. I went to take leave of him, but I missed him, and a day or two later he was gone.

I note these particulars, as may easily be imagined, wholly for their reference to himself—for the emphasized occasion they give to remembrance and regret. Yet even remembrance and regret, in such a case, have a certain free relief, for our final thought of James Russell Lowell is that what he consistently lived for remains of him. There is nothing ineffectual in his name and fame—they stand for large and delightful things. He is one of the happy figures of literature. He had his trammels and his sorrows, but he drank deep of the tonic draught, and he will long count as an erect fighting figure on the side of optimism and beauty. He was strong without narrowness, he was wise without bitterness and glad without fatuity. That appears for the most part the temper of those who speak from the quiet English heart, the steady pulses of which were the sufficient rhythm of his eloquence. This source of influence will surely not forfeit its long credit in the world so long as we continue occasionally to know it by what is so rich in performance and so stainless in character.

1891.

FRANCES ANNE KEMBLE[1]

Mrs. Kemble used often to say of people who met her during the later years of her life, " No wonder they were surprised and bewildered, poor things— they supposed I was dead!" Dying January 15th, 1893, in her eighty-third year, she had outlived a whole order of things, her "time," as we call it, and in particular so many of her near contemporaries, so many relations and friends, witnesses and admirers, so much, too, of her own robust and ironic interest in life, that the event, as regards attention excited, may well be said to have introduced her to unconscious generations. To that little group of the faithful for whom she had represented rare things, and who stood by with the sense of an emptier and vulgarer world when, at Kensal Green, her remains were laid in the same earth as her father's, the celebrity of an age almost antediluvian—to these united few the form in which the attention I speak of roused itself was for the most part a strange revelation of ignorance. It was in so many cases—I allude, though perhaps I ought not, to some of the newspapers—also a revelation of flippant ill-nature trying to pass as information, that the element of perplexity was added to the element of surprise. Mrs. Kemble all her life was so great a figure for those who were not in ignorance, the distinction and interest of her character were, among them, so fundamental an article of faith, that such persons were startled at finding themselves called to be, not combative in the cause of her innumerable strong features (they were used to that), but insistent in respect to her eminence. No common attachment probably ever operated as a more genial bond, a more immediate password, than an appreciation of this extraordinary woman; so that inevitably, to-day, those who had the privilege in the evening of her life of knowing her better will have expressed to each other the hope for some commemoration more proportionate. The testimony of such of them as might have hesitated will certainly in the event have found itself singularly quickened. The better word will yet be spoken, and indeed if it should drop from all the lips to which it has risen with a rush, Mrs. Kemble's fine memory would become the occasion of a lively literature. She was an admirable subject for the crystallization of anecdote, for encompassing legend. If we have a definite after-life in the amount of illustration that may gather about us, few vivid names ought to fade more slowly.

As it was not, however, the least interesting thing in her that she was composed of contrasts and opposites, so the hand that should attempt a living portrait would be conscious of some conflicting counsel. The public and the private were both such inevitable consequences of her nature that we take perforce into account the difficulty of reconciling one with the other.

If she had had no public hour there would have been so much less to admire her for; and if she had not hated invasion and worldly noise we should not have measured her disinterestedness and her noble indifference. A prouder nature never affronted the long humiliation of life, and to few persons can it have mattered less on the whole how either before or after death the judgment of men was likely to sound. She had encountered publicity as she had encountered bad weather; but the public, on these occasions, was much more aware of her, I think, than she was aware of the public. With her immense sense of comedy she would have been amused at being vindicated, and leaving criticism far behind, would have contributed magnificent laughable touches—in the wonderful tone in which she used to read her Falstaff or even her Mrs. Quickly—to any picture of her peculiarities. She talked of herself in unreserved verses, in published records and reminiscences; but this overflow of her conversation, for it was nothing more, was no more directed at an audience than a rural pedestrian's humming of a tune. She talked as she went, from wealth of animal spirits. She had a reason for everything she did (not always, perhaps, a good one), but the last reason she would have given for writing her books was the desire to see if people would read them. Her attitude towards publication was as little like the usual attitude in such a matter as possible —which was true indeed of almost any relation in which she happened to find herself to any subject. Therefore if it is impossible to say for her how large she was without going into the details, we may remember both her own aloofness and her own spontaneity, and above all, that every impulse to catch her image before it melts away is but a natural echo of her presence. That intense presence simply continues to impose itself.

Not the least of the sources of its impressiveness in her later years was the historic value attached to it—its long backward reach into time. Even if Mrs. Kemble had been a less remarkable person she would have owed a distinction to the far-away past to which she gave continuity, would have been interesting from the curious contacts she was able, as it were, to transmit. She made us touch her aunt Mrs. Siddons, and whom does Mrs. Siddons not make us touch? She had sat to Sir Thomas Lawrence for her portrait, and Sir Thomas Lawrence was in love with Sir Joshua's Tragic Muse. She had breakfasted with Sir Walter Scott, she had sung with Tom Moore, she had listened to Edmund Kean and to Mademoiselle Mars. These things represented a privilege of which the intensity grew with successive years, with the growth of a modernness in which she found herself—not in the least plaintively indeed—expatriated. The case was the more interesting that the woman herself was deeply so; relics are apt to be dead, and Mrs. Kemble, for all her antecedents, was a force long unspent. She could communicate the thrill if her auditor could receive it; the want of vibration was much more likely to be in the auditor. She had been, in short, a celebrity in the twenties, had attracted the town while the century was still almost as immature as herself. The great thing was that from the first she had abundantly lived and, in more than one meaning of the word, acted—felt, observed, imagined, reflected, reasoned, gathered in her passage the abiding impression, the sense and suggestion of things. That she was the last of the greater Kembles could never be a matter of indifference, even to those of her friends who had reasons less abstract for being fond of her; and it was a part of her great range and the immense variety of the gifts by which she held attention, whisked it from one kind of subjugation to another, that the "town" she had astonished in her twentieth year was, for the London-lover, exactly the veritable town, that of the old books and prints, the old legends and landmarks. Her own love for London, like her endurance of Paris, was small; she treated her birthplace at best—it was the way she treated many things—as an alternative that would have been impossible if she had cared; but the great city had laid its hand upon her from the first (she was born in that Newman Street which had a later renown, attested by Thackeray, as the haunt of art-students and one of the boundaries of Bohemia), playing a large part in her mingled experience and folding her latest life in an embrace which could be grandmotherly even for old age.

She had figured in the old London world, which lived again in her talk and, to a great degree, in her habits and standards and tone. This background, embroidered with her theatrical past, so unassimilated, but so vivid in her handsome hereditary head and the unflagging drama of her manner, was helped by her agitated, unsettled life to make her what I have called historic. If her last twenty years were years of rest, it was impossible for an observer of them not to feel from how many things she was resting—from how long a journey and how untempered a fate, what an expenditure of that rich personality which always moved all together and with all its violent force. Whatever it was, at any rate, this extraordinary mixture of incongruous things, of England and France in her blood, of America and England in her relationships, of the footlights and the glaciers in her activity, of conformity and contumacy in her character, and tragedy and comedy in her talk —whatever it was, there was always this strangeness and this amusement for the fancy, that the beginning of it had been anything so disconnected as the elder Covent Garden, the Covent Garden of Edmund Kean (I find his name on a playbill of the year of her first appearance), and a tremendous success as Juliet in 1829. There was no convenient and handy formula for Mrs. Kemble's genius, and one had to take her career, the juxtaposition of her interests, exactly as one took her disposition, for a remarkably fine cluster of inconsistencies. But destiny had turned her out a Kemble, and had taken for granted of a Kemble certain things—especially a theatre and a tone; in this manner she was enabled to present as fine an example as one could wish of submission to the general law at the sacrifice of every approach, not to freedom, which she never could forego, but to the superficial symmetry that enables critics to classify. This facility her friends enjoyed with her as little as they enjoyed some others; but it was a small drawback in the perception of that variety, the result of many endowments, which made other company by contrast alarmingly dull and yet left one always under the final impression of her sincerity. It was her character, in its generosity and sincerity, that was simple; it was her great gifts and her intelligence that banished the insular from her attitude and even, with her rich vein of comedy, made a temptation for her of the bewilderment of the simple.

Since it was indeed, however, as the daughter of the Kembles, the histrionic figure, the far-away girlish Juliet and Julia, that the world primarily regarded her and that her admirably mobile face and expressive though not effusive manner seemed, with however little intention, to present her, this side of her existence should doubtless be disposed of at the outset of any attempted sketch of her, even should such a sketch be confined by limits permitting not the least minuteness. She left it behind her altogether as she went, very early in life indeed, but her practice of theatrical things is a point the more interesting as it threw a strong light not only on many of those things themselves, but on the nature of her remarkable mind. No such mind and no such character were surely in any other case concerned with them. Besides having an extreme understanding of them, she had an understanding wholly outside of them and larger than any place they can fill; and if she came back to them in tone, in reminiscence, in criticism (she was susceptible to playhouse beguilement to her very latest years), it was a return from excursions which ought logically to have resulted in alienation. Nobody connected with the stage could have savored less of the "shop." She was a reactionary Kemble enough, but if she got rid of her profession she could never get rid of her instincts, which kept her dramatic long after she ceased to be theatrical. They existed in her, as her unsurpassable voice and facial play existed, independently of ambition or cultivation, of disenchantment or indifference. She never ceased to be amusing on the subject of that vivid face which was so much more scenic than she intended, and always declined to be responsible for her manner, her accents, her eyes. These things, apart from family ties, were her only link with the stage, which she had from the first disliked too much to have anything so submissive as a taste about it. It was a convenience for her which heredity made immediate, just as it was a convenience to write, offhand, the most entertaining books, which from the day they went to the publisher she never thought of again nor listened to a word about; books inspired by her spirits, really, the high spirits and the low, by her vitality, her love of utterance and of letters, her natural positiveness. She took conveniences for granted in life, and, full as she was of ideas and habits, hated pretensions about personal things and fine names for plain ones. There never was any felicity in approaching her on the ground of her writings, or indeed in attempting to deal with her as a woman professedly "intellectual," a word that, in her horror of *coteries* and current phrases, she always laughed to scorn.

All these repudiations together, however, didn't alter the fact that when the author of these pages was a very small boy the reverberation of her first visit to the United States, though it had occurred years before, was still in the air: I allude to the visit of 1832, with her father, of which her first "Journal," published in 1835, is so curious, so amusing, and, with its singular testimony to the taste of the hour, so living a specimen. This early book, by the way, still one of the freshest pictures of what is called a "brilliant girl" that our literature possesses, justifies wonderfully, with its spontaneity and gayety, the sense it gives of variety and vitality, of easy powers and overtopping spirits, the great commotion she produced in her youth. Marie Bashkirtseff was in the bosom of the future, but as a girlish personality she had certainly been anticipated; in addition to which it may be said that a comparison of the two diaries would doubtless lead to considerations enough on the difference between health and disease. However this may be, one of the earliest things that I remember with any vividness is a drive in the country, near New York, in the course of which the carriage passed a lady on horseback who had stopped to address herself with some vivacity to certain men at work by the road. Just as we had got further one of my elders exclaimed to the other, "Why, it's Fanny Kemble!" and on my inquiring who was the bearer of this name, which fell upon my ear for the first time, I was informed that she was a celebrated actress. It was added, I think, that she was a brilliant reader of Shakespeare, though I am not certain that the incident occurred after she had begun her career of reading. The American cities, at any rate, were promptly filled with the glory of this career, so that there was a chance for me to be vaguely perplexed as to the bearing on the performance, which I heard constantly alluded to, of her equestrian element, so large a part of her youth. Did she read on horseback, or was her acting one of the attractions of the circus? There had been something in the circumstances (perhaps the first sight of a living Amazon—an apparition comparatively rare then in American suburbs) to keep me from forgetting the lady, about whom gathered still other legends than the glamour of the theatre; at all events she was planted from that moment so firmly in my mind that when, as a more developed youngster, after an interval of several years, I was taken for education's sake to hear her, the occasion was primarily a relief to long suspense. It became, however, and there was another that followed it, a joy by itself and an impression ineffaceable.

This was in London, and I remember even from such a distance of time every detail of the picture and every tone of her voice. The two readings—

one was of *King Lear*, the other of *A Midsummer-Night's Dream* — took place in certain Assembly Rooms in St. John's Wood, which, in immediate contiguity to the Eyre Arms tavern, appear still to exist, and which, as I sometimes pass, I even yet never catch a glimpse of without a faint return of the wonder and the thrill. The choice of the place, then a "local centre," shows how London ways have altered. The reader dressed in black velvet for *Lear* and in white satin for the comedy, and presented herself to my young vision as a being of formidable splendor. I must have measured in some degree the power and beauty of her performance, for I perfectly recall the sense of irreparable privation with which a little later I heard my parents describe the emotion produced by her *Othello*, given at the old Hanover Square Rooms and to which I had not been conducted. I have seen both the tragedy and the "Dream" acted several times since then, but I have always found myself waiting vainly for any approach to the splendid volume of Mrs. Kemble's "Howl, howl, howl!" in the one, or to the animation and variety that she contributed to the other. I am confident that the most exquisite of fairy-tales never was such a "spectacle" as when she read, I was going to say mounted, it. Is this reminiscence of the human thunder-roll that she produced in *Lear* in some degree one of the indulgences with which we treat our childhood? I think not, in the light of innumerable subsequent impressions. These showed that the force and the imagination were still there; why then should they not, in the prime of their magnificent energy, have borne their fruit? The former of the two qualities, leaving all the others, those of intention and discrimination, out of account, sufficed by itself to excite the astonishment of a genius no less energetic than Madame Ristori, after she had tasted for a couple of hours of the life that Mrs. Kemble's single personality could impart to a Shakespearean multitude. "Che forza, ma che forza, che forza!" she kept repeating, regarding it simply as a feat of power.

It is always a torment to the later friends of the possessor of a great talent to have to content themselves with the supposition and the hearsay; but in Mrs. Kemble's society there were precious though casual consolations for the treacheries of time. She was so saturated with Shakespeare that she had made him, as it were, the air she lived in, an air that stirred with his words whenever she herself was moved, whenever she was agitated or impressed, reminded or challenged. He was indeed her utterance, the language she spoke when she spoke most from herself. He had said the things that she would have wished most to say, and it was her greatest happiness, I think, that she could always make him her obeisance by the same borrowed words that expressed her emotion. She was as loyal to him — and it is saying not a little — as she was to those most uplifted Alps which gave her the greater part of the rest of her happiness and to which she paid her annual reverence with an inveteracy, intensely characteristic, that neither public nor private commotions, neither revolutions nor quarantines, neither war nor pestilence nor floods, could disconcert. Therefore one came in for many windfalls, for echoes and refrains, for snatches of speeches and scenes. These things were unfailing illustrations of the great luxury one had been born to miss. Moreover, there were other chances — the chances of anecdote, of association, and that, above all, of her company at the theatre, or rather on the return from the theatre, to which she often went, occasions when, on getting, after an interval of profound silence, to a distance — never till then — some train of quotation and comparison was kindled. As all roads lead to Rome, so all humor and all pathos, all quotation, all conversation, it may be said, led for Mrs. Kemble to the poet she delighted in and for whose glory it was an advantage — one's respect needn't prevent one from adding — that she was so great a talker.

Twice again, after these juvenile evenings I have permitted myself to recall, I had the opportunity of hearing her read whole plays. This she did repeatedly, though she had quitted public life, in one or two American cities after the civil war; she had never been backward in lending such aid to "appeals," to charitable causes, and she had a sort of American patriotism, a strange and conditioned sentiment of which there is more to be said, a love for the United States which was a totally different matter from a liking, and which, from 1861 to 1865, made her throb with American passions. She returned to her work to help profusely the Sanitary Commission or some other deserving enterprise that was a heritage of the war-time. One of the plays I speak of in this connection was *The Merchant of Venice*, the other was *Henry V.* No Portia was so noble and subtle as that full-toned Portia of hers — such a picturesque great lady, such a princess of poetry and comedy. This circumstance received further light on an occasion — years afterwards, in London — of my going to see the play with her. If the performance had been Shakespearean there was always an epilogue that was the real interest of the evening—a beautiful rally, often an exquisite protest, of all her own instinct, in the brougham, in the Strand, in the Brompton Road. Those who sometimes went with her to the play in the last years of her life will remember the Juliets, the Beatrices, the Rosalinds whom she could still make vivid without an accessory except the surrounding London uproar. There was a Beatrice in particular, one evening, who seemed to have stepped with us into the carriage in pursuance of her demonstration that this charming creature, all rapidity and resonance of wit, should ring like a silver bell. We might have been to the French comedy—the sequel was only the more interesting, for, with her love of tongues and her ease in dealing with them, her gift of tone was not so poor a thing as to be limited to her own language. Her own language indeed was a plural number; French rose to her lips as quickly and as racily as English, and corresponded to the strong strain she owed to the foreignness of her remarkable mother, a person as to whom, among the many persons who lived in her retrospects, it was impossible, in her company, not to feel the liveliest curiosity; so natural was it to be convinced of the distinction of the far-away lady whose easy gift to the world had been two such daughters as Fanny Kemble and Adelaide Sartoris. There were indeed friends of these brilliant women —all their friends of alien birth, it may be said, and the list was long—who were conscious of a very direct indebtedness to the clever and continental Mrs. Charles Kemble, an artist, recordedly, and a character. She had in advance enlarged the situation, multiplied the elements, contributed space and air. Had she not notably interposed in the interest of that facility of intercourse to which nothing ministers so much as an imagination for the difference of human races and the variety of human conditions?

This imagination Mrs. Kemble, as was even more the case with her eminent sister, had in abundance; her conversation jumped gayly the Chinese wall, and if she " didn't like foreigners " it was not, as many persons can attest, because she didn't understand them. She declared of herself, freely—no faculty for self-derision was ever richer or droller—that she was not only intensely English, but the model of the British Philistine. She knew what she meant, and so assuredly did her friends; but somehow the statement was always made in French; it took her foreignness to support it: "*Ah, vous savez, je suis Anglaise, moi —la plus Anglaise des Anglaises!*" That happily didn't prevent the voice of Mademoiselle Mars from being still in her ear, nor, more importunately yet, the voice of the great Rachel, nor deprive her of the ability to awaken these wonderful echoes. Her memory was full of the great speeches of the old French drama, and it was in her power especially to console, in free glimpses, those of her interlocutors who languished under the sorrow of having come too late for Camille and Hermione. The moment at which, however, she remembered Rachel's deep voice most gratefully was that of a certain grave "*Bien, très bien!*" dropped by it during a private performance of *The Hunchback*, for a charity, at Bridgewater House, I think, when the great actress, a spectator, happened to be seated close to the stage, and the Julia, after one of her finest moments, caught the words. She could repeat, moreover, not only the classic *tirades*, but all sorts of drolleries, couplets and prose, from long-superseded vaudevilles — witness Grassot's shriek, "*Approchez-vouz plus loin!*" as the scandalized daughter of Albion in *Les Anglaises pour Rire*. I scarcely know whether to speak or to be silent — in connection with such remembrances of my own — on the subject of a strange and sad attempt, one evening, to sit through a performance of *The Hunchback*, a play in which, in her girlhood, she had been, and so triumphantly, the first representative of the heroine, and which, oddly enough, she had never seen from "in front." She had gone, reluctantly and sceptically, only because something else that had been planned had failed at the last, and the sense of responsibility became acute on her companion's part when, after the performance had begun, he perceived the turn the affair was likely to take. It was a vulgar and detestable rendering, and the distress of it became greater than could have been feared: it brought back across the gulf of years her different youth and all the ghosts of the dead, the first interpreters — her father, Charles Kemble, the Sir Thomas Clifford, Sheridan Knowles himself, the Master Walter, the vanished Helen, the vanished Modus: they seemed, in the cold, half-empty house and before the tones of their successors, to interpose a mute reproach—a reproach that looked intensely enough out of her eyes when at last, under her breath, she turned to her embarrassed neighbor with a tragic, an unforgettable "How could you bring me to see this thing?"

I have mentioned that *Henry V.* was the last play I heard her read in public, and I remember a declaration of hers that it was the play she loved best to read, better even than those that yielded poetry more various. It was gallant and martial and intensely English, and she was certainly on such evenings the "*Anglaise des Anglaises*" she professed to be. Her splendid tones and her face, lighted like that of a war-goddess, seemed to fill the performance with the hurry of armies and the sound of battle; as in her rendering of *A Midsummer-Night's Dream*, so the illusion was that of a multitude and a pageant. I recall the tremendous ring of her voice, somewhat diminished as it then was, in the culminating "God for Harry, England, and Saint George!" a voice the immense effect of which, in her finest years—the occasion, for instance, of her brief return to the stage in 1847—an old friend just illustrates to me by a reminiscence. She was acting at that period at the Princess's Theatre, with Macready, in whom my informant, then a very young man and an unfledged journalist, remembers himself to have been, for some reason, "surprisingly disappointed." It all seems very ancient history. On one of the evenings of *Macbeth* he was making his way, by invitation, to Douglas Jerrold's box—Douglas Jerrold had a newspaper—when, in the passage, he was arrested by the sense that Mrs. Kemble was already on the stage, reading the letter with which Lady Macbeth makes her entrance. The manner in which she read it, the tone that reached his ears, held him motionless and spellbound till she had finished. To nothing more beautiful had he ever listened, nothing more beautiful was he ever to hear again. This was the sort of impression commemorated in Longfellow's so sincere sonnet, "Ah, precious evenings, all too swiftly sped!" Such evenings for the reader herself sped swiftly as well, no doubt; but they proceeded with a regularity altogether, in its degree, characteristic of her, and some of the rigidities of which she could relate with a drollery that yielded everything but the particular point. The particular point she never yielded—she only yielded afterwards, in overwhelming profusion, some other quite different, though to herself possibly much more inconvenient one: a characteristic of an order that one of her friends probably had in mind in declaring that to have a difference with her was a much less formidable thing than to make it up.

Her manner of dealing with her readings was the despair of her agents and managers, whom she profoundly commiserated, whom she vividly imitated, and who, in their wildest experience of the "temperament of genius" and the oddities of the profession, had never encountered her idiosyncrasies. It threw, indeed, the strongest light upon the relation in which her dramatic talent, and the faculty that in a different nature one would call as a matter of course her artistic sense stood to the rest of her mind, a relation in which such powers, on so great a scale, have probably never but in that single instance found themselves. On the artistic question, in short, she was unique; she disposed of it by a summary process. In other words, she would none of it at all, she recognized in no degree its application to herself. It once happened that one of her friends, in a moment of extraordinary inadvertence, permitted himself to say to her in some argument, "Such a clever woman as you!" He measured the depth of his fall when she challenged him with one of her facial flashes and a "How dare you call me anything so commonplace?" This could pass; but no one could have had the temerity to tell her she was an artist. The chance to discriminate was too close at hand; if *she* was an artist, what name was left for her sister Adelaide, of musical fame, who, with an histrionic equipment scarcely inferior to her own, lived in the brightest air of æsthetics? Mrs. Kemble's case would have been an exquisite one for a psychologist interested in studying the constitution of sincerity. That word expresses the special light by which she worked, though it doubtless would not have solved the technical problem for her if she had not had the good-fortune to be a Kemble. She was a moralist who had come out of a theatrical nest, and if she read Shakespeare in public it was very much because she loved him, loved him in a way that made it odious to her to treat him so commercially. She read straight through the list of his plays—those that constituted her repertory, offering them in a succession from which no consideration of profit or loss ever induced her to depart. Some of them "drew" more than others, *The Merchant of Venice* more than *Measure for Measure*, *As You Like It* more than *Coriolanus*, and to these her men of business vainly tried to induce her either to confine herself or to give a more frequent place: her answer was always her immutable order, and her first service was to her master. If on a given evening the play didn't fit the occasion, so much the worse for the occasion: she had spoken for her poet, and if he had more variety than the "public taste," this was only to his honor.

Like all passionate workers, Mrs. Kemble had her own convictions about the public taste, and those who knew her, moreover, couldn't fail to be acquainted with the chapter — it was a large one — of her superlative Quixotisms. During her American visits, before the war, she would never read in the Southern

States: it was a part of the consistency with which she disapproved of sources of payment proceeding from the "peculiar institution." This was a large field of gain, closed to her, for her marriage to Mr. Butler, her residence in Georgia and the events which followed it, culminating in her separation, had given her, in the South, a conspicuity, a *retentissement*, of the kind that an impresario rejoices in. What would have been precisely insupportable to her was that people should come not for Shakespeare but for Fanny Kemble, and she simply did everything she could to prevent it. Comically out of his reckoning was one of these gentlemen with whom she once happened to talk of a young French actress whose Juliet, in London, had just been a nine days' wonder. "Suppose," she said, with derision, "that, *telle que vous me voyez*, I should go over to Paris and appear as Célimène!" Mrs. Kemble had not forgotten the light of speculation kindled in her interlocutor's eye as he broke out, with cautious and respectful eagerness, "You're not, by chance—a—*thinking* of it, madam?" The only thing that, during these busy years, she had been "thinking of" was the genius of the poet it was her privilege to interpret, in whom she found all greatness and beauty, and with whom for so long she had the great happiness (except her passion for the Alps the only really secure happiness she knew) of living in daily intimacy. There had been other large rewards which would have been thrice as large for a person without those fine perversities that one honored even while one smiled at them, but above all there had been that one. "Think," she often said in later years, "think, if you please, what *company!*" It befell, on some occasion of her being in one of her frequent and admirable narrative moods, that a friend was sufficiently addicted to the perpetual puzzle of art to ask her what preparation, in a series of readings, what degree of rehearsal, as it were, she found necessary for performances so arduous and so complex. "Rehearsal?"—she was, with all the good faith in the world, almost scandalized at the idea. "I may have read over the play, and I think I kept myself quiet." "But was nothing determined, established in advance? weren't your lines laid down, your points fixed?" This was an inquiry which Mrs. Kemble could treat with all the gayety of her irony, and in the light of which her talent exhibited just that disconcerting wilfulness I have already spoken of. She would have been a capture for the disputants who pretend that the actor's emotion must be real, if she had not been indeed, with her hatred both of enrolment and of tea-party æsthetics, too dangerous a recruit for any camp. Priggishness and pedantry excited her ire; woe therefore to those who collectively might have presumed she was on their "side."

She was artistically, I think, a very fine anomaly, and, in relation to the efficacity of what may be called the natural method, the operation of pure sincerity, a witness no less interesting than unconscious. An equally active and fruitful love of beauty was probably never accompanied with so little technical curiosity. Her endowment was so rich, her spirit so proud, her temper so high, that, as she was an immense success, they made her indifference and her eccentricity magnificent. From what she would have been as a failure the imagination averts its face; and if her only receipt for "rendering" Shakespeare was to live with him and try to be worthy of him, there are many aspirants it would not have taken far on the way. Nor would one have expected it to be the precursor of performances masterly in their finish. Such simplicities were easy to a person who had Mrs. Kemble's organ, her presence, and her rare perceptions. I remember going many years ago, in the United States, to call on her in company with a lady who had borrowed from her a volume containing one of Calderon's plays translated by Edward Fitzgerald. This lady had brought the book back, and knowing her sufficiently well (if not sufficiently ill!) to venture to be pressing, expressed her desire that she should read us one of the great Spaniard's finest passages. Mrs. Kemble, giving reasons, demurred, but finally suffered herself to be persuaded. The scene struck me at the time, I remember, as a reproduction of some anecdotic picture I had carried in my mind of the later days of Mrs. Siddons — Mrs. Siddons reading Milton in her mob-cap and spectacles. The sunny drawing-room in the country, the morning fire, the "Berlin wools" of the hostess and her rich old-English quality, which always counted double beyond the seas, seemed in a manner a reconstitution, completed, if I am not mistaken, by the presence of Sir Thomas Lawrence's magnificent portrait of her grandmother, Mrs. Roger Kemble—"the old lioness herself," as he, or some one else, had called her, the mother of all the brood. Mrs. Kemble read, then, as she only could read, and, the poetry of the passage being of the noblest, with such rising and visible, such extreme and increasing emotion, that I presently became aware of her having suddenly sought refuge from a disaster in a cry of resentment at the pass she had been brought to, and in letting the book fly from her hand and hurtle across the room. All her "art" was in the incident.

It was just as much and just as little in her talk, scarcely less than her dramatic faculty a part of her fine endowment and, indeed, scarcely at all to be distinguished from it. Her conversation opened its doors wide to all parts of her mind, and all expression, with her, was singularly direct and immediate. Her great natural resources put a premium, as it were, on expression, so that there might even have been ground for wondering to what exaggeration it would have tended had not such perfect genuineness been at the root. It was exactly this striking natural form, the channel open to it, that made the genuineness so unembarrassed. Full as she was, in reflection, of elements that might have excluded each other, she was at the same time, socially and in action, so much of one piece, as the phrase is, that her different gifts were literally portions of each other. As her talk was part of her drama, so, as I have intimated, her writing was part of her talk. It had the same free sincerity as her conversation, and an equal absence of that quality which may be called in social intercourse diplomacy and in literature preoccupation or even ambition or even vanity. It cannot often have befallen her in her long life to pronounce the great word Culture—the sort of term she invariably looked at askance; but she had acted in the studious spirit without knowing that it had so fine a name. She had always lived with books and had the habit and, as it were, the hygiene of them; never, moreover (as a habit would not have been hers without some odd intensity), laying down a volume that she had begun, or failing to read any that was sent her or lent her. Her friends were often witnesses of heroic, of monstrous feats of this kind. "I read everything that is given me, except the newspaper—and from beginning to end," she was wont to say with that almost touching docility with which so many of her rebellions were lovably underlaid. There was something of the same humility in her fondness for being read to, even by persons professing no proficiency in the art—an attitude indeed that, with its great mistress for a listener, was the only discreet one to be assumed. All this had left her equally enriched and indifferent; she never dreamed of being a woman of letters—her wit and her wisdom relieved her too comfortably of such pretensions. Her various books, springing in every case but two or three straight from the real, from experience; personal and natural, humorous and eloquent, interesting as her character and her life were interesting, have all her irrepressible spirit or, if the word be admissible, her spiritedness. The term is not a critical one, but the geniality (in the Germanic sense) of her temperament makes everything she wrote what is called good reading. She wrote exactly as she talked, observing, asserting, complaining, confiding, contradicting, crying out and bounding off, always effectually communicating. Last, not least, she uttered with her pen as well as with her lips the most agreeable, uncontemporary, self-respecting English, as idiomatic as possible and just as little common. There were friends to whom she was absolutely precious, with a preciousness historic, inexpressible, to be kept under glass, as one of the rare persons (how many of her peers are left in the world?) over whom the trail of the newspaper was not. I never saw a newspaper in her house, nor in the course of many years heard her so much as allude to one; and as she had the habit, so she had the sense (a real touchstone for others) of English undefiled. French as she was, she hated Gallicisms in the one language as much as she winced at Anglicisms in the other, and she was a constant proof that the richest colloquial humor is not dependent for its success upon slang, least of all (as this is a matter in which distance gilds) upon that of the hour. I won't say that her lips were not occasionally crossed gracefully enough by that of 1840. Her attitude towards Americanisms may be briefly disposed of—she confounded them (when she didn't think, as she mostly did, that Americans made too many phrases—then she was impelled to be scandalous) with the general modern madness for which the newspaper was responsible.

Her prose and her poetical writings are alike unequal; easily the best of the former, I think, are the strong, insistent, one-sided "Journal of a Residence on a Georgia Plantation" (the most valuable account — and as a report of strong emotion scarcely less valuable from its element of *parti-pris*—of impressions begotten by that old Southern life which we are too apt to see to-day as through a haze of Indian summer), and the copious and ever-delightful "Records of a Girlhood" and "Records of Later Life," which form together one of the most animated autobiographies in the language. Her poetry, all passionate and melancholy and less prized, I think, than it deserves, is perfectly individual and really lyrical. Much of it is so off-hand as to be rough, but much of it has beauty as well as reality, such beauty as to make one ask one's self (and the question recurs in turning the leaves of almost any of her books) whether her aptitude for literary expression had not been well worth her treating it with more regard. That she might have cared for it more is very certain — only as certain, however, as it is doubtful if any circumstances could have made her care. You can neither take vanity from those who have it nor give it to those who have it not. She really cared only for things higher and finer and fuller and happier than the shabby compromises of life, and the polishing of a few verses the more or the less would never have given her the illusion of the grand style. The matter comes back, moreover, to the terrible question of "art"; it is difficult after all to see where art can be squeezed in when you have such a quantity of nature. Mrs. Kemble would have said that she had all of hers on her hands. A certain rude justice presides over our affairs, we have to select and to pay, and artists in general are rather spare and thrifty folk. They give up for their security a great deal that Mrs. Kemble never could give up; security was her dream, but it remained her dream: practically she passed her days in peril. What she had in verse was not only the lyric impulse but the genuine lyric need; poetry, for her, was one of those moral conveniences of which I have spoken and which she took where she found them. She made a very honest use of it, inasmuch as it expressed for her what nothing else could express — the inexpugnable, the fundamental, the boundless and generous sadness which lay beneath her vitality, beneath her humor, her imagination, her talents, her violence of will and integrity of health. This note of suffering, audible to the last and pathetic, as the prostrations of strength are always pathetic, had an intensity all its own, though doubtless, being so direct and unrelieved, the interest and even the surprise of it were greatest for those to whom she was personally known. There was something even strangely simple in that perpetuity of pain which the finest of her sonnets commemorate and which was like the distress of a nature conscious of its irremediable exposure and consciously paying for it. The great tempest of her life, her wholly unprosperous marriage, had created waves of feeling which, even after long years, refused to be stilled, continued to gather and break.

Twice only, after her early youth, she tried the sort of experiment that is supposed most effectually to liberate the mind from the sense of its own troubles —the literary imagination of the troubles of others. She published, in 1863, the fine, sombre, poetical, but unmanageable play called *An English Tragedy* (written many years previous); and at the age of eighty she, for the first time, wrote and put forth a short novel. The latter of these productions, "Far Away and Long Ago," shows none of the feebleness of age; and besides the charm, in form, of its old decorous affiliation (one of her friends, on reading it, assured her in perfect good faith that she wrote for all the world like Walter Scott), it is a twofold example of an uncommon felicity. This is, on the one hand, to break ground in a new manner and so gracefully at so advanced an age (did *any* one else ever produce a first fiction at eighty?), and on the other, to revert successfully, in fancy, to associations long outlived. Interesting, touching must the book inevitably be, from this point of view, to American readers. There was nothing finer in Mrs. Kemble's fine mind than the generous justice of which she was capable (as her knowledge grew, and after the innocent impertinences of her girlish "Journal") to the country in which she had, from the first, found troops of friends and intervals of peace as well as depths of disaster. She had a mingled feeling and a sort of conscientious strife about it, together with a tendency to handle it as gently with one side of her nature as she was prompted to belabor it with the other. The United States commended themselves to her liberal opinions as much as they disconcerted her intensely conservative taste; she relished every obligation to them but that of living in them; and never heard them eulogized without uttering her reserves or abused without speaking her admiration. They had been the scene of some of her strongest friendships, and, eventually, among the mountains of Massachusetts, she had for many years, though using it only in desultory ways, enjoyed the least occasional of her homes. Late in life she looked upon this region as an Arcadia, a happy valley, a land of woods and waters and upright souls; and in the light of this tender retrospect, a memory of summer days and loved pastimes, of plentiful riding and fishing, recounted her romantic anecdote, a retarded stroke of the literary clock of 1840. *An English Tragedy* seems to sound from a still earlier timepiece, has in it an echo of the great Elizabethans she cherished.

Compromised by looseness of construction, it has nevertheless such beauty and pathos as to make us wonder why, with her love of poetry (which she widely and perpetually quoted) and her hereditary habit of the theatre, she should not oftener have tried her strong hand at a play. This reflection is particularly suggested by a sallow but robust pamphlet which lies before me, with gilt edges and " Seventh Edition " stamped in large letters on its cover; an indication doubly significant in connection with the words " Five shillings and sixpence " (a very archaic price for the form) printed at the bottom. " Miss Fanny

Kemble's Tragedy," *Francis the First*, was acted, with limited success indeed, in the spring of 1832, and afterwards published by Mr. John Murray. She appeared herself, incongruously, at the age of twenty-three, as the queen-mother, Louisa of Savoy (she acted indeed often at this time with her father parts the most mature); and the short life of the play, as a performance, does not seem to have impaired the circulation of the book. Much ventilated in London lately has been the question of the publication of acted plays; but even those authors who have hoped most for the practice have probably not hoped for seventh editions. It was to some purpose that she had been heard to describe herself as having been in ancient days "a nasty scribbling girl." I know not how many editions were attained by *The Star of Seville*, her other youthful drama, which I have not encountered. Laxity in the formative direction is, however, the weakness that this species of composition least brooks. If Mrs. Kemble brushed by, with all respect, the preoccupation of "art," it was not without understanding that the form in question is simply, and of necessity, *all* art, a circumstance that is at once its wealth and its poverty. Therefore she forbore to cultivate it; and as for the spirit's refuge, the sovereign remedy of evocation, she found this after all in her deep immersion in Shakespeare, the multitude of whose characters she could so intensely, in theatrical parlance, create.

Any brief account of a character so copious, a life so various, is foredoomed to appear to sin by omissions; and any attempt at coherence is purchased by simplifications unjust, in the eyes of observers, according to the phase or the period with which such observers happen to have been in contact. If, as an injustice less positive than some others, we dwell, in speaking to unacquainted readers, on Mrs. Kemble's "professional" career, we seem to leave in the shade the other, the personal interest that she had for an immense and a constantly renewed circle and a whole later generation. If we hesitate to sacrifice the testimony offered by her writings to the vivacity of her presence in the world, we are (besides taking a tone that she never herself took) in danger of allotting a minor place to that social charm and more immediate empire which might have been held in themselves to confer eminence and lift the individual reputation into the type. These certainly were qualities of the private order; but originality is a question of degree, and the higher degrees carry away one sort of barrier as well as another. It is vain to talk of Mrs. Kemble at all, if we are to lack assurance in saying, for those who had not the privilege of knowing her as well as for those who had, that she was one of the rarest of women. To insist upon her accomplishments is to do injustice to that human largeness which was the greatest of them all, the one by which those who admired her most knew her best. One of the forms, for instance, taken by the loyalty she so abundantly inspired was an ineradicable faith in her being one of the first and most original of talkers. To that the remembering listener returns as on the whole, in our bridled race, the fullest measure and the brightest proof. Her talk was everything, everything that she was, or that her interlocutor could happen to want; though, indeed, it was often something that he couldn't possibly have happened to expect. It was herself, in a word, and everything else at the same time. It may well have never been better than, with so long a past to flow into it, during the greater part of the last twenty years of her life. So at least is willing to believe the author of these scanted reminiscences, whose memory carries him back to Rome, the ancient, the adored, and to his first nearer vision of the celebrated lady, still retaining in aspect so much that had made her admirably handsome (including the marked splendor of apparel), as she rolled, in the golden sunshine, always alone in her high carriage, through Borghese villas and round Pincian hills. This expression had, after a short interval, a long sequel in the quiet final London time, the time during which she willingly ceased to wander and indulged in excursions only of memory and of wit.

These years of rest were years of anecdote and eloquence and commentary, and of a wonderful many-hued retrospective lucidity. Her talk reflected a thousand vanished and present things; but there were those of her friends for whom its value was, as I have hinted, almost before any other documentary. The generations move so fast and change so

much that Mrs. Kemble testified even more than
she affected to do, which was much, to antique manners and a closed chapter of history. Her conversation swarmed with people and with criticism of
people, with the ghosts of a dead society. She
had, in two hemispheres, seen every one and known
every one, had assisted at the social comedy of her
age. Her own habits and traditions were in themselves a survival of an era less democratic and more
mannered. I have no room for enumerations, which
moreover would be invidious; but the old London
of her talk—the direction I liked it best to take—
was in particular a gallery of portraits. She made
Count d'Orsay familiar, she made Charles Greville
present; I thought it wonderful that she could be
anecdotic about Miss Edgeworth. She reanimated
the old drawing-rooms, relighted the old lamps, retuned the old pianos. The finest comedy of all,
perhaps, was that of her own generous whimsicalities. She was superbly willing to amuse, and on
any terms, and her temper could do it as well as her
wit. If either of these had failed, her eccentricities
were always there. She had, indeed, so much finer
a sense of comedy than any one else that she herself knew best, as well as recked least, how she
might exhilarate. I remember that at the play she
often said, "Yes, they're funny; but they don't begin to know how funny they might be!" Mrs. Kemble always knew, and her good-humor effectually
forearmed her. She had more "habits" than most
people have room in life for, and a theory that to a

person of her disposition they were as necessary as the close meshes of a strait-waistcoat. If she had not lived by rule (on her showing), she would have lived infallibly by riot. Her rules and her riots, her reservations and her concessions, all her luxuriant theory and all her extravagant practice, her drollery that mocked at her melancholy, her imagination that mocked at her drollery, and her rare forms and personal traditions that mocked a little at everything—these were part of the constant freshness which made those who loved her love her so much. "If my servants can live with me a week they can live with me forever," she often said; "but the first week sometimes kills them." I know not what friends it may also have killed, but very fully how many it spared; and what dependants, what devotees, what faithful and humble affections clung to her to the end and after. A domestic who had been long in her service quitted his foreign-home the instant he heard of her death, and, travelling for thirty hours, arrived travel-stained and breathless, like a messenger in a romantic tale, just in time to drop a handful of flowers into her grave.

The Alpine guides loved her—she knew them all, and those for whom her name offered difficulties identified her charmingly as "*la dame qui va chantant par les montagnes.*" She had sung, over hill and dale, all her days (music was in her blood); but those who had not been with her in Switzerland while she was still alert never knew what admirable nonsense she could talk, nor with what originality and gayety she could invite the spirit of mirth, flinging herself, in the joy of high places, on the pianos of mountain inns, joking, punning, botanizing, encouraging the lowly and abasing the proud, making stupidity everywhere gape (that was almost her mission in life), and startling infallibly all primness of propriety. Punctually on the first of June, every year, she went to Switzerland; punctually on the first of September she came back. During the interval she roamed as far and as high as she could; for years she walked and climbed, and when she could no longer climb she rode. When she could no longer ride she was carried, and when her health ceased to permit the *chaise-à-porteurs* it was as if the great warning had come. Then she moved and mounted only with wistful, with absolutely tearful eyes, sitting for hours on the balconies of high-perched hotels, and gazing away at her paradise lost. She yielded the ground only inch by inch, but towards the end she had to accept the valleys almost altogether and to decline upon paltry compromises and Italian lakes. Nothing was more touching at the last than to see her caged at Stresa or at Orta, still slowly circling round her mountains, but not trusting herself to speak of them. I remember well the melancholy of her silence during a long and lovely summer drive, after the turn of the tide, from one of the places just mentioned to the other; it was so little what she wanted to be doing. When, three years before her death, she had to recognize that her last pilgrimage had been performed, this was the knell indeed; not the warning of the end, but the welcome and inexorable term. Those, however, with whom her name abides will see her as she was during the previous years—a personal force so large and sound that it was, in fact, no merely simple satisfaction to be aware of such an abundance of being on the part of one whose innermost feeling was not the love of life. To such uneasy observers, seeking for the truth of personal histories and groping for definitions, it revealed itself as impressive that she had never, at any moment from the first, been in spirit reconciled to existence. She had done what her conditions permitted to become so, but the want of adjustment, cover it up as she might with will or wit, with passions or talents, with laughter or tears, was a quarrel too deep for any particular conditions to have made right. To know her well was to ask one's self what conditions could have fallen in with such an unappeasable sense—I know not what to call it, such arrogance of imagination. She was more conscious of this infirmity than those who might most have suffered from it could ever be, and all her generosities and sociabilities, all her mingled insistence and indifference were, as regards others, a magnificently liberal penance for it. Nothing indeed could exceed the tenderness of her conscience and the humility of her pride. But the contempt for conditions and circumstances, the grandeur preconceived, were essentially there; she was, in the ancient sense of the word, indomitably, incorruptibly superb. The greatest pride of all is to be proud of nothing, the pride not of pretension but of renunciation; and this was of course her particular kind. I remember her saying once, in relation to the difficulty of being pleased, that nature had so formed her that she was ever more aware of the one fault something beautiful might have than of all the beauties that made it what it was. The beauty of life at best has a thousand faults; this was therefore still more the case with that of a career in the course of which two resounding false notes had ministered to her characteristic irony. She detested the stage, to which she had been dedicated while she was too young to judge, and she had failed conspicuously to achieve happiness or tranquillity in marriage. These were the principal among many influences that made that irony defensive. It was exclusively defensive, but it was the first thing that her interlocutors had to meet. To a lady who had been brought, wonderingly, to call upon her, and who the next day caused inquiry to be made whether she had not during the visit dropped a purse in the house, she requested answer to be returned that she was sorry her ladyship had had to pay so much more to see her than had formerly been the case. To a very loquacious actress who, coming to "consult" her, expatiated on all the parts she desired to play, beginning with Juliet, the formidable authority, after much patience, replied, "Surely the part most marked out for you is that of Juliet's nurse!"

But it was not these frank humors that most distinguished her, nor those legendary *brusqueries* into which her flashing quickness caused her to explode under visitations of dulness and density, which, to save the situation, so often made her invent, for arrested interlocutors, retorts at her own expense to her own sallies, and which, in her stall at the theatre, when comedy was helpless and heavy, scarcely permitted her (while she instinctively and urgingly clapped her hands to a faster time) to sit still for the pity of it; it was her fine, anxious humanity, the generosity of her sympathies, and the grand line and mass of her personality. This elevation no smallness, no vanity, no tortuosity nor selfish precaution defaced, and with such and other vulgarities it had neither common idiom nor possible intercourse. Her faults themselves were only noble, and if I have ventured to allude to one of the greatest of them, this is merely because it was, in its conscious survival, the quality in her nature which arouses most tenderness of remembrance. After an occasion, in 1885, when such an allusion had been made in her own presence, she sent the speaker a touching, a revealing sonnet, which, as it has not been published, I take the liberty of transcribing :

> " Love, joy and hope, honor and happiness,
> And all that life could precious count beside,
> Together sank into one dire abyss.
> Think you there was too much of *any* pride
> To fill so deep a pit, a gap so wide,
> Sorrow of such a dismal wreck to hide,
> And shame of such a bankruptcy's excess?

> Oh, friend of many lonely hours, forbear
> The sole support of such a weight to chide!
> It helps me all men's pity to abide,
> Less beggar'd than I am still to appear,
> An aspect of some steadfastness to wear,
> Nor yet how often it has bent confess
> Beneath the burden of my wretchedness!"

It is not this last note, however, that any last word about her must sound. Her image is composed also of too many fairer and happier things, and in particular of two groups of endowment, rarely found together, either of which would have made her interesting and remarkable. The beauty of her deep and serious character was extraordinarily brightened and colored by that of her numerous gifts, and remains splendidly lighted by the memory of the most resonant and most personal of them all.

GUSTAVE FLAUBERT

In the year 1877 Gustave Flaubert wrote to a friend: "You speak of Balzac's letters. I read them when they appeared, but with very little enthusiasm. The man gains from them, but not the artist. He was too much taken up with business. You never meet a general idea, a sign of his caring for anything beyond his material interests. . . . What a lamentable life!" At the time the volumes appeared (the year before) he had written to Edmond de Goncourt: "What a preoccupation with money and how little love of art! Have you noticed that he never *once* speaks of it? He strove for glory, but not for beauty."

The reader of Flaubert's own correspondence,* lately given to the world by his niece, Madame Commanville, and which, in the fourth volume, is brought to the eve of his death — the student of so much vivid and violent testimony to an intensely exclusive passion is moved to quote these words for the sake of contrast. It will not be said of the writer that he himself never once speaks of art; it will be said of

* "Correspondance de Gustave Flaubert." Quatrième Série. Paris, 1893.

him with a near approach to truth that he almost never once speaks of anything else. The effect of contrast is indeed strong everywhere in this singular publication, from which Flaubert's memory receives an assault likely to deepen the air of felicity missed that would seem destined henceforth to hang over his personal life. "May I be skinned alive," he writes in 1854, "before I ever turn my private feelings to literary account." His constant refrain in his letters is the impersonality, as he calls it, of the artist, whose work should consist exclusively of his subject and his style, without an emotion, an idiosyncrasy that is not utterly transmuted. Quotation does but scanty justice to his rage for this idea; almost all his feelings were such a rage that we wonder what form they would have borrowed from a prevision of such posthumous betrayal. "It's one of my principles that one must never write down *one's self*. The artist must be present in his work like God in creation, invisible and almighty, everywhere felt, but nowhere seen." Such was the part he allotted to form, to that rounded detachment which enables the perfect work to live by its own life, that he regarded as indecent and dishonorable the production of any impression that was not intensely calculated. "Feelings" were necessarily crude, because they were inevitably unselected, and selection (for the picture's sake) was Flaubert's highest morality.

This principle has been absent from the counsels of the editor of his letters, which have been given to the world, so far as they were procurable, without attenuation and without scruple. There are many, of course, that circumstances have rendered inaccessible, but in spite of visible gaps the revelation is full enough and remarkable enough. These communications would, of course, not have been matter for Flaubert's highest literary conscience; but the fact remains that in our merciless age ineluctable fate has overtaken the man in the world whom we most imagine gnashing his teeth under it. His ideal of dignity, of honor and renown, was that nothing should be known of him but that he had been an impeccable writer. "I feel all the same," he wrote in 1852, "that I shall not die before I've set a-roaring somewhere (*sans avoir fait rugir quelque part*) such a style as hums in my head, and which may very well overpower the sound of the parrots and grasshoppers." This is a grievous accident for one who could write that "the worship of art contributes to pride, and of pride one has never too much." Sedentary, cloistered, passionate, cynical, tormented in his love of magnificent expression, of subjects remote and arduous, with an unattainable ideal, he kept clear all his life of vulgarity and publicity and newspaperism only to be dragged after death into the middle of the marketplace, where the electric light beats fiercest. Madame Commanville's publication hands him over to the Philistines with every weakness exposed, every mystery dispelled, every secret betrayed. Almost the whole of her second volume, to say nothing of a large part of her first, consists of his love-letters to the only woman he appears to have addressed in the accents of passion. His private style, moreover, was as unchastened as his final form was faultless. The result happens to be deeply interesting to the student of the famous "artistic temperament"; it can scarcely be so for a reader less predisposed, I think, for Flaubert was a writers' writer as much as Shelley was a "poets' poet"; but we may ask ourselves if the time has not come when it may well cease to be a leading feature of our homage to a distinguished man that we shall sacrifice him with sanguinary rites on the altar of our curiosity. Flaubert's letters, indeed, bring up with singular intensity the whole question of the rights and duties, the decencies and discretions of the insurmountable desire to *know*. To lay down a general code is perhaps as yet impossible, for there is no doubt that to know is good, or to want to know, at any rate, supremely natural. Some day or other surely we shall all agree that everything is relative, that facts themselves are often falsifying, and that we pay more for some kinds of knowledge than those particular kinds are worth. Then we shall perhaps be sorry to have had it drummed into us that the author of calm, firm masterpieces, of "Madame Bovary," of "Salammbô," of "Saint-Julien l'Hospitalier," was narrow and noisy, and had not personally and morally, as it were, the great dignity of his literary ideal.

When such revelations are made, however, they are made, and the generous attitude is doubtless at that stage to catch them in sensitive hands. Poor Flaubert has been turned inside out for the lesson, but it has been given to him to constitute practically —on the demonstrator's table with an attentive circle round—an extraordinary, a magnificent "case." Never certainly in literature was the distinctively literary idea, the fury of execution, more passionately and visibly manifested. This rare visibility is probably the excuse that the responsible hand will point to. The letters enable us to note it, to follow it from phase to phase, from one wild attitude to another, through all the contortions and objurgations, all the exaltations and despairs, tensions and collapses, the mingled pieties and profanities of Flaubert's simplified yet intemperate life. Their great interest is that they exhibit an extraordinary singleness of aim, show us the artist not only disinterested, but absolutely dishumanized. They help us to perceive what Flaubert missed almost more than what he gained, and if there are many questions in regard to such a point of view that they certainly fail to settle, they at least cause us to turn them over as we have seldom turned them before. It was the lifelong discomfort of this particular fanatic, but it is our own extreme advantage, that he was almost insanely excessive. "In literature," he wrote in 1861, "the best chance one has is by following out one's temperament and exaggerating it." His own he could scarcely exaggerate; but it carried him so far that we seem to see on distant heights his agitations outlined against the sky. "Impersonal" as he wished his work to be, it was his strange fortune to be the most expressive, the most vociferous, the most spontaneous of men. The record of his temperament is therefore complete, and if his ambiguities make the illuminating word difficult to utter, it is not because the picture is colorless.

Why was such a passion, in proportion to its strength, after all so sterile? There is life, there is blood in a considerable measure in "Madame Bovary," but the last word about its successors can only be, it seems to me, that they are splendidly and infinitely curious. Why may, why *must*, indeed, in certain cases, the effort of expression spend itself, and spend itself in success, without completing the circle, without coming round again to the joy of evocation? How can art be so genuine and yet so unconsoled, so unhumorous, so unsociable? When it is a religion, and therefore an authority, why should it not be, like other authorities, a guarantee? How can it be such a curse without being also a blessing? What germ of treachery lurks in it to make it, not necessarily, but so easily that there is but a hair-line to cross, delusive for personal happiness? Why, in short, when the struggle is success, should the success not be at last serenity? These mysteries and many others pass before us as we listen to Flaubert's loud plaint, which is precisely the profit we derive from his not having, with his correspondents, struck, like Balzac, only the commercial note. Nothing in his agitated and limited life, which began at Rouen in 1821, is more striking than the prompt, straightforward way his destiny picked him out and his conscience handed him over. As most young men have to contend with some domestic disapproval of the muse, so this one had rather to hang back on the easy incline and to turn away his face from the formidable omens. It was only too evident that he would be free to break his heart, to *gueuler*, as he fondly calls it, to spout, to mouth and thresh about, to that heart's content. No career was ever more taken for granted in its intensity, nor any series of tribulations more confidently invited. It was recognized from the first that the tall and splendid youth, green-eyed and sonorous (his stature and aspect were distinguished), was born to *gueuler*, and especially his own large cadences.

His father, a distinguished surgeon, who died early, had purchased near Rouen, on the Seine, the small but picturesque property of Croisset; and it was in a large five-windowed corner room of this quiet old house, his study for forty years, that his life was virtually spent. It was marked by two great events: his journey to the East and return through the south of Europe with Maxime du Camp in 1849, and the publication of "Madame Bovary" (followed by a train of consequences) in 1857. He made a second long journey (to Algeria, Tunis, and the site of Carthage) while engaged in writing "Salammbô"; he had before his father's death taken part in a scanted family pilgrimage to the north of Italy, and he appears once to have spent a few weeks on the Righi, and at another time a few days in London, an episode, oddly enough, of which there is but the faintest, scarcely a recognizable echo in his correspondence. For the rest, and save for an occasional interlarding of Paris, his years were spent at his patient table in the room by the rural Seine. If success in life (and it is the definition open perhaps to fewest objections) consists of achieving in maturity the dreams of one's prime, Flaubert's measure may be said to have been full. M. Maxime du Camp, in those two curious volumes of "Impressions Littéraires," which in 1882 treated a surprised world and a scandalized circle to the physiological explanation of his old friend's idiosyncrasies, declares that exactly as that friend was with intensity at the beginning, so was he with intensity in the middle and at the end, and that no life was ever simpler or straighter in the sense of being a case of growth without change. Doubtful, indeed, were the urgency of M. du Camp's revelation and the apparent validity of his evidence; but whether or no Flaubert was an epileptic subject, and whether or no there was danger in our unconsciousness of the question (danger to any one but M. Maxime du Camp), the impression of the reader of the letters is in complete conformity with the pronouncement to which I allude. The Flaubert of fifty differs from the Flaubert of twenty only in size. The difference between "Bouvard et Pécuchet" and "Madame Bovary" is not a difference of spirit; and it is a proof of the author's essential continuity that his first published work, appearing when he had touched middle life and on which his reputation mainly rests, had been planned as long in advance as if it had been a new religion.

"Madame Bovary" was five years in the writing,

and the "Tentation de Saint-Antoine," which saw the light in 1874, but the consummation of an idea entertained in his boyhood. "Bouvard et Pécuchet," the intended epos of the blatancy, the comprehensive *bêtise*, of mankind, was in like manner the working-out at the end of his days of his earliest generalization. It had literally been his life-long dream to crown his career with a panorama of human ineptitude. Everything in his literary life had been planned and plotted and prepared. One moves in it through an atmosphere of the darkest, though the most innocent, conspiracy. He was perpetually laying a train, a train of which the inflammable substance was "style." His great originality was that the long siege of his youth was successful. I can recall no second case in which poetic justice has interfered so gracefully. He began "Madame Bovary" from afar off, not as an amusement or a profit or a clever novel or even a work of art or a *morceau de vie*, as his successors say to-day, not even, either, as the best thing he could make it; but as a premeditated classic, a masterpiece pure and simple, a thing of conscious perfection and a contribution of the first magnitude to the literature of his country. There would have been every congruity in his encountering proportionate failure and the full face of that irony in things of which he was so inveterate a student. A writer of tales who should have taken the extravagance of his design for the subject of a sad "novelette" could never have permitted himself any termination of such a story but an effective anticlimax.

The masterpiece at the end of years would inevitably fall very flat and the overweening spirit be left somehow to its illusions. The solution, in fact, was very different, and as Flaubert had deliberately sown, so exactly and magnificently did he reap. The perfection of "Madame Bovary" is one of the commonplaces of criticism, the position of it one of the highest a man of letters dare dream of, the possession of it one of the glories of France. No calculation was ever better fulfilled, nor any train more successfully laid. It is a sign of the indefeasible bitterness to which Flaubert's temperament condemned him and the expression of which, so oddly, is yet as obstreperous and boyish as that of the happiness arising from animal spirits—it is a mark of his amusing pessimism that so honorable a first step should not have done more to reconcile him to life. But he was a creature of transcendent dreams and unfathomable perversities of taste, and it was in his nature to be more conscious of one broken spring in the couch of fame, more wounded by a pin-prick, more worried by an assonance, than he could ever be warmed or pacified from within. Literature and life were a single business to him, and the "torment of style," that might occasionally intermit in one place, was sufficiently sure to break out in another. We may polish our periods till they shine again, but over the style of life our control is necessarily more limited.

To such limitations Flaubert resigned himself with the worst possible grace. He polished ferociously, but there was a side of the matter that his process could never touch. Some other process might have been of use; some patience more organized, some formula more elastic, or simply perhaps some happier trick of good-humor; at the same time it must be admitted that in his deepening vision of the imbecility of the world any remedy would have deprived him of his prime, or rather of his sole, amusement. The *bêtise* of mankind was a colossal comedy, calling aloud to heaven for an Aristophanes to match, and Flaubert's nearest approach to joy was in noting the opportunities of such an observer and feeling within himself the stirrings of such a genius Towards the end he found himself vibrating at every turn to this ideal, and if he knew to the full the tribulation of proper speech no one ever suffered less from that of proper silence. He broke it in his letters, on a thousand queer occasions, with all the luxury of relief. He was blessed with a series of correspondents with whom he was free to leave nothing unsaid; many of them ladies, too, so that he had in their company all the inspiration of gallantry without its incidental sacrifices. The most interesting of his letters are those addressed between 1866 and 1876 to Madame George Sand, which, originally collected in 1884, have been re-embodied in Madame Commanville's publication. They are more interesting than ever when read, as we are now able to read them, in connection with Madame Sand's equally personal and much more luminous answers, accessible in the fifth and sixth volumes of her own copious and strikingly honorable "Correspondance." No opposition could have been more of a nature to keep the ball rolling than that of the parties to this candid commerce, who were as united by affection and by common interests as they were divided by temper and their way of feeling about those interests. Living, each of them, for literature (though Madame Sand, in spite of her immense production, very much less exclusively for it than her independent and fastidious friend), their comparison of most of the impressions connected with it could yet only be a lively contrast of temperaments. Flaubert, whose bark indeed (it is the rule) was much worse than his bite, spent his life, especially the later part of it, in a state of acute exasperation; but her unalterable serenity was one of the few irritants that were tolerable to him.

Their letters are a striking lesson in the difference between good humor and bad, and seem to point the moral that either form has only to be cultivated to become our particular kind of intelligence. They compared conditions, at any rate, her expansion with his hard contraction, and he had the advantage of finding in a person who had sought wisdom in ways so many and so devious one of the few objects within his ken that really represented virtue and that he could respect. It gives us the pattern of his experience that Madame Sand should have stood to him for so much of the ideal, and we may say this even under the impression produced by a reperusal of her total correspondence, a monument to her generosity and variety. Poor Flaubert appears to us to-day almost exactly by so much less frustrated as he was beguiled by this happy relation, the largest he ever knew. His interlocutress, who in the evening of an arduous life accepted refreshment wherever she found it and who could still give as freely as she took, for immemorial habit had only added to each faculty, his correspondent, for all her love of well-earned peace, offered her breast to his aggressive pessimism; had motherly, reasoning, coaxing hands for it; made, in short, such sacrifices that she often came to Paris to go to brawling Magny dinners to meet him and wear, to please him, as I have heard one of the diners say, unaccustomed peach-blossom dresses. It contributes to our sense of what there was lovable at the core of his effort to select and his need to execrate that he should have been able to read and enjoy so freely a writer so fluid; and it also reminds us that imagination is, after all, for the heart, the safest quality. Flaubert had excellent honest inconsistencies, crude lapses from purity in which he could like the books of his friends. He was susceptible of painless amusement (a rare emotion with him) when his imagination was touched, as it was infallibly and powerfully, by affection. To make a hard rule never to be corrupted, and then to make a special exception for fondness, is of course the right attitude.

He had several admirations, and it might always be said of him that he would have admired if he could, for he could like a thing if he could be proud of it, and the act adapted itself to his love of magnificence. He could like, indeed, almost any one he could say great colored things about: the ancients, almost promiscuously, for they never wrote in newspapers, and

Shakespeare (of whom he could not say fine things enough) and Rabelais and Montaigne and Goethe and Victor Hugo (his biggest modern enthusiasm) and Leconte de Lisle and Renan and Théophile Gautier. He did scant justice to Balzac and even less to Alfred de Musset. On the other hand, he had an odd and interesting indulgence for Boileau. Balzac and Musset were not, by his measure, "writers," and he maintains that, be it in verse, be it in prose, it is only so far as they "write" that authors live; between the two categories he makes a fundamental distinction. The latter, indeed, the mere authors, simply did not exist for him, and with Mr. Besant's Incorporated Society he would have had nothing whatever to do. He declares somewhere that it is only the writer who survives in the poet. In spite of his patience with the "muse" to whom the majority of the letters in the earlier of the volumes before us were addressed, and of the great invidious *coup de chapeau* with which he could here and there render homage to versification, his relish for poetry as poetry was moderate. Far higher was his estimate of prose as prose, which he held to be much the more difficult art of the two, with more maddening problems and subtler rhythms, and on whose behalf he found it difficult to forgive the "proud-sister" attitude of verse. No man at any rate, to make up for scanty preferences, can have had a larger list of literary aversions. His eye swept the field in vain for specimens untainted with the "modern infection," the plague which had killed Théophile Gautier and to which he considered that he himself had already succumbed. If he glanced at a *feuilleton* he saw that Madame Sarah Bernhardt was "a social expression," and his resentment of this easy wisdom resounded disproportionately through all the air he lived in. One has always a kindness for people who detest the contemporary tone if they have done something fine; but the baffling thing in Flaubert was the extent of his suffering and the inelasticity of his humor. The jargon of the newspapers, the slovenliness of the novelists, the fatuity of Octave Feuillet, to whom he was exceedingly unjust, for that writer's love of magnificence was not inferior to his critic's, all work upon him with an intensity only to be explained by the primary defect of his mind, his want of a general sense of proportion. That sense stopped apparently when he had settled the relation of the parts of a phrase, as to which it was exquisite.

Fortunately he had confidants to whom he could cry out when he was hurt, and whose position, as he took life for the most part as men take a violent toothache, was assuredly no sinecure. To more than one intense friendship were his younger and middle years devoted; so close was his union with Louis Bouilhet, the poet and dramatist, that he could say in 1870: "I feel no longer the need to write, because I wrote especially for a being who is no more. There's no taste in it now—the impulse has gone." As he wrote for Bouilhet, so Bouilhet wrote for him. "There are so few people who like what I like or have an idea of what I care for." That was the indispensable thing for him in a social, a personal relation, the existence in another mind of a love of literature sufficiently demonstrated to relieve the individual from the great and damning charge, the charge perpetually on Flaubert's lips in regard to his contemporaries, the accusation of malignantly hating it. This universal conspiracy he perceived, in his own country, in every feature of manners, and to a degree which may well make us wonder how high he would have piled the indictment if he had extended the inquiry to the manners of ours. We draw a breath of relief when we think to what speedier suffocation he would have yielded had he been materially acquainted with the great English-speaking peoples. When he declared, naturally enough, that liking what he liked was a condition of intercourse, his vision of this community was almost destined, in the nature of things, to remain unachievable; for it may really be said that no one in the world ever liked anything so much as Flaubert liked beauty of style. The mortal indifference to it of empires and republics was the essence of that "modern infection" from which the only escape would have been to *ne faire que de l'art*. Mankind, for him, was made up of the three or four persons, Ivan Turgenieff in the number, who perceived what he was trying for, and of the innumerable millions who didn't. Poor M. Maxime du Camp, in spite of many of the leading characteristics of a friend, was one of this multitude, and he pays terribly in the pages before us for his position. He pays, to my sense, excessively, for surely he had paid enough and exactly in the just and appropriate measure, when, in the introduction contributed to the "definitive " edition of " Madame Bovary," M. Guy de Maupassant, avenging his master by an exquisite stroke, made public the letter of advice and remonstrance addressed to Flaubert by M. du Camp, then editor of the *Revue de Paris*, on the eve of the serial appearance of the former's first novel in that periodical. This incomparable effusion, with its amazing reference to excisions, and its suggestion that the work be placed in the hands of an expert and inexpensive corrector who will prepare it for publication, this priceless gem will twinkle forever in the setting M. de Maupassant has given it, or we may, perhaps, still more figuratively say in the forehead of the masterpiece it discusses. But there was surely a needless, there was surely a nervous and individual ferocity in such a vindictive giving to the world of every passage of every letter in which the author of that masterpiece has occasion to allude to his friend's want of tact. It naturally made their friendship unsuccessful that Flaubert disliked M. du Camp, but it is a monstrous imputation on his character to assume that he was small enough never to have forgiven and forgotten the other's mistake. Great people never should be avenged; it diminishes their privilege. What M. du Camp, so far as an outsider may judge, had to be punished for was the tone of his reminiscences. But the tone is unmistakably the tone of affection. He may have felt but dimly what his old comrade was trying for, and even the latent richness of "L'Education Sentimentale," but he renders full justice to Flaubert's noble independence.

The tone of Flaubert's own allusions is a different thing altogether. It is not unfair to say that all this disproportionate tit-for-tat renders the episode one of the ugliest little dramas of recent literary history. The irony of a friend's learning after long years and through the agency of the press how unsuspectedly another friend was in the habit of talking of him, is an irony too cruel for impartial minds. The disaster is absolute, and our compassion goes straight to the survivor. There are other survivors who will have but little more reason to think that the decencies have presided over such a publication.

It is only a reader here and there in all the wide world who understands to-day, or who ever understood, what Gustave Flaubert tried for; and it is only when such a reader is also a writer, and a tolerably tormented one, that he particularly cares. Poor Flaubert's great revenge, however, far beyond that of any editorial treachery, is that when this occasional witness does care he cares very peculiarly and very tenderly, and much more than he may be able successfully to say. Then the great irritated style-seeker becomes, in the embracing mind, an object of interest and honor; not so much for what he altogether achieved, as for the way he strove and for the inspiring image that he presents. There is no reasoning about him; the more we take him as he is the more he has a special authority. "Salammbô," in which we breathe the air of pure æsthetics, is as hard as stone; "L'Education," for the same reason, is as cold as death; "Saint-Antoine" is a medley of wonderful bristling metals and polished agates, and the drollery of "Bouvard et Pécuchet" (a work as sad as something perverse and puerile done for a wager) about as contagious as the smile of a keeper showing you through the wards of a madhouse. In "Madame Bovary" alone emotion is just sufficiently present to take off the chill. This truly is a qualified report, yet it leaves Flaubert untouched at the points where he is most himself, leaves him master of a province in which, for many of us, it will never be an idle errand to visit him. The way to care for him is to test the virtue of his particular exaggeration, to accept for the sake of his æsthetic influence the idiosyncrasies now revealed to us, his wild gesticulation, his plaintive, childish side, the side as to which one asks one's self what has become of ultimate good-humor, of human patience, of the enduring *man*. He pays and pays heavily for his development in a single direction, for it is probable that no literary effort so great, accompanied with an equal literary talent, ever failed on so large a scale to be convincing. It convinces only those who are converted, and the number of such is very small. It is an appeal so technical that we may say of him still, but with more resignation, what he personally wailed over, that nobody takes his great question seriously. This is indeed why there may be for each of the loyal minority a certain fine scruple against insistence. If he had had in his nature a contradiction the less, if his indifference had been more forgiving, this is surely the way in which he would have desired most to be preserved.

To no one at any rate need it be denied to say that the best way to appreciate him is, abstaining from the clumsy process of an appeal and the vulgar process of an advertisement, exclusively to *use* him, to feel him, to be privately glad of his message. In proportion as we swallow him whole and cherish him as a perfect example, his weaknesses fall into their place as the conditions about which, in estimating a man who has been original, there is a want of tact in crying out. There is, of course, always the answer that the critic is to be suborned only by originalities that fertilize; the rejoinder to which, of equal necessity, must ever be that even to the critics of unborn generations poor Flaubert will doubtless yield a fund of amusement. To the end of time there will be something flippant, something perhaps even "clever" to be said of his immense ado about nothing. Those for some of whose moments, on the contrary, this ado will be as stirring as music, will belong to the group that has dabbled in the same material and striven with the same striving. The interest he presents, in truth, can only be a real interest for fellowship, for initiation of the practical kind; and in that case it becomes a sentiment, a sort of mystical absorption or fruitful secret. The sweetest things in the world of art or the life of letters are the irresponsible sympathies that seem to rest on divination. Flaubert's hardness was only the act of holding his breath in the reverence of his search for beauty; his universal renunciation, the long spasm of his too-fixed attention, was only one of the absurdest sincerities of art.

To the participating eye these things are but details in the little square picture made at this distance of time by his forty years at the battered table at Croisset. Everything lives in this inward vision of the wide room on the river, almost the cell of a monomaniac, but consecrated ground to the faithful, which, as he tried and tried again, must so often have resounded with the pomp of a syntax addressed, in his code, peremptorily to the ear. If there is something tragi-comic in the scene, as of a tenacity in the void or a life laid down for grammar, the impression passes when we turn from the painful process to the sharp and splendid result. Then, since if we like people very much we end by liking their circumstances, the eternal chamber and the dry Benedictine years have a sufficiently palpable offset in the *repoussé* bronze of the books.

An incorruptible celibate and *dédaigneux des femmes* (as, in spite of the hundred and forty letters addressed to Madame Louise Colet, M. de Maupassant styles him and, in writing to Madame Sand, he confesses himself), it was his own view of his career that, as art was the only thing worth living for, he had made immense sacrifices to application—sacrificed passions, joys, affections, curiosities, and opportunities. He says that he shut his passions up in cages, and only at long intervals, for amusement, had a look at them. The *orgie de littérature*, in short, had been his sole form of excess. He knew best, of course, but his imaginations about himself (as about other matters) were, however justly, rich, and to the observer at this distance he appears truly to have been made of the very stuff of a Benedictine. He compared himself to the camel, which can neither be stopped when he is going nor moved when he is resting. He was so sedentary, so averse to physical exercise, which he speaks of somewhere as an *occupation funeste*, that his main alternative to the chair was, even by day, the bed, and so omnivorous in research that the act of composition, with him, was still more impeded by knowledge than by taste. "I have in me," he writes to the imperturbable Madame Sand, "a *fond d'ecclésiastique* that people don't know"—the clerical basis of the Catholic clergy. "We shall talk of it," he adds, "much better *vivâ voce* than by letter"; and we can easily imagine the thoroughness with which between the unfettered pair, when opportunity favored, the interesting subject was treated. At another time, indeed, to the same correspondent, who had given him a glimpse of the happiness of being a grandmother, he refers with touching sincerity to the poignancy of solitude to which the "radical absence of the feminine element" in his life had condemned him. "Yet I was born with every capacity for tenderness. One doesn't shape one's destiny, one undergoes it. I was pusillanimous in my youth—I was *afraid* of life. We pay for everything." Besides, it was his theory that a "man of style" should never stoop to action. If he had been afraid of life in fact, I must add, he was preserved from the fear of it in imagination by that great "historic start," the sensibility to the *frisson historique*, which dictates the curious and beautiful outburst, addressed to Madame Colet, when he asks why it had not been his lot to live in the age of Nero. "How I would have talked with the Greek rhetors, travelled in the great chariots on the Roman roads, and in the evening, in the hostelries, turned in with the vagabond priests of Cybele! . . . I *have* lived, all over, in those directions; doubtless in some prior state of being. I'm sure I've been, under the Roman empire, manager of some troop of strolling players, one of the rascals who used to go to Sicily to buy women to make actresses, and who were at once professors, panders, and artists. These scoundrels have wonderful 'mugs' in the comedies of Plautus, in reading which I seem to myself to remember things."

He was an extreme admirer of Apuleius, and his florid inexperience helps doubtless somewhat to explain those extreme sophistications of taste of which "La Tentation de Saint-Antoine" is so elaborate an example. Far and strange are the refuges in which such an imagination seeks oblivion of the immediate and the ugly. His life was that of a pearl-diver, breathless in the thick element while he groped for the priceless word, and condemned to plunge again and again. He passed it in reconstructing sentences, exterminating repetitions, calculating and comparing cadences, harmonious *chutes de phrase*, and beating about the bush to deal death to the abominable assonance. Putting aside the particular ideal of style which made a pitfall of the familiar, few men surely have ever found it so difficult to deal with the members of a phrase. He loathed the smug face of facility as much as he suffered from the nightmare of toil; but if he had been marked in the cradle for literature it may be said without paradox that this was not on account of any native disposition to write, to write at least as he aspired and as he understood the term. He took long years to finish his books, and terrible months and weeks to deliver himself of his chapters and his pages. Nothing could exceed his endeavor to make them all rich and round, just as nothing could exceed the unetherized anguish in which his successive children were born. His letters, in which, inconsequently for one who had so little faith in any rigor of taste or purity of perception save his own, he takes everybody into his most intimate literary confidence, the pages of the publication before us are the record of everything that retarded him. The abyss of reading answered to the abyss of writing; with the partial exception of "Madame Bovary" every subject that he treated required a rising flood of information. There are libraries of books behind his most innocent sentences. The question of "art" for him was so furiously the question of form, and the question of form was so intensely the question of rhythm, that from the beginning to the end of his correspondence we scarcely ever encounter a mention of any beauty but verbal beauty. He quotes Goethe fondly as to the supreme importance of the "conception," but the conception remains for him essentially the plastic one.

There are moments when his restless passion for form strikes us as leaving the subject out of account altogether, as if he had taken it up arbitrarily, blindly, preparing himself the years of misery in which he is to denounce the grotesqueness, the insanity of his choice. Four times, with his *orgueil*, his love of magnificence, he condemned himself incongruously to the modern and familiar, groaning at every step over the horrible difficulty of reconciling "style" in such cases with truth and dialogue with surface. He wanted to do the battle of Thermopylæ, and he found himself doing "Bouvard et Pécuchet." One of the sides by which he interests us, one of the sides that will always endear him to the student, is his extraordinary ingenuity in lifting without falsifying, finding a middle way into grandeur and edging off from the literal without forsaking truth. This way was open to him from the moment he could look down upon his theme from the position of *une blague supérieure*, as he calls it, the amused freedom of an observer as irreverent as a creator. But if subjects were made for style (as to which Flaubert had a rigid theory: the idea was good enough if the expression was), so style was made for the ear, the last court of appeal, the supreme touchstone of perfection. He was perpetually demolishing his periods in the light of his merciless *gueulades*. He tried them on every one; his *gueulades* could make him sociable. The horror, in particular, that haunted all his years was the horror of the *cliché*, the stereotyped, the thing usually said and the way it was usually said, the current phrase that passed muster. Nothing, in his view, passed muster but freshness, that which came into the world, with all the honors, for the occasion. To use the ready-made was as disgraceful as for a self-respecting cook to buy a tinned soup or a sauce in a bottle. Flaubert considered that the dispenser of such wares' was indeed the grocer, and, producing his ingredients exclusively at home, he would have stabbed himself for shame like Vatel. This touches on the strange weakness of his mind, his puerile dread of the grocer, the *bourgeois*, the sentiment that in his generation and the preceding misplaced, as it were, the spirit of adventure and the sense of honor, and sterilized a whole province of French literature. That worthy citizen ought never to have kept a poet from dreaming.

He had for his delectation and for satiric purposes a large collection of those second-hand and approximate expressions which begged the whole literary question. To light upon a perfect example was his nearest approach to natural bliss. "Bouvard et Pécuchet" is a museum of such examples, the cream of that "Dictionnaire des Idées Reçues" for which all his life he had taken notes and which eventually resolved itself into the encyclopædic exactitude and the lugubrious humor of the novel. Just as subjects were meant for style, so style was meant for images; therefore as his own were numerous and admirable he would have contended, coming back to the source, that he was one of the writers to whom the significance of a work had ever been most present. This significance was measured by the amount of style and the quantity of metaphor thrown up. Poor subjects threw up a little, fine subjects threw up much, and the finish of his prose was the proof of his profundity. If you pushed far enough into language you found yourself in the embrace of thought. There are, doubtless, many persons whom this account of the matter will fail to satisfy, and there will indeed be no particular zeal to put it forward even on the part of those for whom, as a writer, Flaubert most vividly exists. He is a strong taste, like any other that is strong, and he exists only for those who have a constitutional need to feel in some direction the particular æsthetic confidence that he inspires. That confidence rests on the simple fact that he carried execution so far and nailed it so fast. No one will care for him at all who does not care for his metaphors, and those moreover who care most for these will be discreet enough to admit that even a style rich in similes is limited when it renders only the visible. The invisible Flaubert scarcely touches; his vocabulary and all his methods were unadjusted and alien to it. He could not read his French Wordsworth, M. Sully-Prudhomme; he had no faith in the power of the moral to offer a surface. He himself offers such a flawless one that this hard concretion is success. If he is impossible as a companion he is deeply refreshing as a reference; and all that his reputation asks of you is an occasional tap of the knuckle at those firm thin plates of gold which constitute the leaves of his books. This passing tribute will yield the best results when you have been prompted to it by some other prose.

In other words, with all his want of *portée*, as the psychological critics of his own country would say of him, poor Flaubert is one of the artists to whom an artist will always go back. And if such a pilgrim, in the very act of acknowledgment, drops for an instant into the tenderness of compassion, it is a compassion singularly untainted with patronage or with contempt; full, moreover, of mystifications and wonderments, questions unanswered and speculations vain. Why was he so unhappy if he was so active; why was he so intolerant if he was so strong? Why should he not have accepted the circumstance that M. de Lamartine also wrote as his nature impelled, and that M. Louis Enault embraced a convenient opportunity to go to the East? The East, if we listen to him, should have been closed to one of these gentlemen and literature forbidden to the other. Why does the inevitable perpetually infuriate him, and why does he inveterately resent the ephemeral? Why does he, above all, in his private, in other words his continuous epistolary, despair, assault his correspondents with malodorous comparisons? The bad smell of the age was the main thing he knew it by. Naturally therefore he found life a *chose hideuse*. If it was his great merit and the thing we hold on to him for that the artist and the man were welded together, what becomes, in the proof, of a merit that is so little illuminating for life? What becomes of the virtue of the beauty that pretends to be worth living for? Why feel, and feel genuinely, so much about "art," in order to feel so little about its privilege? Why proclaim it on the one hand the holy of holies, only to let your behavior confess it on the other a temple open to the winds? Why be angry that so few people care for the real thing, since this aversion of the many leaves a luxury of space? The answer to these too numerous questions is the final perception that the subject of our observations failed of happiness, failed of temperance, not through his excesses, but absolutely through his barriers. He passed his life in strange oblivion of the circumstance that, however incumbent it may be on most of us to do our duty, there is, in spite of a thousand narrow dogmatisms, nothing in the world that any one is under the least obligation to *like*—not even (one braces one's self to risk the declaration) a particular kind of writing. Particular kinds of writing may sometimes, for their producers, have the good-fortune to please; but these things are windfalls, pure luxuries, not resident even in the cleverest of us as natural rights. Let Flaubert always be cited as one of the devotees and even, when people are fond of the word, as one of the martyrs of the plastic idea; but let him be still more considerately preserved and more fully presented as one of the most conspicuous of the faithless. For it was not that he went too far, it was on the contrary that he stopped too short. He hovered forever at the public door, in the outer court, the splendor of which very properly beguiled him, and in which he seems still to stand as upright as a sentinel and as shapely as a statue. But that immobility and even that erectness were paid too dear. The shining arms were meant to carry further, the other doors were meant to open. He should at least have listened at the chamber of the soul. This would have floated him on a deeper tide; above all it would have calmed his nerves.

1893.

PIERRE LOTI

A few years ago the author of these remarks received from an observant friend then in Paris (not a Frenchman) a letter containing a passage which he ventures to transcribe. His correspondent had been to see a celebrated actress—the most celebrated actress of our time—in a new and successful play.

"She is a wonderful creature, but how a being so intelligent as she can so elaborate what has so little moral stuff in it to work upon I don't comprehend. The play is hard and sinister and horrible without being in the least degree tragic or pathetic; one felt when it was over like an accomplice in some cold-blooded piece of cruelty. I am moved to give up the French and call to my own species to stand from under and let their fate overtake them. Such a disproportionate development of the external perceptions and such a perversion of the natural feelings must work its Nemesis in some way."

These simple lines, on account of their general, not of their special application, have come back to me in reading over the several volumes of the remarkable genius who wears in literature the name of Pierre Loti, as well as in refreshing my recollection of some of the pages of his contemporaries. An achievement in art or in letters grows more interesting when we begin to perceive its connections; and, indeed, it may be said that the study of connections is the recognized function of intelligent criticism. It is a comparatively poor exercise of the attention (for the critic always, I mean) to judge a book all by itself, even if it happen to be a book as independent, as little the product of a school and a fashion, as "Le Mariage de Loti" or "Mon Frère Yves" or "Pêcheur d'Islande." Each of these works is interesting as illustrating the talent and character of the author, but they become still more interesting as we note their coincidences and relations with other works, for then they begin to illustrate other talents and other characters as well: the plot thickens, the whole spectacle expands. We seem to be studying not simply the genius of an individual, but, in a living manifestation, that of a nation or of a conspicuous group; the nation or the group becomes a great figure operating on a great scale, and the drama of its literary production (to speak only of that) a kind of world-drama, lighted by the universal sun, with Europe and America for the public, and the arena of races, the battle-field of their inevitable contrasts and competitions, for the stage. Is not the entertainment, moreover, a particularly good bill, as they say at the theatre, when it is a question of the performances of France? Will not the connoisseur feel much at his ease, in such a case, about the high capacity of the actor, settle himself in his stall with the comfortable general confidence that he is to listen to a professional and not to an amateur? Whatever benefits or injuries that great country may have conferred upon mankind, she has certainly rendered them the service of being always, according to her own expression, *bien en scène*. She commits herself completely and treats us to extreme cases; her cases are test-cases, her experiments heroic and conclusive. She has educated our observation by the finish of her manner, and whether or no she has the best part in the play we feel that she has rehearsed best.

A writer of the ability of Alphonse Daudet, of that of Guy de Maupassant, or of that of the brothers De Goncourt, can never fail to be interesting by virtue of that ability, the successive manifestations of which keep our curiosity alive; but this curiosity is never so great as after we have noted, as I think we almost inveterately do, that the strongest gift of each of them is the strongest gift of all: a remarkable art of expressing the life, of picturing the multitudinous, adventurous experience, of the senses. We recognize this accomplishment with immense pleasure as we read—a pleasure so great that it is not for some time that we make the other observation that inevitably follows on its heels. That observation is somewhat to this effect: that in comparison the deeper, stranger, subtler inward life, the wonderful adventures of the soul, are so little pictured that they may almost be said not to be pictured at all. We end with an impression of want of equilibrium and proportion, and by asking ourselves (so coercive are the results of comparative criticism) whether such a sacrifice be quite obligatory. The value of the few words in the letter I just cited is simply that they offer a fresh, direct, almost startled measure of the intensity of the sacrifice, accompanied with the conviction that it must sooner or later be paid for, like every other extravagance, and that if the payment be on the scale of the aberration it will make an eddy of which those who are wise in time should keep clear. This profuse development of the external perceptions—those of the appearance, the sound, the taste, the material presence and pressure of things, will at any rate, I think, not be denied to be the master-sign of the novel in France as the first among the younger talents show it to us to-day. They carry into the whole business of looking, seeing, hearing, smelling, into all kinds of tactile sensibility and into noting, analyzing, and expressing the results of these acts, a seriousness much greater than that of any other people. Their tactile sensibility is immense, and it may be said in truth to have produced a literature. They are so strong on this side that they seem to me to be easily masters, and I cannot imagine that their supremacy should candidly be contested.

An acute sense of aspect and appearance is not common, for the only sense that most people have is of the particular matter with which, on any occasion, their business, their interest or subsistence is bound up; but it is less uncommon in some societies than in others, and it flourishes conspicuously in France. Such is the witness borne by the very vocabulary of the people, which abounds in words and idioms expressing shades and variations of the visible. I once in Paris, at a café, heard a gentleman at a table next to my own say to a companion, speaking of a lady who had just entered the establishment, "A quoi ressemble-t-elle donc?" "Mon Dieu, à une poseuse de sangsues." The reply struck me as a good example of prompt exactness of specification. If you ask a French hatter which of two hats is the more commendable, he will tell you that one of them *dégage mieux la physionomie.* The judgment of his English congener may be as good (we ourselves perhaps are pledged to think it better), but it will be more dumb and pointless—he will have less to say about disengaging the physiognomy. Half the faculty I speak of in the French is the expressive part of it. The perception and the expression together have been worked to-day (for the idiosyncrasy is noticeably modern) with immense vigor, and from Balzac to Pierre Loti, the latest recruit to the band of painters, the successful workers have been the novelists. There are different ways of working, and Flaubert, Edmond and Jules de Goncourt, Zola, Daudet, Maupaussant, and the writer to whom I more particularly refer, have each had a way of his own. There are story-tellers to-day in France who are not students, or at any rate not painters, of the mere palpable—but then they are not conspicuously anything else. I can think of but one writer whose foremost sign, though his literary quality is of the highest, does not happen to be visual curiosity. M. Paul Bourget looks much more within than without, and notes with extraordinary closeness the action of life on the soul, especially the corrosive and destructive action. Many people in England hold that corrosion and destruction are not worth noting; but it should be added that they are probably not as a general thing people to whom one would go for information on the subject—I mean on the subject of the soul. M. Paul Bourget, however, is peculiar in this, that he is both master and pupil; he is alone, *parmi les jeunes;* and, moreover, there are other directions in which he is not isolated at all, those of tactile sensibility, or isolated only because he follows them so far.

The case was not always as I have here attempted to indicate it, for Madame George Sand had an admirable faculty of looking within and a comparatively small one of looking without. Attempting, some months ago, at Venice, to read over "Consuelo," I was struck on the spot with the very small degree to which the author troubled herself about close representation, the absence of any attempt at it or pretension to it; and I could easily understand the scorn with which that sort of irresponsibility (reaching at times on Madame Sand's part a truly exasperating artlessness) has always filled the votaries of the reproductive method. M. Octave Feuillet turns his polished glass on the life of the spirit, but what he finds in the spirit is little more (as it strikes me) than the liveliest phenomena of the flesh. His heroes and heroines are lined on the under side with the same stuff as on the upper—a curious social silken material, adapted only, as we are constantly reminded, to the contacts of patricians. If the soul, for the moralizing observer, be a romantic, moonlighted landscape, with woods and mountains and dim distances, visited by strange winds and murmurs, for M. Octave Feuillet it is rather a square French salon in white and gold, with portraits of the king and queen and the pope, a luminary in old Sèvres and plenty of *bibelots* and sofas. I hasten to add that it is an apartment in which one may spend an hour most agreeably. Even at present there are distinguished variations, if we look outside the group of novelists. If there were not a poet like Sully-Prudhomme or a moralist like M. Renan, the thesis that the French imagination has none but a sensual conscience would be made simpler than it ever is to prove anything.

We perceive, on the other hand, that the air of initiation fails as soon as the inward barrier is crossed, and the diminution of credit produced by this failure is, I confess, the only Nemesis in which for the present I have confidence. It appears to me, indeed, all-sufficient—it appears ideal; and if the writers I have named deserve chastisement for their collective sin against proportion (since sin it shall be held), I know not how a more terrible one could have been invented. The penalty they pay is the heaviest that can be levied, the most summary writ that can be served, upon a great talent — great talents having, as a general thing, formidable defences—and consists simply in the circumstance that, when they lay their hands upon the spirit of man, they cease to seem expert. This would be a great humiliation if they recognized it. They rarely do, however, so far as may be observed; which is a proof that their defences *are* formidable. There is a distinct transition, at any rate, in the case I mention, and assuredly a distinct descent. As painters they go straight to the mark, as analysts they only scratch the surface. We leave authority on one side of the line, and encounter on the other a curiously complacent and unconscious provincialism. Such is the impression we gather in every case, though there are some cases in which the incongruity is more successfully dissimulated than in others. What makes it grow, when once we perceive it, is the large and comprehensive pretensions of the writers—the sense they give us of camps and banners, war-cries and watch-fires. The "Journal" of the brothers De Goncourt, of which two volumes have lately been put forth, is a very interesting publication and suggests many thoughts; but the first remark to be made about it is that it makes a hundred claims to penetration, to profundity. At the same time it is a perfect revelation of the visual passion and of the way it may flourish (not joyously indeed in this case, but with an air of jealous, nervous, conscious tension), at the expense of other passions and even other faculties. Perhaps the best illustration of all would be the difference between the superiority of Gustave Flaubert as a painter of aspects and sensations, and his lapses and limitations, his general insignificance, as a painter of ideas and moral states. If you feel the talent that abides in his style very much (and some people feel it immensely and as a sort of blinding glory), you are bribed in a measure to overlook the inequality; but there comes a moment when the bribe, large as it is, is ineffectual. His imagination is so fine that we take some time to become conscious that almost none of it is moral or even human. "Bouvard et Pécuchet," even as an unfinished work, has merits of execution that could only spring from a great literary energy; but "Bouvard et Pécuchet" is surely, in the extreme juvenility of its main idea, one of the oddest productions for which a man who had lived long in the world was ever responsible. Flaubert, indeed, was the very apostle of surface, and an extraordinary example of a sort of transposition of the conscience. If for "perversion of the natural feelings" (the phrase of the letter I quoted) we read inaction rather, and inexperience and indifference in regard to the phenomena of character and the higher kinds of sensibility, he will appear to represent the typical disparity at its maximum. The brothers De Goncourt strike us as knowing as little about these matters as he, but somehow it is not suggested to us in the same degree that they might have known more. His gift is not their gift, and it is his gift that makes us measure him by a high standard. "Germinie Lacerteux," indeed, without being so fine as "Madame Bovary," has great ability; but nothing else they have written has an equal ability with "Germinie Lacerteux."

One of the consequences of the generalization I have ventured to make is that when a new French talent mounts above the horizon we watch with a kind of anxiety to see whether it will present itself in a subversive and unaccommodating manner. M. Pierre Loti is a new enough talent for us still to feel something of the glow of exultation at his having not contradicted us. He has in fact done exactly the opposite. He has added more than we had dared to hope to the force of our generalization and removed every scruple of a magnanimous sort that we might have felt in making it. By scruples of a magnanimous sort I mean those that might have been engendered by a sense of favors intensely enjoyed. At the moment we are under the spell of such a talent as Alphonse Daudet's or Emile Zola's or Guy de Maupassant's or (to give variety to the question) that of so rare and individual a genius as this exquisite Loti, it takes no great sophistry to convince us of the indelicacy, of the ingratitude even, of turning an invidious eye on anything so irrelevant as deficiencies. But the spell is foredoomed to fluctuations, to lapses, and we end by seeming to perceive with perplexity that even literary figures so brilliant as these may have too happy, too insolent a lot. Are they after all to enjoy their honors without paying for them? How *we* should have to pay for them if *we* were to succeed in plucking them and wearing them! The fortunate Frenchmen give us the sense of a kind of fatuity in impunity, a kind of superficiality in distinction, a kind of irritating mastery of the trick of eating your cake and having it. Such is one of the reflections to which Pierre Loti eventually leads us. In common with his companions he performs so beautifully as to kick up a fine golden dust over the question of what he contains—or of what he doesn't. The agility of all their movements makes up for the thinness of so much of their inspiration. To be so constituted as to expose one's self to the charge of vulgarity of spirit and yet to have a charm that successfully snaps its fingers at all "charges," is to be so lucky that those who work in harder conditions surely may allow themselves the solace of small criticisms. It may be said that if we indulge in small criticisms we resist our author's charm after all; but the answer to this is that the effort to throw off our enthralment even for an hour is an almost heroic struggle with a sweet superstition. The whole second-rate element in Loti, for instance, becomes an absolute stain if we think much about it. But practically (and this is his first-rate triumph) we *don't* think much about it, so unreserved is our surrender to irresistible illusion and contagious life.

To be so rare that you can be common, so good that you can be bad without loss of caste, be a mere sponge for sensations and yet not forfeit your human character—secure, on the contrary, sympathy and interest for it whenever you flash *that* facet into the sun—and then on top of all write, as Goldsmith wrote, like an angel — that surely is to wear the amulet to some purpose, the literary feather with a swagger that becomes pardonable. This rarity of the mixture, which makes such a literary unity of such a personal duality, is altogether in Pierre Loti a source of fascination. He combines aptitudes which seldom sit down to the same table, and combines them with singular facility and naturalness, an air of not caring whether he combines them or not. He may not be as ignorant of literature as he pretends (he protests perhaps a little too much that he never opens a book), but it is very clear that what is at the bottom of his effect is not (in a degree comparable at least to the intensity of the effect) the study of how to produce it. What he studies is a very different matter, and I know no case in which literature, left to come off as it can, comes off so beautifully. To be such a rover of the deep, such a dabbler in adventure as would delight the soul of Mr. Robert Louis Stevenson, and yet to have at one's command a sensitive and expressive apparatus separated by the whole scale from that of Jim Hawkins and John Silver, is to have little need of "cultivating" originality, as M. Guy de Maupassant the other day recommended us to do. An officer in the French navy, perpetually circumnavigating the globe, M. Loti has spent most of his life (though its duration, I believe, has not yet been considerable) in strange waters and far lands, and his taste for foreign contacts and free manners, for the natural, personal life, has led him to cultivate most of his opportunities. That taste and those opportunities are among soldiers and sailors common enough; but what is not so in the same connection is the spirit of the artist, which in M. Loti is as natural as all the rest. There is a reflection in regard to the distribution of earthly advantages which is probably familiar to most men of letters, and which at any rate often occurs to the writer of these lines. The persons who see the great things are terribly apt not to be persons who can write or even talk about them; and the persons who can write about them, reproduce them in some way, are terribly apt not to be persons who see them. The "chance" is with the blind or the dumb, and the immortal form, waiting for a revelation that doesn't come, is with the poor sedentary folk who bewail the waste of chances. Many an artist will have felt his heart sink on questioning some travelled friend in vain. The travelled friend has not noticed or has nothing to say about things which must have had an inestimable suggestiveness. So we frame a sort of ideal of success, in which the man of action and the man of observation melt into each other. The transcendent result is a precious creature who knows the sea as well as Captain Marryat, and writes about it as well — I can only say as well as Pierre Loti.

"She flew before the weather, the *Marie* [a fishing-boat in the Icelandic waters], flew faster and faster, and the weather flew as well, as before something mysterious and terrible. The gale, the sea, the *Marie* herself, were all taken with the same madness of flight and speed in the same direction. What scurried the fastest was the wind; then the great surges of the swell, slower and heavier, rushing after it; then the *Marie*, borne along in the universal motion. The waves pursued her with their blanched crests, rolling in a perpetual fall, and she, forever caught, forever left behind, got away from them, all the same, by the clever furrow she made in her wake, which sucked their rage away. And in this flying pace what they were conscious of above all was the sense of lightness; they felt themselves spring, without trouble or effort. When the *Marie* rose on the billows it was without a shock, as if the wind had lifted her; and then her descent was like a slide. ... She seemed to be sliding backwards, the fleeing mountain falling away from under her to rush onward, while she dropped into one of the great hollows that were also rushing. She touched its terrible bottom without a hurt, in a splash of water which didn't even wet her, but which fled like all the rest—fled and fainted ahead, like smoke, like nothing. In the depth of these hollows it was darker, and after each wave had passed they watched the next coming on behind — the next bigger and higher, green and transparent, which hurried up with furious contortions, scrolls almost closing over and seeming to say, 'Wait till I catch you—till I swallow you up!' But it didn't catch you; it only lifted you as you lift a feather in shrugging your shoulders, and you felt it pass under you almost gently, with its gushing foam, the crash of a cascade."

"Mon Frère Yves" and "Pêcheur d'Islande" are full of pages as vivid as that, which seem to us to place the author among the very first of sea-painters.

"You made out thousands of voices [in the huge clamor of a storm in Northern seas], those above either shrill or deep and seeming distant from being so big: that was the wind, the great soul of the uproar, the invisible power that carried on the whole thing. It was dreadful, but there were other sounds as well, closer, more material, more bent on destruction, given out by the torment of the water, which crackled as if on live coals. And it grew and still grew. In spite of their flying pace the sea began to cover them, to 'eat them up,' as they said; first the spray, whipping them from aft, then great bundles of water hurled with a force that might smash everything. The waves grew higher and still crazily higher, and yet they were ravelled as they came and you saw them hanging about in great green tatters, which were the falling water scattered by the wind. It fell in heavy masses on the deck, with the sound of a whack, and then the *Marie* shuddered all over, as if in pain. Now you could make out nothing more, on account of this drift of white slobber; when the gusts groaned afresh you saw it borne in thicker clouds, like the dust on the roads in summer. A heavy rain which had come on now passed aslant, almost horizontal, and all these things hissed together, lashing and wounding like stripes."

The English reader may see in such passages as these what the English reader is rather apt to see in any demonstrative view of difficulty or danger, any tendency to insist that a storm is bad or a mountain steep — a nervous exaggeration, the emotion of one who is not as Englishmen are. But Pierre Loti has many other things to say of the ocean than that it is a terrible place, and of strange countries than that it is a mercy one ever gets there, and the descriptions I have quoted are chosen at hazard. "It always came to an end suddenly [the hot, tropical rain]; the black curtain drew away slowly, dragging its train over the turquoise-tinted sea; the splendid light came forth more astounding after the darkness, and the great equatorial sun drank up fast all the water we had taken; the sails, the wood of the ship, the awnings recovered their whiteness in the sunshine; the *Sibyl* put on altogether the bright color of a dry thing in the midst of the great blue monotony that stretched around her." (Pierre Loti speaks better than of anything else of the ocean, the thing in the world that, after the human race, has most intensity and variety of life; but he renders with extraordinary felicity all the poetry of association, all the touching aspects and suggestions in persons, places, and objects connected with it, whose essential character is that they are more or less its sport and its victims. There is always a charming pity and a kind of filial passion in his phrase when it rests upon the people and things of his wind-swept and wave-washed Brittany. The literature of our day contains nothing more beautiful than the Breton passages, as they may be called, of "Mon Frère Yves" and "Pêcheur d'Islande." There is a sentence in the former of these tales, in reference to the indefinable sweetness of the short-lived Breton summer, which constitutes a sort of image of the attraction of his style. "A compound of a hundred things; the charm of the long, mild days, rarer than elsewhere and sooner gone; the deep, fresh grasses, with their extreme profusion of pink flowers; and then the sense of other years which sleeps there, spread through everything." All this is in Pierre Loti, the mildness and sadness, the profusion of pink flowers, and that implication of *other* conditions at any moment, which is the innermost note of the voice of the sea. When Gaud, in "Pêcheur d'Islande," takes her walk to the dreary promontory where she hopes she may meet her lover, "there were no more trees at all now, nothing but the bare heath, with its green furze, and here and there the divine crucified cutting out the great arms of their crosses against the sky and making the whole region look like an immense place of justice." Too long to quote in their fulness are the two admirable pages in the early part of the history of Gaud and Yann about the winter festival of the *pardon* of the fishermen, with Paimpol full of "the sound of bells and the chant of priests, the rude and monotonous songs of the taverns — old airs to cradle sailors, old *complaintes* brought from the sea, brought from I know not where, from the deep night of time"; full of "old granite houses, shutting in the swarm of the crowd; old roofs that told the story of their centuries of struggle against the west winds, the salt spray, the rains, everything that the sea brings to bear; the story, too, of the warm episodes they had sheltered, old adventures of daring and love." Easier to reproduce, in its concision, is the description of the day, the last day, before Yann Gaos goes forth on the ill-starred expedition from which he never returns:

"There was no wind from any quarter. The sea had turned very gentle; it was everywhere of the same pale blue and remained perfectly quiet. The sun shone with a great white brightness, and the rough Breton land soaked itself in the light as in something fine and rare; it seemed to feel a cheer and a refreshment even to its far-away distances. The air was deliciously tepid and smelt of summer; you would have said that it had stilled itself forever, that there never again would be dark days or tempests. The capes, the bays, without the changing shadows of the clouds, drew out in the sunshine their great motionless lines. They, too, appeared given up to endless rest and tranquillity. . . . On the edges of the ways you saw little hasty flowers, primroses and violets, pale and without scent."

"Madame Chrysanthème," the history of a summer spent in very curious conditions at Nagasaki, the latest of the author's productions and the most distinctively amusing, has less spontaneity than its predecessors, and seems more calculated, more made to order; but it abounds in unsurpassable little vignettes, of which the portrait of certain Japanese ladies of quality whom he met at the photographer's is a specimen:

"I couldn't satiate my desire to look at these two creatures; they captivated me like incomprehensible things that one had never seen. Their fragile bodies, outlandishly graceful in posture, are drowned in stiff materials and redundant sashes, of which the ends droop like tired wings. They make me think, I don't know why, of great, rare insects; the extraordinary patterns on their garments have something of the dark bedizenment of night-butterflies. Above all, there is the mystery of their quite small eyes, drawn back and up so far that the lids are tight and they can scarcely open; the mystery of their expression, which seems to denote inner thoughts of a cold, vague complacency of absurdity — a world of ideas absolutely closed to ourselves."

It may be that many an English reader will not recognize Pierre Loti as a man of action who happens to have a genius for literary expression, the account he himself gives of his exploits not being such as we associate with that character. The term action has a wide signification, but there are some kinds of life which it represents to us certainly much less than others. The exploits of the author of "Madame Chrysanthème," of "Ayizadé," of "Rarahu," of "Le Roman d'un Spahi," and "Pasquala Ivanovitch," are—I hardly know what to call them, for we scarcely mention achievements of this order in English—more relaxing on the whole than tonic. An author less tonic than Pierre Loti can indeed not well be imagined, and the English reader ought already to have been notified (the plainest good faith requires it and I have delayed much too long) that a good deal of what he has to tell us relates mainly to his successes among the ladies. We have a great and I think a just dislike to the egotistic-erotic, to literary confidences on such points, and when a gentleman abounds in them the last thing we take him for is a real man of action. It must be confessed that Pierre Loti abounds, though his two best books are not autobiographical, and there is simply nothing to reply to any English reader who on ascertaining this circumstance may declare that he desires to hold no commerce with him; nothing, that is, but the simple remark that such a reader will lose a precious pleasure. This warning, however, is a trifle to the really scandalized. I maintain my epithet, at any rate, and I should desire no better justification for it than such an admirable piece as the "Corvée Matinale," in the volume entitled "Propos d'Exil," which describes how the author put off at dawn from a French ship of war, in a small boat with a handful of men, to row up a river on the coast of Anam and confer, with a view of bringing them promptly to terms, with the authorities of the queerest of little Asiatic towns. A writer is to my sense quite man of action enough when he has episodes like that to relate; they give a sufficient perfection to the conjunction of the "chance" and the pictorial view. Danger has nothing to do with it; the manner in which M. Loti gives us on this occasion the impression of an almost grotesque absence of danger, of ugly mandarins superfluously frightened as well as of the color and temperature of the whole scene, the steaming banks of the river, with flat Asiatic faces peeping out of the rushes, the squalid, fetid crowds, the shabby, contorted pagodas, with precious little objects glimmering in the shade of their open fronts—the vividness of all these suggestions is the particular sign of this short masterpiece. The same remark applies to the "Pagodes Souterraines," in the same volume—the story, told with admirable art, of an excursion, while the ship lingers exasperatingly on the same hot, insufferable coast, to visit certain marvellous old tombs and temples, hewn out of a mountain of pink marble, filled with horrible monstrous effigies and guarded by bonzes almost as uncanny. The appreciation of the exotic, which M. Jules Lemaître marks as Loti's distinguishing sign, finds perfect expression in such pages as these.

There are many others of the same sort in the "Propos d'Exil," which is a chaplet of pearls; but perhaps the book is above all valuable for the sketch entitled "Un Vieux"—the picture of the old age, dreary and lamentable, of a worn-out mariner who has retired on his pension to a cottage in the suburbs of Brest. It has delicate sentiment as well as an extraordinary objective reality; but it is not sentimental, for it is characterized by an ineffable pessimism and a close, fascinated notation of the inexorable stages by which lonely and vacant old age moulders away, with its passions dying, dying very hard. "Un Vieux" is singularly ugly, and "Pêcheur d'Islande" is singularly beautiful; but I should be tempted to say that in Pierre Loti's work "Un Vieux" is the next finest thing to "Pêcheur d'Islande." "Mon Frère Yves" is full of beauty, but it carries almost to a maximum the author's characteristic defect, the absence of composition, the *décousu* quality which makes each of his productions appear at first a handful of flying leaves. "Un Vieux" has a form as a whole, though it occurs to me that, perhaps, it is surpassed in this respect by another gem of narration or description, the best pages of the "Fleurs d'Ennui." (We hesitate for a word when it is a question mainly of rendering, as Loti renders it, the impression, of giving the material illusion, of a strange place and strange manners.) I leave to the impartial reader to judge whether "Les Trois Dames de la Kasbah," the gem in question (it has been extracted from the "Fleurs d'Ennui" and published in a pretty little volume by itself), is more or only is less ugly than "Un Vieux." That will depend a good deal on whether he be shocked by the cynicism of the most veracious of all possible representations of the adventures of a band of drunken sailors during a stuffy night at Algiers. Such, and nothing more (the adventures are of the least edifying, and the *dénoûment* is not even mentionable to ears polite), is the subject of

"Les Trois Dames de la Kasbah, Conte Oriental"; and yet the life, the spirit, the color, the communicative tone, the truth and poetry of this little production are such that one cannot conscientiously relegate it (one wishes one could) to a place even of comparative obscurity.

If our author's ruling passion is the appreciation of the exotic, it is not in his first works that he confines his quest to funny calls on nervous mandarins, to the twilight gloom of rheumatic old sailors or the vulgar pranks of reckless young ones. "Le Roman d'un Spahi," "Ayizadé," and "Rarahu" each contain the history of a love-affair with a primitive woman or a combination of primitive women. There is a kind of complacent animalism in them which makes it difficult to speak of them as the perfection of taste, and I profess to be able to defend them on the ground of taste only so long as they are not attacked. The great point is that they will not be attacked by any one who is capable of feeling the extraordinary power of evocation of (for instance) "Le Mariage de Loti" (another name for "Rarahu"), at the same time that he recognizes the abnormal character of such a performance, a character the more marked as the feeling of youth is strong in these early volumes, and the young person has rarely M. Loti's assurance as a *viveur*. He betrays a precocity of depravity which is disconcerting. I write the gross word depravity because we must put the case against him (so many English readers would feel it that way) as strongly as it can be put. It doesn't put it strongly enough to say that the serene surrender to polygamous practices among coral-reefs and in tepid seas is a sign much rather of primitive innocence, for there is an element in the affair that vitiates the argument. This is simply that the serenity (which, I take it, most makes the innocence) cannot under the circumstances be adequate. The pen, the talent, the phrase, the style, the note-book take care of that and change the whole situation; they invalidate the plea of the primitive. They introduce the conscious element, and that is the weak side of Loti's spontaneities and pastorals. What saves him is that his talent never falters, and this is but another illustration of his interesting double nature. His customs and those of his friends at Tahiti, at Stamboul, on the east coast of the Adriatic, or again, according to his latest work, at Nagasaki, are not such as we associate in the least with high types; and yet when we close these various records of the general activity known as the attitude of "conquest," the impression that abides with us is one of surpassing delicacy. The facts are singularly vulgar, in spite of the exotic glow that wraps them up; but the subjective side of the business, the author's imagination, has an extraordinary light. Few things could suggest more the value that we instinctively attach to a high power of evocation—the degree to which we regard it as precious in itself.

What makes the facts vulgar, what justifies us in applying to Loti's picture of himself an ironic epithet or two, is his almost inveterate habit of representing the closest and most intimate personal relations as unaccompanied with any moral feeling, any impulse of reflection or reaction. He has so often the air of not seeming to talk of affection when he talks of love—that oddest of all French literary characteristics, and one to which we owe the circumstance that whole volumes have been written on the latter of these principles without an allusion to the former. There is a moral feeling in the singular friendship of which "Mon Frère Yves" is mainly a masterly commemoration, and also a little in the hindered passion which at last unites, for infinite disaster, alas! the hero and heroine of "Pêcheur d'Islande." These are the exceptions; they are admirable and reassuring. The closer, the more intimate is a personal relation the more we look in it for the human drama, the variations and complications, the note of responsibility for which we appeal in vain to the loves of the quadrupeds. Failing to satisfy us in this way, such a relation is not, as Mr. Matthew Arnold says of American civilization, *interesting*. M. Pierre Loti is too often guilty of the simplicity of assuming that when exhibited on his own part it *is* interesting. I should make a point of parenthesizing that the picture of the passion which holds together in an immortal embrace the two great figures of "Pêcheur d'Islande" is essentially a picture of affection. "Rarahu" is a wonderful extension of the reader's experience—a study of the *nonchalance* of the strange, attractive Maori race and the private life of Polynesia. The impression is irresistible and the transfusion of our consciousness, as one may say, effected without the waste of a drop. The case is the same with "Ayizadé," and the transfusion this time is into a more capacious recipient. "Ayizadé" relates the adventures of a French naval officer who spends a winter, at Salonica and Constantinople, in the tolerably successful effort to pass (not only in the eyes of others but in his very own) for a Turk, and a Turk of the people moreover, with the ingrained superstitions and prejudices. He secures in this experiment the valuable assistance of sundry unconventional persons (for his ideal is the Bohemian Turk, if the expression may be used), foremost of whom is the lady, the wife of a rich and respectable Mussulman, who gives her name to the book. It is for M. Loti himself to have judged whether the results were worth the trouble; the great point is that his reader feels that *he* has them, in their reality, without the trouble, and is beholden to the author accordingly for one of the greatest of literary pleasures. M. Jules Lemaitre, whom it is difficult not to quote in speaking of any writer of whom he has spoken, gives "Ayizadé" the high praise of being the finest case of enlarged sympathy that he knows, and the most successful effort at changing one's skin. Commendation of this order it doubtless deserves, equally with "Le Mariage de Loti," in spite of the infirmity I have hinted at, the fact that the interest is supposed largely to be attached to a close personal relation which is not quite human, which is too simplified, too much like the loves of the quadrupeds. The desire to change his skin is frequent with M. Loti, and it has this oddity that his preference is almost always for a dusky one. We rarely see him attempt to assume the complexion of one of the fairer races—of the English for instance, the fairest perhaps of all. He indulges indeed in the convenient fiction that the personage of whom Loti was originally the *nom de guerre* is Mr. Harry Grant, a midshipman in her Majesty's service; but this device is perfunctory and the identity is not maintained. Nothing could illustrate more our author's almost impertinent amateurishness and laxity of composition, as well as the circumstance that we forgive it at every step, than the artless confusion which runs through all his volumes in regard to such identities. They don't signify, and it is all, as his own idiom has it, sewn with white thread. Loti is at once the pseudonym of M. Julien Viaud and the assumed name of the hero of a hundred more or less scandalous anecdotes. Suddenly he ceases to be Harry Grant and becomes an officer in the French navy. The brother Yves is one person in the charming book which bears his name, and another (apparently) in "Madame Chrysanthème." The name becomes generic and represents any convivial Breton sailor. A curious shadow called Plumkett—a naval comrade—wanders vaguely in and out of almost all the books, in relations incompatible with each other. The odd part of it is that this childish confusion does not only not take from our pleasure, but does not even take from our sense of the author's talent. It is another of the things which prove Loti's charm to be essentially a charm absolute, a charm outside of the rules, outside of logic, and independent of responsibility.

In "Madame Chrysanthème" the periodical experiment is Japanese, the effort on Loti's part has been to saturate with the atmosphere of Nipon that oft-soaked sponge to which I have ventured to compare his imagination. His success has not been so great as in other cases, for the simple reason that the Japanese have not rubbed off on him as freely as the Turks and the Tahitans. The act of sympathy has not taken place, the experiment is comparatively a failure. The wringing-out of the sponge leaves rather a turbid deposit. The author's taste is for the primitive and beautiful, the large and free, and the Japanese strike him as ugly and complicated, tiny and conventional. His attitude is more profane than our own prejudice can like it to be; he quite declines to take them seriously. The reproach, in general, to which many people would hold him to be most open, is that he takes seriously people and things which deserve it less. I may be altogether mistaken, but we treat ourselves to the conviction that he fails of justice to the wonderful little people who have renewed, for Europe and America, the whole idea of Taste. It occurs to us for the first time that he is partially closed, slightly narrow, he whose very profession it is to be accessible to extreme strangeness, and we feel, as devoted readers, a certain alarm.

We ask ourselves whether the sponge has been so often dipped that it has lost its retentive property, and with an anxious desire for reassurance on this point we await his next production.

It is, however, singularly out-of-place to talk of what Pierre Loti may next produce when I have not interrupted my general remarks to mention in detail the high claims of "Mon Frère Yves" and "Pêcheur d'Islande." It is of these things above all the friendly critic must speak if he wishes to speak to friendly ears. If our author had written his other books and not written these he would have been a curious and striking figure in literature; but the two volumes I have last named give him a different place altogether, and if I had not read and re-read them I should not have put forth this general plea. "Mon Frère Yves" is imperfect (it is notably, for what it is, too long), and "Pêcheur d'Islande" is to my sense perfect, yet they have almost an equal part in contributing to their author's name an association of supreme beauty. The history of Marguerite Mével and Yann Gaos strikes me as one of the very few works of imagination of our day completely and successfully beautiful. The singular thing is that these two tales, with their far finer effect, differ only in degree from their predecessors, differ not at all in kind. The part of them that deals with the complicated heart is still the weakest element; it is still, as in the others, the senses that vibrate most (to every impression of air and climate and color and weather and season); the feeling is always the feeling of the great earth—the navigator's earth—as a constant physical solicitation. But the picture in each case has everything that gives a lift to that susceptibility and nothing that draws it down, and the susceptibility finds a language which fits it like a glove. The impulse to be human and reflective—the author has felt it, indeed, strongly in each case; but it is still primitive humanity that fascinates him most, and if Yves and Yann and Silvestre and Gaud and the old grandmother Moan are more complicated than Ayizadé and Samuel and Achmet and Fatou-gaye and Rarahu, they are infinitely less so than the young people of either sex who supply the interest of most valid works of fiction. "Pêcheur d'Islande" is the history of a passion, but of a passion simplified, in its strength, to a sort of community with the winds and waves, the blind natural forces hammering away at the hard Breton country where it is enacted. "Mon Frère Yves" relates the history of an incorrigible drunkard and *coureur*, a robust, delightful Breton sailor who, in his better moments, reads "Le Marquis de Villemer" and weeps over it. (There is a sort of mystification, I should remark, in this production, for the English reader at least, the book being in a large degree the representation of an intimate friendship between the sailor and his superior officer, the spectator of his career and chronicler of his innumerable relapses. Either the conditions which permit of this particular variation of discipline are not adequately explained or the rigor of the hierarchy is less in the French service than in others.) What strikes me in "Pêcheur d'Islande" is the courage which has prompted him to appeal to us on behalf of a situation worn so smooth by generations of novelists that there would seem to be nothing left in it to hook our attention to, not to mention the scarcely less manifest fact that it is precisely this artless absence of suspicion that he was attempting a *tour de force* which has drawn down the abundance of success. Yann Gaos is a magnificent young fisherman — magnificent in stature and strength, and shy and suspicious in temper—whose trade is to spend his summer hauling up millions of cod in the cold and dangerous waters of the North. He meets among the coast-folk of his home a very clever and pretty girl who receives from him an even deeper impression than she gives, but with whom he completely fails to come to an understanding. The understanding is delayed for two years (thanks largely to an absence of "manner" on either side), during which the girl's heart comes near to breaking. At last, quite suddenly, they find themselves face to face, she confessing her misery and he calling himself a dolt. They are married in a hurry, to have a short honeymoon before he starts for his annual cruise (the idea of which fills her with an irresistible foreboding), and he sails away to Iceland with his mates. She waits in vain for his return, and he never, never comes back. This is all the tale can boast in the way of plot; it is the old-fashioned "love-story" reduced to a paucity of terms. I am sure M. Loti has no views nor theories as to what constitutes and does not constitute a plot; he has taken no precautions, he has not sacrificed to any irritated divinity, and yet he has filled the familiar, the faded materials with freshness and meaning. He has appealed to us on "eternal" grounds, and besides the unconscious *tour de force* of doing so in this particular case successfully we impute to him the even more difficult feat of having dispensed with the aid of scenery. His scenery is exactly the absence of scenery; he has placed his two lovers in the mere immensity of sea and sky, so that they seem suspended in a gray, windy void. We see Yann half the time in the perfect blank of fog and darkness. A writer with a story to tell that is not very fresh usually ekes it out by referring as much as possible to surrounding objects. But in this misty medium there are almost no surrounding objects to refer to, and their isolation gives Yann and Gaud a kind of heroic greatness. I hasten to add that, of course, the author would not have conjured so well had he not been an incomparable painter of the sea. The book closes with a passage of strange and admirable eloquence, which it seems to me that no critic speaking of it has a right to omit to quote. I should say, as a preliminary, that in the course of the tale Yann Gaos, "chaffed" by his comrades on the question of his having a sweetheart and marrying her, has declared that for him there is no woman, no wife, no bride, none but the ocean to which he is already betrothed. Also that a vivid and touching incident (as the figure is also itself wonderfully charming) is that of the young fisherman Sylvestre Moan, a cousin of Gaud and a great friend, though younger, of Yann, who, called to serve in the navy, is mortally wounded at Tonquin, and, on the fetid transport that brings him home, dies, suffocating, in the tropics. The author relates how he is buried on the way, in a rank, bright cemetery, during a short disembarkment at Singapore.

"Yann never came home. One August night, out there off the coast of Iceland, in the midst of a great fury of sound, were celebrated his nuptials with the sea—with the sea who of old had also been his nurse. She had made him a strong and broad-chested youth, and then had taken him in his magnificent manhood for herself alone. A deep mystery had enveloped their monstrous nuptials. Dusky veils all the while had been shaken above them, curtains inflated and twisted, stretched there to hide the feast ; and the bride gave voice continually, made her loudest horrible noise to smother the cries. He, remembering Gaud, his wife of flesh, had defended himself, struggling like a giant, against this spouse who was the grave, until the moment when he let himself go, his arms open to receive her, with a great, deep cry like the death-roar of a bull, his mouth already full of water, his arms open, stretched and stiff forever. And they were all at his wedding—all those whom he had bidden of old, all except Sylvestre, who, poor fellow, had gone off to sleep in enchanted gardens far away on the other side of the earth."

If it be then a matter of course in France that a fresh talent should present its possessor mainly as one more *raffiné* in the observation of external things, and also, I think I may add, as one more pessimist in regard to the nature of man and of woman, and if such a presumption appears to have been confirmed by an examination of Pierre Loti, in spite of the effort of poor Yves to cultivate his will. and of the mutual

tenderness of Yann and Gaud, our conclusion, all the
same, will not have escaped the necessity of taking
into account the fact that there still seems an inexhaustible life for writers who obey this particular inspiration. The Nemesis remains very much what I
attempted to suggest its being at the beginning of
these remarks, but somehow the writers over whom
it hovers enjoy none the less remarkable health on
the side on which they are strong. If they have almost nothing to show us in the way of the operation
of character, the possibilities of conduct, the part
played in the world by the *idea* (you would never
guess, either from Pierre Loti or from M. Guy de
Maupassant, that the idea has any force or any credit
in the world); if man, for them, is the simple sport
of fate, with suffering for his main sign—either suffering or one particular satisfaction, always the same
—their affirmation of all this is still, on the whole,
the most complete affirmation that the novel at present offers us. They have on their side the accident,
if accident it be, that they never cease to be artists.
They will keep this advantage till the optimists of
the hour, the writers for whom the life of the soul is
equally real and visible (lends itself to effects and triumphs, challenges the power to "render"), begin to
seem to them formidable competitors. On that day
it will be very interesting to see what line they take,
whether they will throw up the battle, surrendering
honorably, or attempt a change of base. Many intelligent persons hold that for the French a change of
base is impossible and that they are either what they

incessantly show themselves or nothing. This view, of course, derives sanction from that awkward condition which I have mentioned as attached to the work of those among them who are most conspicuous—the fact that their attempts to handle the life of the spirit are comparatively so ineffectual. On the other hand, it is terribly compromising when those who do handle the life of the spirit with the manner of experience fail to make *their* affirmation complete, fail to make us take them seriously as artists, and even go so far (some of them are capable of that) as to introduce the ruinous suggestion that there is perhaps some essential reason (I scarcely know how to say it) why observers who are of that way of feeling should be a little weak in the conjuring line. To be even a little weak in representation is, of course, practically and for artistic purposes, to be what schoolboys call a duffer, and I merely glance, shuddering, at such a possibility. What would be *their* Nemesis, what penalty would such a group have incurred in their failure to rebut triumphantly so damaging an imputation? Who would then have to stand from under? It is not Pierre Loti, at any rate, who makes the urgency of these questions a matter only for the materialists (as it is convenient to call them) to consider. He only adds to our suspicion that, for good or for evil, they have still an irrepressible life, and he does so the more notably that, in his form and seen as a whole, he is a renovator, and, as I may say, a refresher. He plays from his own bat, imitating no one, not even nearly or remotely, to my sense—though

I have heard the charge made—Châteaubriand. He arrives with his bundle of impressions, but they have been independently gathered in the world, not in the school, and it is a coincidence that they are of the same order as the others, expressed in their admirable personal way and with an indifference to the art of transitions which is at once one of the most striking cases of literary irresponsibility that I know and one of the finest of ingratiation. He has settled the question of his own *superficies* (even in the pathos of the sacred reunion of his lovers in "Pêcheur d'Islande" there is something inconvertibly carnal), but he has not settled the other, the general question of how long and how far accomplished and exclusive —practically exclusive—impressionism will yet go, with its vulture on its back and feeding on it. I hope I appear not to speak too apocalyptically in saying that the problem is still there to minister to our interest and perhaps even a little to our anxiety.

1888.

THE JOURNAL OF THE BROTHERS DE GONCOURT

I CAN scarcely forbear beginning these limited remarks on an interesting subject with a regret—the regret that I had not found the right occasion to make them two or three years ago. This is not because since that time the subject has become less attaching, but precisely because it has become more so, has become so absorbing that I am oppressively conscious of the difficulty of treating it. It was never, I think, an easy one; inasmuch as for persons interested in questions of literature, of art, of form, in the general question of the observation of life for an artistic purpose, the appeal and the solicitation of Edmond and Jules de Goncourt were essentially not simple and soothing. The manner of this extraordinary pair, their temper, their strenuous effort and conscious system, suggested anything but a quick solution of the problems that seemed to hum in our ears as we read; suggested it almost as little indeed as their curious, uncomfortable style, with its multiplied touches and pictorial verbosity, was apt to evoke an immediate vision of the objects to which it made such sacrifices of the synthetic and the rhythmic.

None the less, if one liked them well enough to persist, one ended by making terms with them; I allude to the liking as conditional, because it appears to be a rule of human relations that it is by no means always a sufficient bond of sympathy for people to care for the same things: there may be so increasing a divergence when they care for them in different ways. The great characteristic of the way of the brothers De Goncourt was that it was extraordinarily "modern"; so illustrative of feelings that had not yet found intense expression in literature that it made at last the definite standpoint, the common ground and the clear light for taking one's view of them. They bristled (the word is their own) with responsible professions, and took us farther into the confidence of their varied sensibility than we always felt it important to penetrate; but the formula that expressed them remained well in sight. They were historians and observers who were painters; they composed biographies, they told stories, with the palette always on their thumb.

Now, however, all that is changed and the case is infinitely more complicated. M. Edmond de Goncourt has published, at intervals of a few months, the Journal kept for twenty years by his brother and himself, and the Journal makes all the difference. The situation was comparatively manageable before, but now it strikes us as extremely embarrassing. M. Edmond de Goncourt has mixed the cards in the most extraordinary way; he has shifted his position with a carelessness of consequences of which I know no other example. Who can recall an instance of an artist's having it in his power to deprive himself of the advantage of the critical perspective in which he stands, and being eager to use that power?

That MM. de Goncourt should have so faithfully carried on their Journal is a very interesting and remarkable fact, as to which there will be much to say; but it has almost a vulgarly usual air in comparison with the circumstance that one of them has judged best to give the document to the light. If it be true that the elder and surviving brother has held a part of it back, that only adds to the judicious, responsible quality of the act. He has selected, and that indicates a plan and constitutes a presumption of sanity. There has been, so to speak, a method in M. Edmond de Goncourt's madness. I use the term madness because it so conveniently covers most of the ground. How else indeed should one express it when a man of talent defaces with his own hand not only the image of himself that public opinion has erected on the highway of literature, but also the image of a loved and lost partner who can raise no protest and offer no explanation? If instead of publishing his Journal M. de Goncourt had burned it up we should have been deprived of a very curious and entertaining book; but even with that consciousness we should have remembered that it would have been impertinent to expect him to do anything else. Barely conceivable would it have been had he withheld the copious record from the flames for the perusal of a posterity who would pass judgment on it when he himself should be dust. That would have been an act of high humility—the sacrifice of the finer part of one's reputation; but, after all, a man can commit suicide only in his lifetime, and the example would have had its distinction on the part of a curious mind moved by sympathy with the curiosity of a coming age.

If I suggest that if it were possible to us to hear Jules de Goncourt's voice to-day it might convey an explanation, this perhaps represents an explanation as more possible than we see it as yet. Certainly it is difficult to see it as graceful or as conciliatory. There is scarcely any account we can give of the motive of the act that doesn't make it almost less an occasion for complacency than the act itself. (I still refer, of course, to the publication, not to the composition, of the Journal. The composition, for nervous, irritated, exasperated characters, may have been a relief—though even in this light its operation appears to have been slow and imperfect. Indeed, it occurs to one that M. Edmond de Goncourt may have felt the whimsical impulse to expose the fond remedy as ineffectual.) If the motive was not humility, not mortification, it was something else—something that we can properly appreciate only by remembering that it is not enough to be proud, and that the question inevitably comes up of what one's pride is about. If MM. de Goncourt were two almost furious *névrosés*, if the infinite vibration of their nerves and the soreness of their sentient parts were the condition on which they produced many interesting books, the fact was pathetic and the misfortune great, but the legitimacy of the whole thing was incontestable. People are made as they are made, and some are weak in one way and some in another. What passes our comprehension is the state of mind in which their weakness appears to them a source of glory or even of dolorous general interest. It may be an inevitable, or it may even for certain sorts of production be an indispensable, thing to be a *névrosé;* but in what particular juncture is it a communicable thing? M. de Goncourt not only communicates the case, but insists upon it; he has done personally what M. Maxime du Camp did a few years ago for Gustave Flaubert (in his " Souvenirs Littéraires ") when he made known to the world that the author of " Madame Bovary " had epileptic fits. The differences are great, however, for if we are disposed to question M. du Camp's right to put another person's secret into circulation, we must admit that he does so with compunction and mourning. M. de Goncourt, on the other hand, waves the banner of the infirmity that his *collaborateur* shared with him and invites all men to listen to the details. About his right, I hasten to add, so far as he speaks for himself, there is nothing dubious, and this puts us in a rare position for reading and enjoying his book. We are not accomplices and our honor is safe. People are betrayed by their friends, their enemies, their biographers, their critics, their editors, their publishers, and so far as we give ear in these cases we are not quite without guilt; but it is much plainer sailing when the burden of defence rests on the very sufferers. What would have been thought of a friend or an editor, what would have been thought even of an enemy, who should have ventured to print the Journal of MM. de Goncourt?

The reason why it must always be asked in future, with regard to any appreciation of these gentlemen, "Was it formed before the Journal or after the Journal?" is simply that this publication has obtruded into our sense of their literary performance the disturbance of a revelation of personal character. The scale on which the disturbance presents itself is our ground for surprise, and the nature of the character exhibited our warrant for regret. The complication is simply that if to-day we wish to judge the writings of the brothers De Goncourt freely, largely, historically, the feat is almost impossible. We have to reckon with a prejudice—a prejudice of our own. And that is why a critic may be sorry to have missed the occasion of testifying to a liberal comprehension before the prejudice was engendered. Almost impossible, I say, but fortunately not altogether; for is it not the very function of criticism and the sign of its intelligence to acquit itself honorably in embarrassing conditions and track the idea with patience just in proportion as it is elusive? The good method is always to sacrifice nothing. Let us therefore not regret too much either that MM. de Goncourt did not burn their Journal if they wished their novels to be liked, or that they did not burn their novels if they wished their Journal to be forgotten. The difficult point to deal with as regards this latter produc-

tion is that it is a journal of pretensions; for is it not a sound generalization to say that when we speak of pretensions we always mean pretensions exaggerated? If the Journal sets them forth, it is in the novels that we look to see them justified. If the justification is imperfect, that will not disgust us, for what does the disparity do more than help to characterize our authors? The importance of their being characterized depends largely on their talent (for people engaged in the same general effort and interested in the same questions), and of a poverty of talent even the reader most struck with the unamiable way in which, as diarists, they for the most part use their powers will surely not accuse MM. de Goncourt. They express, they represent, they give the sense of life; it is not always the life that such and such a one of their readers will find most interesting, but that is his affair and not theirs. Theirs is to vivify the picture. This art they unmistakably possess, and the Journal testifies to it still more than "Germinie Lacerteux" and "Manette Salomon"; infinitely more, I may add, than the novels published by M. Edmond de Goncourt since the death of his brother.

I do not pronounce for the moment either on the justice or the generosity of the portrait of Sainte-Beuve produced in the Journal by a thousand small touches, entries made from month to month and year to year, and taking up so much place in the whole that the representation of that figure (with the Princess Mathilde, Gavarni, Théophile Gautier, and Gustave Flaubert thrown in a little behind) may almost

be said to be the main effect of the three volumes.
What is incontestable is the intensity of the vision,
the roundness of the conception, and the way that
the innumerable little parts of the image hang together.
The Sainte-Beuve of MM. de Goncourt may not
be the real Sainte-Beuve, but he is a wonderfully possible
and consistent personage. He is observed with
detestation, but at least he is observed, and the faculty
is welcome and rare. This is what we mean by talent
—by having something fresh to contribute. Let us be
grateful for anything at all fresh so long as our gratitude
is not chilled—a case in which it has always the
resource of being silent. It is obvious that this check
is constantly at hand in our intercourse with MM. de
Goncourt, for the simple reason that, with the greatest
desire in the world to see all round, we cannot
rid ourselves of the superstition that, when all is said
and done, art is most in character when it most shows
itself amiable. It is not amiable when it is narrow
and exclusive and jealous, when it makes the deplorable
confession that it has no secret for resisting exasperation.
It is not the sign of a free intelligence or
a rich life to be hysterical because somebody's work
whom you don't like affirms itself in opposition to
that of somebody else whom you do; but this condition
is calculated particularly little to please when
the excitement springs from a comparison more personal.
It is almost a platitude to say that the artistic
passion will ever most successfully assuage the popular
suspicion that there is a latent cruelty in it when
it succeeds in not appearing to be closely connected

with egotism. The uncalculated trick played by our authors upon their reputation was to suppose that their name could bear such a strain. It is tolerably clear that it can't, and this is the mistake we should have to forgive them if we proposed to consider their productions as a whole. It doesn't cover all the ground to say that the injury of their mistake is only for themselves: it is really in some degree for those who take an interest in the art they practise. Such eccentrics, such passionate seekers, may not, in England and America, be numerous; but even if they are a modest band, their complaint is worth taking account of. No one can ever have been nearly so much interested in the work of Edmond and Jules de Goncourt as these gentlemen themselves; their deep absorption in it, defying all competition, is one of the honorable sides of their literary character. But the general brotherhood of men of letters may very well have felt humiliated by the disclosure of such wrath in celestial, that is, in analogous minds. It is, in short, rather a shock to find that artists who could make such a miniature of their Sainte-Beuve have not carried their delicacy a little further. It is always a pain to perceive that some of the qualities we prize don't imply the others.

What makes it important not to sacrifice the Journal (to speak for the present only of that) is this very illustration of the degree to which, for the indefatigable diarists, the things of literature and art are the great realities. If every genuine talent is for the critic a "case" constituted by the special mixture of elements and faculties, it is not difficult to put one's finger on the symptoms in which that of these unanimous brothers resides. It consists in their feeling life so exclusively as a theme for descriptive pictorial prose. Their exclusiveness is, so far as I know, unprecedented; for if we have encountered men of erudition, men of science as deeply buried in learning and in physics, we have never encountered a man of letters (our authors are really one in their duality) for whom his profession was such an exhaustion of his possibilities. Their friend and countryman Flaubert doubtless gave himself up to "art" with as few reservations, but our authors have over him exactly the superiority that the Journal gives them: it is a proof the more of their concentration, of their having drawn breath only in the world of subject and form. If they are not more representative, they are at least more convenient to refer to. Their concentration comes in part from the fact that it is the meeting of two natures, but this also would have counted in favor of expansion, of leakage. "Collaboration" is always a mystery, and that of MM. de Goncourt was probably close beyond any other; but we have seen the process successful several times, so that the real wonder is not that in this case the parties to it should have been able to work together, to divide the task without dividing the effect, but rather that nature should have struck off a double copy of a rare original. An original is a conceivable thing, but a pair of originals who are original in exactly the same way is a phenomenon embodied so far as I know only in the authors of "Manette Salomon." The relation borne by their feelings on the question of art and taste to their other feelings (which they assure us were very much less identical), this peculiar proportion constitutes their originality. In whom was ever the group of "other feelings" proportionately so small? In whom else did the critical vibration (in respect to the things cared for, limited in number, even very limited, I admit) represent so nearly the totality of emotion? The occasions left for MM. de Goncourt to vibrate differently were so few that they scarcely need be counted.

The manifestation of life that most appeals to them is the manifestation of Watteau, of Lancret, of Boucher, of Fragonard; they are primarily critics of pictorial art (with sympathies restricted very much to a period) whose form of expression happens to be literary, but whose sensibility is the sensibility of the painter and the sculptor, and whose attempt, allowing for the difference of the instrument, is to do what the painter and the sculptor do. The most general stricture to be made on their work is probably that they have not allowed enough for the difference of the instrument, have persisted in the effort to render impressions that the plastic artist renders better, neglecting too much those he is unable to render. From time to time they have put forth a volume which is really an instructive instance of misapplied ingenuity. In "Madame Gervaisais," for example, a picture of the visible, sketchable

Rome of twenty-five years ago, we seem to hear the voice forced to sing in a register to which it doesn't belong, or rather (the comparison is more complete) to attempt effects of sound that are essentially not vocal. The novelist competes with the painter and the painter with the novelist, in the treatment of the aspect and figure of things; but what a happy tact each of them needs to keep his course straight, without poaching on the other's preserves! In England it is the painter who is apt to poach most, and in France the writer. However this may be, no one probably has poached more than have MM. de Goncourt.

Whether it be because there is something that touches us in pious persistence in error, or because even when it prevails there may on the part of a genuine talent be the happiest hits by the way, I will not pretend to declare; certain it is that the manner in which our authors abound in their own sense and make us feel that they would not for the world care for anything but what exactly they do care for, raises the liveliest presumption in their favor. If literature is kept alive by a passion loyal even to narrowness, MM. de Goncourt have rendered real services. They may look for it on the one side in directions too few, and on the other in regions thankless and barren; their Journal, at all events, is a signal proof of their good faith. Wonderful are such courage and patience and industry; fatigued, displeased, disappointed, they never intermit their chronicle nor falter in their task. We owe to this remarkable feat the vivid reflection of their life for twenty years, from the *coup d'état* which produced the Second Empire to the death of the younger brother on the eve of the war with Germany; the history of their numerous books, their articles, their studies, studies on the social and artistic history of France during the latter half of the last century— on Mme. de Pompadour, Mme. du Barry, and the other mistresses of Louis XV., on Marie Antoinette, on society and *la femme* during the Revolution and the Directory; the register, moreover, of their adventures and triumphs as collectors (collectors of the furniture, tapestries, drawings of the last century), of their observations of every kind in the direction in which their nature and their *milieu* prompt them to observe, of their talks, their visits, their dinners, their physical and intellectual states, their projects and visions, their ambitions and collapses, and, above all, of their likes and dislikes. Above all of their dislikes, perhaps I should say, for in this sort of testimony the Journal is exceedingly rich. The number of things and of people obnoxious to their taste is extremely large, especially when we consider the absence of variety, as the English reader judges variety, in their personal experience. What strikes an English reader, curious about a society in which acuteness has a high development and thankful for a picture of it, is the small surface over which the career of MM. de Goncourt is distributed. It seems all to take place in a little ring, a coterie of a dozen people. Movement, exercise, travel, other countries, play no part in it; the same persons, the same places, names, and occasions perpetually recur; there is scarcely any change of scene or any enlargement of horizon. The authors rarely go into the country, and when they do they hate it, for they find it *bête*. To the English mind that item probably describes them better than anything else. We end with the sensation of a closed room, of a want of ventilation; we long to open a window or two and let in the air of the world. The Journal of MM. de Goncourt is mainly a record of resentment and suffering, and to this circumstance they attribute many causes; but we suspect at last that the real cause is for them too the inconvenience from which we suffer as readers—simply the want of space and air.

Though the surface of the life represented is, as I have said, small, it is large enough to contain a great deal of violent reaction, an extraordinary quantity of animadversion, indignation, denunciation. Indeed, as I have intimated, the simplest way to sketch the relation of disagreement of our accomplished diarists would be to mention the handful of persons and things excepted from it. They are "down" absolutely on Sainte-Beuve and strongly on MM. Taine and Schérer. But I am taking the wrong course. The great exceptions then, in addition to the half-dozen friends I have mentioned (the Princess, Gavarni, Théophile Gautier, Flaubert, and Paul de Saint-Victor, though the two last named with restrictions which finally become in the one case considerable and in the other very marked), are the artistic production of the reign of Louis XV. and some of the literary, notably that of Diderot, which they oppose with a good deal of acrimony to that of Voltaire. They have also no quarrel with the wonderful figure of Marie Antoinette, unique in its evocation of luxury and misery, as is proved by the elaborate monograph which they published in 1858. This list may appear meagre, but I think it really exhausts their positive sympathies, so far as the Journal enlightens us. That is precisely the interesting point and the fact that arrests us, that the Journal, copious as a memorandum of the artistic life, is in so abnormally small a degree a picture of enjoyment. Such a fact suggests all sorts of reflections, and in particular an almost anxious one as to whether the passionate artistic life necessarily excludes enjoyment. I say the passionate because this makes the example better; it is only passion that gives us revelations and notes. If the artist is necessarily sensitive, does that sensitiveness form in its essence a state constantly liable to shade off into the morbid? Does this liability, moreover, increase in proportion as the effort is great and the ambition intense? MM. de Goncourt have this ground for expecting us to cite their experience in the affirmative, that it is an experience abounding in revelations. I don't mean to say that they are all, but only that they are preponderantly, revelations of suffering. In the month of March, 1859, in allusion to their occupations and projects, they make the excellent remark, the fruit of acquired wisdom, that

"In this world one must do a great deal, one must intend a great deal." That is refreshing, that is a breath of air. But as a general thing what they commemorate as workers is the simple break-down of joy.

"Tell us," they would probably say, "where you will find an analysis equally close of the cheerfulness of creation, and then we will admit that our testimony is superficial. Many a record of a happy personal life, yes; but that is not to the point. The question is how many windows are opened, how many little holes are pierced, into the consciousness of the artist. Our contention would be that we have pierced more little holes than any other gimlet has achieved. Doubtless there are many people who are not curious about the consciousness of the artist and who would look into our little holes — if the sense of a kind of indelicacy, even of indecency in the proceeding were not too much for them — mainly with some ulterior view of making fun of them. Of course the better economy for such people is to let us alone. But if you *are* curious (there are a few who happen to be), where will you get to the same degree as in these patient pages the particular sensation of having your curiosity stimulated and fed? Will you get it in the long biography of Scott, in that of Dickens, in the autobiography of Trollope, in the letters of Thackeray? An intimation has reached us that in reading the letters of Thackeray you are moved, on the contrary, to wonder by what trick certain natural little betrayals of the consciousness of the artist have been conjured away. Very likely (we see you mean it) such betrayals are 'natural' only when people have a sense of responsibility. This sense may very well be a fault, but it is a fault to which the world owes some valuable information. Ah! of course if you don't think our information valuable, there is no use talking." The most convenient answer to this little address would probably be the remark that valuable information is supplied by the artist in more ways than one, and that we must look for it in his finished pieces as well as in his note-books. If we should see a flaw in this supposititious plea of our contentious friends it would be after turning back to "Germinie Lacerteux" and "Manette Salomon." Distinguished and suggestive as these performances are, they do not illustrate the artistic view so very much more than the works of those writers whose neglect of the practice of keeping a diary of protest lays them open to the imputation of levity.

In reading the three volumes pencil in hand, I have marked page after page as strongly characteristic, but I find in turning them over that it would be difficult to quote from them without some principle of selection. The striking passages or pages range themselves under three or four heads—the observation of persons, the observation of places and things (works of art, largely), the report of conversations, and the general chapter of the subjective, which, as I have hinted, is the general chapter of the *saignant*. "During dinner," I read in the second volume, "*nous avons l'agacement* of hearing

Sainte-Beuve, the fine talker, the fine connoisseur in letters, talk art in a muddled manner, praise Eugène Delacroix as a philosophical painter," etc. These words, *nous avons l'agacement*, might stand as the epigraph of the Journal at large, so exact a translation would they be of the emotion apparently most frequent with the authors. On every possible and impossible occasion they have the annoyance. I hasten to add that I can easily imagine it to have been an annoyance to hear the historian of Port Royal talk, and talk badly, about Eugène Delacroix. But on whatever subject he expressed himself he seems to have been to the historians of Manette Salomon even as a red rag to a bull. The aversion they entertained for him, a plant watered by frequent intercourse and protected by punctual notes, has brought them good luck; in this sense, I mean, that they have made a more living figure of him than of any name in their work. The taste of the whole evocation is, to my mind and speaking crudely, atrocious; there is only one other case (the portrait of Madame de Païva) in which it is more difficult to imagine the justification of so great a license. Nothing of all this is quotable by a cordial admirer of Sainte-Beuve, who, however, would resent the treachery of it even more than he does if he were not careful to remember that the scandalized reader has always the resource of opening the "Causeries du Lundi." MM. de Goncourt write too much as if they had forgotten that. The thirty volumes of that wonderful work contain a sufficiently substantial answer to their account of the figure he cut when they dined with him as his invited guests or as fellow-members of a brilliant club. Impression for impression, we have that of the Causeries to set against that of the Journal, and it takes the larger hold of us. The reason is that it belongs to the finer part of Sainte-Beuve; whereas the picture from the Goncourt gallery (representing him, for instance, as a *petit mercier de province en partie fine*) deals only with his personal features. These are important, and they were unfortunately anything but superior; but they were not so important as MM. de Goncourt's love of art, for art makes them, nor so odious surely when they were seen in conjunction with the nature of his extraordinary mind. Upon the nature of his extraordinary mind our authors throw no more light than his washerwoman or his shoemaker might have done. They may very well have said, of course, that this was not their business, and that the fault was the eminent critic's if his small and ugly sides were what showed most in his conversation. Their business, they may contend, was simply to report that conversation and its accompaniment of little, compromising personal facts as minutely and vividly as possible; to attempt to reproduce for others the image that moved before them with such infirmities and limitations. Why for others? the reader of these volumes may well ask himself in this connection as well as in many another; so clear does it appear to him that *he* must have been out of the question of Sainte-Beuve's private relations—just as he feels that he was never included in that of Madame de Païva's or the Princess Mathilde's. We are confronted afresh with the whole subject of critical discretion, the responsibility of exposure, and the strange literary manners of our day. The Journal of MM. de Goncourt will have rendered at least the service of fortifying the blessed cause of occasional silence. If their ambition was to make Sainte-Beuve odious, it has suffered the injury that we are really more disagreeably affected by the character of the attack. That is more odious even than the want of private dignity of a demoralized investigator. And in this case the question the reader further asks is, Why even for themselves? and what superior interest was served by the elaboration week by week of this minute record of an implacable animosity? Keeping so patiently-written, so crossed and dotted and dated a register of hatred is a practice that gives the queerest account of your own nature, and indeed there are strange lights thrown throughout these pages on that of MM. de Goncourt. There is a kind of ferocity in the way the reporter that abides in them (how could they have abstained from kicking him out of doors with a "You're very clever, but you're really a bird of night"?) pursues the decomposing *causeur* to the end, seeking effects of grotesqueness in the aspects of his person and the misery of his disease.

All this is most unholy, especially on the part of a pair of *délicats*. MM. de Goncourt, I know, profess a perfect readiness to relinquish this title in certain conditions; they consider that there is a large delicacy and a small one, and they remind us of the fact that they could never have written "Germinie Lacerteux" if they had been afraid of being called coarse. In fact they imply, I think, that for people of masculine observation the term has no relevancy at all; it is simply non-observant in its associations and exists for the convenience of the ladies—a respectable function, but one of which the importance should not be overrated. This idea is luminous, but it will probably never go far without plumping against another, namely, that there is a reality in the danger of *feeling* coarsely, that the epithet represents also a state of perception. Does it come about, the danger in question, in consequence of too prolonged a study, however disinterested, of the uglinesses and uncleannesses of life? It may occur in that fashion and it may occur in others; the point is that we recognize its ravages when we encounter them, and that they are a much more serious matter than the accident—the source of some silly reproach to our authors—of having narrated the history of an hysterical servant-girl. That is a detail ("Germinie Lacerteux" is a very brilliant experiment), whereas the catastrophe I speak of is of the very essence. We know it has taken place when we begin to notice that the artist's instrument has parted with the quality which is supposed to make it most precious— the fineness to which it owed its sureness, its exemption from mistakes. The spectator's disappointment is great, of course, in proportion as his confidence was high. The fine temper of MM. de Goncourt had inspired us with the highest; their whole attitude had been a protest against vulgarity. Mere prettiness of subject—we were aware of the very relative place they give to that; but, on the other hand, had they not mastered the whole gamut of the shades of the aristocratic sense? Was not a part of the charm of execution of "Germinie Lacerteux" the glimpse of the taper fingers that wielded the brush? It was not perhaps the brush of Vandyck, but might Vandyck not have painted the white hand that held it?· It is no white hand that holds, alas, this uncontrollably querulous and systematically treacherous pen. "Mémoires de la Vie Littéraire" is the sub-title of their Journal; but what sort of a life will posterity credit us with having led and for what sort of chroniclers will they take the two gentlemen who were assiduous attendants at the Diner Magny only to the end that they might smuggle in, as it were, the uninvited (that is, you and me who read), and entertain them at the expense of their colleagues and comrades? The Diner Magny was a club, the club is a high expression of the civilization of our time; but the way in which MM. de Goncourt interpret the institution makes them singular participants of that civilization. It is a strange performance, when one thinks of the performers—celebrated representatives of the refinement of their age. "If this was the best society," our grandchildren may say, "what could have been the *procédés* in that which was not so good?"

It is the firm conviction of many persons that

literature is not doing well, that it is even distinctly on the wane, and that before many years it will have ceased to exist in any agreeable form, so that those living at that period will have to look far back for any happy example of it. May it not occur to us that if they look back to the phase lately embodied by MM. de Goncourt it will perhaps strike them that their loss is not cruel, since the vanished boon was, after all, so far from guaranteeing the amenities of things? May the moral not appear pointed by the authors of the Journal rather than by the *confrères* they have sacrificed? We of the English tongue move here already now in a region of uncertain light, where our proper traditions and canons cease to guide our steps. The portions of the work before us that refer to Madame de Païva, to the Princess Mathilde Bonaparte, leave us absolutely without a principle of appreciation. If it be correct according to the society in which they live, we have only to learn the lesson that we have no equivalent for some of the ideas and standards of that society. We read on one page that our authors were personal friends of Madame de Païva, her guests, her interlocutors, recipients of her confidence, partakers of her hospitality, spectators of her splendor. On the next we see her treated like the last of the last, with not only her character but her person held up to our irreverent inspection, and the declaration that "elle s'est toute crachée," in a phrase which showed one day that she was purse-proud. Is it because the lady owed her great wealth to the favors of which she had been lavish that MM. de Goncourt hold themselves free to turn her friendship to this sort of profit? If Madame de Païva was good enough to dine, or anything else, with, she was good enough either to speak of without brutality or to speak of not at all. Does not this misdemeanor of MM. de Goncourt perhaps represent, where women are concerned, a national as well as a personal tendency — a tendency which introduces the strangest of complications into the French theory of gallantry? Our Anglo-Saxon theory has only one face, while the French appears to have two; with "Make love to her," as it were, on one side, and "Tue-la" on the other. The French theory, in a word, involves a great deal of killing, and the ladies who are the subject of it must often ask themselves whether they do not pay dearly for this advantage of being made love to. By "killing" I allude to the exploits of the pen as well as to those of the directer weapons so ardently advocated by M. Dumas the younger. On what theory has M. Edmond de Goncourt handed over to publicity the whole record of his relations with the Princess Mathilde? He stays in her house for days, for weeks together, and then portrays for our entertainment her person, her clothes, her gestures, and her *salon*, repeating her words, reproducing her language, relating anecdotes at her expense, describing the freedom of speech used towards her by her *convives*, the racy expressions that passed her own lips. In one place he narrates (or is it his brother?) how the Princess was unable to resist the impulse to place a kiss upon his brow. The liberty taken is immense, and the idea of gallantry here has undergone a transmutation which lifts it quite out of measurement by any scale or scruple of ours. I repeat that the plea is surely idle that the brothers are accomplished reporters to whom an enterprising newspaper would have found it worth while to pay a high salary; for that cleverness, that intelligence, are simply the very standard by which we judge them. The betrayal of the Princess is altogether beyond us.

Would Théophile Gautier feel that he is betrayed? Probably not, for Théophile Gautier's feelings, as represented by MM. de Goncourt, were nothing if not eccentric, his judgment nothing if not perverse. His two friends say somewhere that the sign of his conversation was *l'énormité dans le paradoxe*. He certainly then would have risen to the occasion if it were a question of maintaining that his friends had rendered a service to his reputation. This to my mind is contestable, though their intention (at least in publishing their notes on him) was evidently to do so, for the greater part of his talk, as they repeat it, owes most of its relief to its obscenity. That is not fair to a man really clever—they should have given some other examples. But what strongly strikes us, however the service to Gautier may be estimated, is that they have rendered a questionable service to themselves. He is the finest mind in their pages, he is ever the object of their sympathy and applause. That is very graceful, but it enlightens us as to their intellectual perspective, and I say this with a full recollection of all that can be urged on Gautier's behalf. He was a charming genius, he was an admirable, a delightful writer. His vision was all his own and his brush was worthy of his vision. He knew the French color-box as well as if he had ground the pigments, and it may really be said of him that he did grind a great many of them. And yet with all this he is not one of the first, for his poverty of ideas was great. *Le sultan de l'épithète* our authors call him, but he was not the emperor of thought. To be light is not necessarily a damning limitation. Who was lighter than Charles Lamb, for instance, and yet who was wiser for our immediate needs? Gautier's defect is that he had veritably but one idea: he never got beyond the superstition that real literary greatness is to bewilder the *bourgeois*. Flaubert sat, intellectually, in the same everlasting twilight, and the misfortune is even greater for him, for his was the greater spirit. Gautier had other misfortunes as well—the struggle that never came to success, the want of margin, of time to do the best work, the conflict, in a hand-to-mouth, hackneyed literary career, between splendid images and peculiarly sordid realities. Moreover, his paradoxes were usually genial and his pessimism was amiable —in the poetic glow of many of his verses and sketches you can scarcely tell it from optimism. All this makes us tender to his memory, but it does not blind us to the fact that MM. de Goncourt classify themselves when they show us that in the literary circle of their time they find him the most typical figure. He has the supreme importance, he looms largest and covers most ground. This leaves Gautier very much where he was, but it tickets his fastidious friends.

"Théophile Gautier, who is here for some days, talks opera-dancers," they note in the summer of 1868. "He describes the white satin shoe which, for each of them, is strengthened by a little cushion of silk in the places where the dancer feels that she bears and presses most; a cushion which would indicate to an expert the name of the dancer. And observe that this work is always done by the dancer herself." I scarcely know why, but there is something singularly characteristic in this last injunction of MM. de Goncourt, or of MM. de Goncourt and Théophile Gautier combined: "Et remarquez —!" The circumstance that a ballet-girl cobbles her shoes in a certain way has indeed an extreme significance. "Gautier begins to rejudge *The Misanthrope*, a comedy for a Jesuit college on the return from the holidays. Ah! the pig—what a language! it *is* ill-written!" And Gautier adds that he can't say this in print; people would abuse him and it would take the bread out of his mouth. And then he falls foul of Louis XIV. "A hog, pockmarked like a colander, and short! He was not five feet high, the great king. Always eating and — " My quotation is nipped in the bud: an attempt to reproduce Gautier's conversation in English encounters obstacles on the threshold. In this case we must burn pastilles even to read the rest of the sketch, and we cannot translate it at all. "*Les bourgeois*—why, the most enormous things go on *chez les bourgeois*," he remarks on another occasion. "I have had a glimpse of a few interiors. It is the sort of thing to make you veil your face." But again I must stop. M. Taine on this occasion courageously undertakes the defence of the *bourgeois*, of their decency, but M. Paul de Saint-Victor comes to Gautier's support with an allusion impossible even to paraphrase, which apparently leaves those gentlemen in possession of the field. The effort of our time has been, as we know, to disinter the details of history, to see the celebrities of the past, and even the obscure persons, in the small facts as well as in the big facts of their lives. In his realistic evocation of Louis XIV. Gautier was in agreement with this fashion; the historic imagination operated in him by the light of the rest of his mind. But it is through the nose even more than through the eyes that it appears to have operated, and these flowers of his conversation suggest that, though he was certainly an animated talker, our wonder at such an anomaly as that MM. de Goncourt should apparently have sacrificed almost every one else to their estimate of him is not without its reasons.

There are lights upon Flaubert's conversation which are somewhat of the same character (though not in every case) as those projected upon Gautier's. Gautier himself furnishes one of the most interesting of them when he mentions that the author of "Madame Bovary" had said to him of a new book, "It is finished; I have a dozen more pages to write, but I have the fall of every phrase." Flaubert had the religion of rhythm, and when he had caught the final cadence of each sentence — something that might correspond, in prose, to the rhyme — he filled in the beginning and middle. But Gautier makes the distinction that his rhythms were addressed above all to the ear (they were "mouthers," as the author of "Le Capitaine Fracasse" happily says); whereas those that he himself sought were ocular, not intended to be read aloud. There was no style worth speaking of for Flaubert but the style that required reading aloud to give out its value; he *mouthed* his passages to himself. This was not in the least the sort of prose that MM. de Goncourt themselves cultivated. The reader of their novels will perceive that harmonies and cadences are nothing to them, and that their rhythms are, with a few rare exceptions, neither to be sounded nor to be seen. A page of "Madame Gervaisais," for instance, is an almost impossible thing to read aloud. Perhaps this is why poor Flaubert ended by giving on their nerves when on a certain occasion he invited them to come and listen to a manuscript. They could endure the structure of his phrase no longer, and they alleviate themselves in their diary. It accounts for the great difference between their treatment of him and their treatment of Gautier: they accept the latter to the end, while with the author of "Salammbô" at a given moment they break down.

It may appear that we *have* sacrificed MM. de Goncourt's Journal, in contradiction to the spirit professed at the beginning of these remarks; so that we must not neglect to give back with the other hand something presentable as the equivalent of what we have taken away. The truth is our authors are, in a very particular degree, specialists, and the element of which, as they would say, *nous avons l'agacement* in this autobiographic publication is largely the result of a disastrous attempt, undertaken under the circumstances with a strangely good conscience, to be more general than nature intended them. Constituted in a remarkable manner for receiving impressions of the external, and resolving them into pictures in which each touch looks fidgety, but produces none the less its effect— for conveying the suggestion (in many cases, perhaps in most, the derisive or the invidious suggestion) of scenes, places, faces, figures, objects, they have not been able to deny themselves in the page directly before us the indulgence of a certain yearning for the abstract, for conceptions and ideas. In this direction they are not happy, not general and serene; they have a way of making large questions small, of thrusting in their petulance, of belittling even the religion of literature. *Je vomis mes contemporains*, one of them somewhere says, and there is always danger for them that an impression will act as an emetic. But when we meet them on their own ground, that of the perception of feature and expression, that of translation of the printed and published text of life, they are altogether admirable.

It is mainly on this ground that we meet them in their novels, and the best pages of the Journal are those in which they return to it. There are, in fact, very few of these that do not contain some striking illustration of the way in which every combination of objects about them makes a picture for them, and a picture that testifies vividly to the life led in the midst of it. In the year 1853 they were legally prosecuted as authors of a so-called indecent article in a foolish little newspaper; the prosecution was puerile, and their acquittal was a matter of course. But they had to select a defender, and they called upon a barrister who had been recommended to them as "safe." "In his drawing-room he had a flower-stand of which the foot consisted of a serpent in varnished wood climbing in a spiral up to a bird's nest. When I saw this flower-stand I felt a chill in my back. I guessed the sort of advocate that was to be our lot." The object, rare or common, has on every occasion the highest importance for them; when it is rare it gives them their deepest pleasure, but when it is common it represents and signifies, and it is ever the thing that signifies most.

Théophile Gautier's phrase about his own talent has attained a certain celebrity ("Critics have been so good as to reason about me overmuch—I am simply a man for whom the visible world exists"), but MM. de Goncourt would have had every bit as good a right to utter it. People for whom the visible world doesn't "exist" are people with whom they have no manner of patience, and their conception of literature is a conception of something in which such people have no part. Moreover, oddly enough, even as specialists they pay for their intensity by stopping short in certain directions; the country is a considerable part of the visible world, but their Journal is full of little expressions of annoyance and disgust with it. What they like is the things they can do something with, and they can do nothing with woods and fields, nothing with skies that are not the ceiling of crooked streets or the "glimmering square" of windows. However, we must, of course, take men for what they have, not for what they have not, and the good faith of the two brothers is immensely fruitful when they project it upon their own little plot. What an amount of it they have needed, we exclaim as we read, to sustain them in such an attempt as "Madame Gervaisais"—an attempt to trace the conversion of a spirit from scepticism to Catholicism through contact with the old marbles and frescos, the various ecclesiastical bric-à-brac of Rome. Nothing could show less the expert, the habitual explorer of the soul than the purely pictorial plane of the demonstration. Of the attitude of the soul itself, of the combinations, the agitations, of which it was traceably the scene, there are no picture and no notation at all. When the great spiritual change takes place for their heroine, the way in which it seems to the authors most to the purpose to represent it is by a wonderful description of the confessional, at the Gesù, to which she goes for the first time to kneel. A deep Christian mystery has been wrought within her, but the account of it in the novel is that

"The confessional is beneath the mosaic of the choir, held and confined between the two supports carried by the heads of angels, with the shadow of the choir upon its brown wood, its little columns, its escutcheoned front, the hollow of its blackness detaching itself dark from the yellow marble of the pilasters, from the white marble of the wainscot. It has two steps on the side for the knees of the penitent; at the height for leaning a little square of copper trellis-work, in the middle of which the whisper of lips and the breath of sins has made a soiled, rusty circle; and above this, in a poor black frame, a meagre print, under which is stamped *Gesù muore in croce*, and the glass of which receives a sort of gleam of blood from the flickering fire of a lamp suspended in the chapel beside it."

The weakness of such an effort as "Madame Gervaisais" is that it has so much less authority as the history of a life than as the exhibition of a palette. On the other hand, it expresses some of the aspects of the most interesting city in the world with an art altogether peculiar, an art which is too much, in places, an appeal to our patience, but which says a hundred things to us about the Rome of our senses a hundred times better than we could have said them for ourselves. At the risk of seeming to attempt to make characterization an affair of as many combined and repeated touches as MM. de Goncourt themselves, or as the cumulative Sainte-Beuve, master of aggravation, I must add that their success, even where it is great, is greatest for those readers who are submissive to description and even to enumeration. The process, I say, is an appeal to our patience, and I have already hinted that the image, the evocation, is not immediate, as it is, for instance, with Guy de Maupassant: our painters believe, above all, in shades, deal essentially with shades, have a horror of anything like rough delineation. They arrive at the exact, the particular; but it is, above all, on a second reading that we see them arrive, so that they perhaps suffer a certain injustice from those who are unwilling to give more than a first. They select, but they see so much in things that even their selection contains a multiplicity of items. The Journal, none the less, is full of aspects caught in the fact. In 1867 they make a stay in Auvergne, and their notes are perhaps precisely the more illustrative from the circumstance that they find everything odious.

"Return to Clermont. We go up and down the town. Scarcely a passer. The flat Sabbatical gloom of *la province*, to which is added here the mourning of the horrible stone of the country, the slate-stone of the Volvic, which resembles the stones of dungeons in the fifth act of popular melodramas. Here and there a *campo* which urges suicide, a little square with little pointed paving-stones and the grass of the court of a seminary growing between them, where the dogs yawn as they pass. A church, the cathedral of colliers, black without, black within, a law-court, a black temple of justice, an Odeon-theatre of the law, academically funereal, from which one drops into a public walk where the trees are so bored that they grow thin in the wide, mouldy shade. Always and everywhere the windows and doors bordered with black, like circulars conveying information of a demise. And sempiternally, on the horizon, that eternal Puy de Dôme, whose bluish cone reminds one so, grocer-fashion, of a sugar-loaf wrapped in its paper."

A complete account of MM. de Goncourt would not close without some consideration of the whole question of, I will not say the legitimacy, but the discretion, of the attempt on the part of an artist whose vehicle is only collocations of words to be nothing if not plastic, to do the same things and achieve the same effects as the painter. Our authors offer an excellent text for a discourse on that theme, but I may not pronounce it, as I have not in these limits pretended to do more than glance in the direction of that activity in fiction on which they appear mainly to take their stand. The value of the endeavor I speak of will be differently rated according as people like to "see" as they read, and according as in their particular case MM. de Goncourt will appear to have justified by success a manner of which it is on every occasion to be said that it was handicapped at the start. My own idea would be that they have given this manner unmistakable life. They have had an observation of their own, which is a great thing, and it has made them use language in a light of their own. They have attempted an almost impossible feat of translation, but there are not many passages they have altogether missed. Those who feel the spectacle as they feel it will always understand them enough, and any writer—even those who risk less—may be misunderstood by readers who have not that sympathy. Of course the general truth remains that if you wish to compete with the painter prose is a roundabout vehicle, and it is simpler to adopt the painter's tools. To this MM. de Goncourt would doubtless have replied that there is *no* use of words that is not an endeavor to "render," that lines of division are arrogant and arbitrary, that the point at which the pen should give way to the brush is a matter of appreciation, that the only way to see what it can do, in certain directions of ingenuity, is to try, and that they themselves have the merit of having tried and found out. What they have found out, what they show us, is not certainly of the importance that all the irritation, all the envy and uncharitableness of their Journal would seem to announce for compositions brought forth in such throes; but the fact that they themselves make too much of their genius should not lead us to make too little. Artists will find it difficult to forgive them for introducing such a confusion between æsthetics and ill-humor. That is compromising to the cause, for it tends to make the artistic spirit synonymous with the ungenerous. When one has the better thoughts one doesn't print the worse. We have never been ignorant of the fact that talent may be considerable even when character is peevish; that is a mystery which we have had to accept. It is a poor reward for our philosophy that Providence should appoint MM. de Goncourt to insist upon the converse of the proposition during three substantial volumes.

1888.

BROWNING IN WESTMINSTER ABBEY

The lovers of a great poet are the people in the world who are most to be forgiven a little wanton fancy about him, for they have before them, in his genius and work, an irresistible example of the application of the imaginative method to a thousand subjects. Certainly, therefore, there are many confirmed admirers of Robert Browning to whom it will not have failed to occur that the consignment of his ashes to the great temple of fame of the English race was exactly one of those occasions in which his own analytic spirit would have rejoiced and his irrepressible faculty for looking at human events in all sorts of slanting colored lights have found a signal opportunity. If he had been taken with it as a subject, if it had moved him to the confused yet comprehensive utterance of which he was the great professor, we can immediately guess at some of the sparks he would have scraped from it, guess how splendidly, in the case, the pictorial sense would have intertwined itself with the metaphysical. For such an occasion would have lacked, for the author of "The Ring and the Book," none of the complexity and convertibility that were dear to him. Passion and ingenuity, irony and solemnity, the impressive and the unexpected, would each have forced their way through; in a word, the author would have been sure to take the special, circumstantial view (the inveterate mark of all his speculation) even of so foregone a conclusion as that England should pay her greatest honor to one of her greatest poets. At any rate, as they stood in the Abbey on Tuesday last those of his admirers and mourners who were disposed to profit by his warrant for inquiring curiously, may well have let their fancy range, with its muffled step, in the direction which *his* fancy would probably not have shrunk from following, even perhaps to the dim corners where humor and the whimsical lurk. Only, we hasten to add, it would have taken Robert Browning himself to render the multifold impression.

One part of it on such an occasion is, of course, irresistible — the sense that these honors are the greatest that a generous nation has to confer, and that the emotion that accompanies them is one of the high moments of a nation's life. The attitude of the public, of the multitude, at such hours, is a great expansion, a great openness to ideas of aspiration and achievement; the pride of possession and of bestowal, especially in the case of a career so complete as Mr. Browning's, is so present as to make regret a minor matter. We possess a great man most when we begin to look at him through the glass plate of death; and it is a simple truth, though containing an apparent contradiction, that the Abbey never strikes us so benignantly as when we have a valued voice to commit to silence there. For the silence is articulate after all, and in worthy instances the preservation great. It is the other side of the question that would pull most the strings of irresponsible reflection—all those conceivable postulates and hypotheses of the poetic and satiric mind to which we owe the picture of how the bishop ordered his tomb in St. Praxed's. Macaulay's "temple of silence and reconciliation"—and none the less perhaps because he himself is now a presence there—strikes us, as we stand in it, not only as local but as social—a sort of corporate company; so thick, under its high arches, its dim transepts and chapels, is the population of its historic names and figures. They are a company in possession, with a high standard of distinction, of immortality, as it were; for there is something serenely inexpugnable even in the position of the interlopers. As they look out, in the rich dusk, from the cold eyes of statues and the careful identity of tablets, they seem, with their converging faces, to scrutinize decorously the claims of each new recumbent glory, to ask each other how he is to be judged as an accession. How difficult to banish the idea that Robert Browning would have enjoyed prefiguring and disintegrating the mystifications, the reservations, even perhaps the slight buzz of scandal in the Poets' Corner, to which his own obsequies might give rise! Would not his great relish, in so characteristic an interview with his crucible, have been his perception of the bewildering modernness, to much of the society, of the new candidate for a niche? That is the interest and the fascination, from what may be termed the inside point of view, of Mr. Browning's having received, in this direction of becoming a classic, the only official assistance that is ever conferred upon English writers.

It is as classics on one ground and another — some members of it perhaps on that of not being anything else — that the numerous assembly in the Abbey holds together, and it is as a tremendous and incomparable modern that the author of "Men and Women" takes his place in it. He introduces to his predecessors a kind of contemporary individualism which surely for many a year they had not been reminded of with any such force. The tradition of the poetic character as something high, detached, and simple, which may be assumed to have prevailed among them for a good while, is one that Browning has broken at every turn; so that we can imagine his new associates to stand about him, till they have got used to him, with rather a sense of failing measures. A good many oddities and a good many great writers have been entombed in the Abbey; but none of the odd ones have been so great and none of the great ones so odd. There are plenty of poets whose right to the title may be contested, but there is no poetic head of equal power — crowned and recrowned by almost importunate hands—from which so many people would withhold the distinctive wreath. All this will give the marble phantoms at the base of the great pillars and the definite personalities of the honorary slabs something to puzzle out until, by the quick operation of time, the mere fact of his lying there among the classified and protected makes even Robert Browning lose a portion of the bristling surface of his actuality.

For the rest, judging from the outside and with his contemporaries, we of the public can only feel that his very modernness — by which we mean the all-touching, all-trying spirit of his work, permeated with accumulations and playing with knowledge — achieves a kind of conquest, or at least of extension, of the rigid pale. We cannot enter here upon any account either of that or of any other element of his genius, though surely no literary figure of our day seems to sit more unconsciously for the painter. The very imperfections of this original are fascinating, for they never present themselves as weaknesses — they are boldnesses and overgrowths, rich roughnesses and humors—and the patient critic need not despair of digging to the primary soil from which so many disparities and contradictions spring. He may finally even put his finger on some explanation of the great mystery, the imperfect conquest of the poetic form by a genius in which the poetic passion had such volume and range. He may successfully say how it was that a poet without a lyre — for that is practically Browning's deficiency: he had the scroll, but not often the sounding strings—was nevertheless, in his best hours, wonderfully rich in the magic of his art, a magnificent master of poetic emotion. He will justify on behalf of a multitude of devotees the great position assigned to a writer of verse of which the nature or the fortune has been (in proportion to its value and quantity) to be treated rarely as quotable. He will do all this and a great deal more besides; but we need not wait for it to feel that something of our latest sympathies, our latest and most restless selves, passed the other day into the high part — the show-part, to speak vulgarly — of our literature. To speak of Mr. Browning only as he was in the last twenty years of his life, how quick such an imagination as his would have been to recognize all the latent or mystical suitabilities that, in the last resort, might link to the great Valhalla by the Thames a figure that had become so conspicuously a figure of London! He had grown to be intimately and inveterately of the London world; he was so familiar and recurrent, so responsive to all its solicitations, that, given the endless incarnations he stands for to-day, he would have been missed from the congregation of worthies whose memorials are the special pride of the Londoner. Just as his great sign to those who knew him was that he was a force of health, of temperament, of tone, so what he takes into the Abbey is an immense expression of life — of life rendered with large liberty and free experiment, with an unprejudiced intellectual eagerness to put himself in other people's place, to participate in complications and consequences — a restlessness of psychological research that might well alarm any pale company for their formal orthodoxies.

But the illustrious whom he rejoins may be reassured, as they will not fail to discover: in so far as they are representative it will clear itself up that, in spite of a surface unsuggestive of marble and a reckless individualism of form, he is quite as representative as any of them. For the great value of Browning is that at bottom, in all the deep spiritual and human essentials, he is unmistakably in the great tradition—is, with all his Italianisms and cosmopolitanisms, all his victimization by societies organized to talk about him, a magnificent example of the best and least dilettantish English spirit. That constitutes indeed the main chance for his eventual critic, who will have to solve the refreshing problem of how, if subtleties be not what the English spirit most delights in, the author of, for instance, "Any Wife to Any Husband" made them his perpetual pasture and yet remained typically of his race. He was, indeed, a wonderful mixture of the universal and the alembicated. But he played with the curious and the special, they never submerged him, and it was a sign of his robustness that he could play to the end. His voice sounds loudest, and also clearest, for the things that, as a race, we like best—the fascination of faith, the acceptance of life, the respect for its mysteries, the endurance of its charges, the vitality of the will, the validity of character, the beauty of action, the seriousness, above all, of the great human passion. If Browning had spoken for us in no other way, he ought to have been made sure of, tamed, and chained as a classic, on account of the extraordinary beauty of his treatment of the special relation between man and woman. It is a complete and splendid picture of the matter, which somehow places it at the same time in the region of conduct and responsibility. But when we talk of Robert Browning's speaking "for us," we go to the end of our privilege, we say all. With a sense of security, perhaps even a certain complacency, we leave our sophisticated modern conscience, and perhaps even our heterogeneous modern vocabulary, in his charge among the illustrious. There will possibly be moments in which these things will seem to us to have widened the allowance, made the high abode more comfortable for some of those who are yet to enter it.

1890

HENRIK IBSEN

I

ON THE OCCASION OF *HEDDA GABLER*

WHETHER or no Henrik Ibsen be a master of his art, he has had a fortune that, in the English-speaking world, falls not always even to the masters—the fortune not only of finding himself the theme of many pens and tongues, but the rarer privilege and honor of acting as a sort of register of the critical atmosphere, a barometer of the intellectual weather. Interesting or not in himself (the word on this point varies from the fullest affirmation to the richest denial), he has sounded in our literary life a singularly interesting hour. At any rate, he himself constitutes an episode, an event, if the sign of such action be to have left appearances other than you found them. He has cleared up the air we breathe and set a copy to our renouncement; has made many things wonderfully plain and quite mapped out the prospect. Whenever such service is rendered, the attentive spirit is the gainer; these are its moments of amplest exercise. Illusions are sweet to the dreamer, but not so to the observer, who has a horror of a fool's paradise. Henrik Ibsen will have led him inexorably into the rougher road. Such recording and illuminating agents are precious; they tell us where we are in the thickening fog of life, and we feel for them much of the grateful respect excited in us at sea, in dim weather, by the exhibition of the mysterious instrument with which the captain takes an observation. We have held *Ghosts*, or *Rosmersholm*, or *Hedda Gabler* in our hand, and *they* have been our little instrument — they have enabled us to emulate the wary mariner; the consequence of which is that we know at least on what shores we may ground or in what ports we may anchor. The author of these strange works has, in short, performed a function which was doubtless no part of his purpose. This was to tell us about his own people; yet what has primarily happened is that he has brought about an exhibition of ours.

It is a truly remarkable show, for as to where *nous en sommes*, as the phrase goes, in the art of criticism and the movement of curiosity, as to our accumulations of experience and our pliancy of intelligence, our maturity of judgment and our distinction of tone, our quick perception of quality and (peculiar glory of our race) our fine feeling for shades, he has been the means of our acquiring the most copious information. Whether or no we may say that as a sequel to this we know Dr. Ibsen better, we may at least say that we know more about ourselves. We glow with the sense of how we may definitely look to each other to take things, and that is an immense boon, representing in advance a wonderful economy of time, a saving of useless effort and vain appeal. The great clarifying fact has been that, with *Hedda Gabler* and *Ghosts* and all the rest, we have stood in an exceptionally agitated way in the presence of the work of art, and have gained thereby a peculiarly acute consciousness of how we tend to consider it. It has been interesting to perceive that we consider the work of art with passion, with something approaching to fury. Under its influence we sweep the whole keyboard of emotion, from frantic enjoyment to ineffable disgust. Resentment and reprobation happen to have been indeed in the case before us the notes most frequently sounded; but this is obviously an accident, not impairing the value of the illustration, the essence of which is that our critical temper remains exactly the *naïf* critical temper, the temper of the spectators in the gallery of the theatre who howl at the villain of the play.

It has been the degree, in general, of the agitation that has been remarkable in the case before us, as may conveniently be gathered from a glance at the invaluable catalogue of denouncements drawn up by Mr. William Archer after perusal of the articles lately dedicated by the principal London journals to a couple of representations of Ibsen: that, if I mistake not, of *Ghosts* and that of *Rosmersholm*. This catalogue is a precious document, one of those things that the attentive spirit would not willingly let die. It is a thing, at any rate, to be kept long under one's hand, as a mine of suggestion and reference; for it illuminates, in this matter of the study of Ibsen, the second characteristic of our emotion (the first, as I have mentioned, being its peculiar intensity): the fact that that emotion is conspicuously and exclusively moral, one of those cries of outraged purity which have so often and so pathetically resounded through the Anglo-Saxon world.

We have studied our author, it must be admitted, under difficulties, for it is impossible to read him without perceiving that merely book in hand we but half know him—he addresses himself so substantially to representation. This quickens immensely our consideration for him, since in proportion as we become conscious that he has mastered an exceedingly difficult form are we naturally reluctant, in honor, to judge him unaccompanied by its advantages, by the benefit of his full intention. Considering how much Ibsen has been talked about in England and America, he has been lamentably little seen and heard. Until *Hedda Gabler* was produced in London six weeks ago, there had been but one attempt to represent its predecessors that had consisted of more than a single performance. This circumstance has given a real importance to the undertaking of the two courageous young actresses who have brought the most recent of the author's productions to the light, and who have promptly found themselves justified in their talent as well as in their energy. It was a proof of Ibsen's force that he had made us chatter about him so profusely without the aid of the theatre; but it was even more a blessing to have the aid at last. The stage is to the prose drama (and Ibsen's later manner is the very prose of prose) what the tune is to the song or the concrete case to the general law. It immediately becomes apparent that he needs the test to show his strength and the frame to show his picture. An extraordinary process of vivification takes place; the conditions seem essentially enlarged. Those of the stage in general strike us for the most part as small enough, so that the game played in them is often not more inspiring than a successful sack-race. But Ibsen reminds us that if they do not in themselves confer life they can at least receive it when the infusion is artfully attempted. Yet how much of it they were doomed to receive from *Hedda Gabler* was not to be divined till we had seen *Hedda Gabler* in the frame. The play, on perusal, left one comparatively muddled and mystified, fascinated, but—in one's intellectual sympathy —snubbed. Acted, it leads that sympathy over the straightest of roads with all the exhilaration of a superior pace. Much more, I confess, one doesn't get from it; but an hour of refreshing exercise is a reward in itself. The sense of being moved by a scientific hand as one sits in one's stall has not been spoiled for us by satiety.

Hedda Gabler then, in the frame, is exceedingly vivid and curious, and a part of its interest is in the way it lights up in general the talent of the author. It is doubtless not the most complete of Ibsen's plays, for it owes less to its subject than to its form; but it makes good his title to the possession of a real method, and in thus putting him before us as a master it exhibits at the same time his irritating, his bewildering incongruities. He is nothing, as a literary personality, if not positive; yet there are moments when his great gift seems made up of negatives, or at any rate when the total seems a contradiction of each of the parts. I premise, of course, that we hear him through a medium not his own, and I remember that translation is a shameless falsification of color. Translation, however, is probably not wholly responsible for three appearances inherent in all his prose work, as we possess it, though in slightly differing degrees, and yet quite unavailing to destroy in it the expression of life; I mean, of course, the absence of humor, the absence of free imagination, and the absence of style. The absence of style, both in the usual and in the larger sense of the word, is extraordinary, and all the more mystifying that its place is not usurped, as it frequently is in such cases, by vulgarity. Ibsen is massively common and "middle-class," but neither his spirit nor his manner is small. He is never trivial and never cheap, but he is in nothing more curious than in owing to a single source such distinction as he retains. His people are of inexpressive race; they give us essentially the *bourgeois* impression; even when they are furiously nervous and, like Hedda, more than sufficiently fastidious, we recognize that they live, with their remarkable creator, in a world in which selection has no great range. This is perhaps one reason why they none of them, neither the creator nor the creatures, appear to feel much impulse to *play* with the things of life. This impulse, when it breaks out, is humor, and in the scenic genius it usually breaks out in one place or another. We get the feeling, in Ibsen's plays, that such whims are too ultimate, too much a matter of luxury and leisure for the stage of feeling at which his characters have arrived. They are all too busy learning to live—humor will come in later, when they know how. A certain angular irony they frequently manifest, and some of his portraits are strongly satirical, like that, to give only two instances, of Tesman, in *Hedda Gabler* (a play indeed suffused with irrepressible irony), or that of Hialmar Ekdal, in *The Wild Duck*. But it is the ridicule without the smile, the dance without the music, a sort of sarcasm that is nearer to tears than to laughter. There is nothing very droll in the world, I think, to Dr. Ibsen; and nothing is more interesting than to see how he makes up his world without a joke. Innumerable are the victories of talent, and art is a legerdemain.

It is always difficult to give an example of an absent quality, and, if the romantic is even less present in Ibsen than the comic, this is best proved by the fact that everything seems to us inveterately observed. Nothing is more puzzling to the readers of his later work than the reminder that he is the great dramatic poet of his country, or that the author of *The Pillars of Society* is also the author of *Brand* and *Peer Gynt*, compositions which, we are assured, testify to an audacious imagination and abound in complicated fantasy. In his satiric studies of contemporary life, the impression that is strongest with us is that the picture is infinitely *noted*, that all the patience of the constructive pessimist is in his love of the detail of character and of conduct, in his way of accumulating the touches that illustrate them. His recurrent ugliness of surface, as it were, is a sort of proof of his fidelity to the real in a spare, strenuous, democratic community; just as the same peculiarity is one of the sources of his charmless fascination — a touching vision of strong forces struggling with a poverty, a bare provinciality, of life. I call the fascination of Ibsen charmless (for those who feel it at all), because he holds us without bribing us; he squeezes the attention till he almost hurts it, yet with never a conciliatory stroke. He has as little as possible to say to our taste; even his large, strong form takes no account of that, gratifying it without concessions. It is the oddity of the mixture that makes him so individual — his perfect practice of a difficult and delicate art, combined with such æsthetic density. Even in such a piece as *The Lady from the Sea* (much the weakest, to my sense, of the whole series), in which he comes nearer than in others — unless indeed it be in *Hedda Gabler* — to playing with an idea from the simple instinct of sport, nothing could be less picturesque than the general effect, with every inherent incentive to have made it picturesque. The idea might have sprung from the fancy of Hawthorne, but the atmosphere is the hard light of Ibsen. One feels that the subject should have been tinted and distanced; but, in fact, one has to make an atmosphere as one reads, and one winces considerably under *Doctor Wangel* and the pert daughters.

For readers without curiosity as to their author's point of view (and it is doubtless not a crime not to have it, though I think it is a misfortune, an open window the less), there is too much of *Doctor Wangel* in Ibsen altogether—using the good gentleman's name for what it generally represents or connotes. It represents the ugly interior on which his curtain inexorably rises, and which, to be honest, I like for the queer associations it has taught us to respect: the hideous carpet and wall-paper and curtains (one may answer for them), the conspicuous stove, the lonely centre-table, the "lamps with green shades," as in the sumptuous first act of *The Wild Duck*, the pervasive air of small interests and standards, the sign of limited local life. It represents the very clothes, the inferior fashions, of the figures that move before us, and the shape of their hats and the tone of their conversation and the nature of their diet. But the oddest thing happens in connection with this effect—the oddest extension of sympathy or relaxation of prejudice. What happens is that we feel that whereas, if Ibsen were weak or stupid or vulgar, this parochial or suburban stamp would only be a stick to beat him with; it acts, as the case stands, and in the light of his singular masculinity, as a sort of substitute — a little clumsy, if you like — for charm. In a word, it becomes touching, so that practically the *blasé* critical mind enjoys it as a refinement. What occurs is very analogous to what occurs in our appreciation of the dramatist's remarkable art, his admirable talent for producing an intensity of interest by means incorruptibly quiet, by that almost demure preservation of the appearance of the usual in which we see him juggle with difficulty and danger and which constitutes, as it were, his only coquetry. There are people who are indifferent to these mild prodigies; there are others for whom they will always remain the most charming privilege of art.

Hedda Gabler is doubtless as suburban as any of its companions; which is indeed a fortunate circumstance, inasmuch as if it were less so we should be deprived of a singularly complete instance of a phenomenon difficult to express, but which may perhaps be described as the operation of talent without glamour. There is notoriously no glamour over the suburbs, and yet nothing could be more vivid than Dr. Ibsen's account of the incalculable young woman into whom Miss Robins so artistically projects herself. To "like" the play, as we phrase it, is doubtless therefore to give one of the fullest examples of our constitutional inability to control our affections. Several of the spectators who have liked it most will probably admit even that, with themselves, this sentiment has preceded a complete comprehension. They would perhaps have liked it better if they had understood it better — as to this they are not sure; but they at any rate liked it well enough. Well enough for what? the question may of course always be in such a case. To be absorbed, assuredly, which is the highest tribute we can pay to any picture of life, and a higher one than most pictures attempted succeed in making us pay. Ibsen is various, and *Hedda Gabler* is probably an ironical pleasantry, the artistic exercise of a mind saturated with the vision of human infirmities; saturated, above all, with a sense of the infinitude, for all its mortal savor, of *character*, finding that an endless romance and a perpetual challenge. Can there have been at the source of such a production a mere refinement of conscious power, an enjoyment of difficulty, and a preconceived victory over it? We are free to imagine that in this case Dr. Ibsen chose one of the last subjects that an expert might have been expected to choose, for the harmless pleasure of feeling and of showing that he was in possession of a method that could make up for its deficiencies.

The demonstration is complete and triumphant, but it does not conceal from us — on the contrary — that his drama is essentially that supposedly undramatic thing, the picture not of an action but of a condition. It is the portrait of a nature, the story of what Paul Bourget would call an *état d'âme*, and of a state of nerves as well as of soul, a state of temper, of health, of chagrin, of despair. *Hedda Gabler* is, in short, the study of an exasperated woman; and it may certainly be declared that the subject was not in advance, as a theme for scenic treatment, to be pronounced promising. There could in fact, however, be no more suggestive illustration of the folly of quarrelling with an artist over his subject. Ibsen has had only to take hold of this one in earnest to make it, against every presumption, live with an intensity of life. One can doubtless imagine other ways, but it is enough to say of this one that, put to the test, it imposes its particular spectacle. Something might have been gained, entailing perhaps a loss in another direction, by tracing the preliminary stages, showing the steps in Mrs. Tesman's history which led to the spasm, as it were, on which the curtain rises and of which the breathless duration — ending in death — is the period of the piece. But a play is above everything a work of selection, and Ibsen, with his curious and beautiful passion for the unity of time (carried in him to a point which almost always implies also that of place), condemns himself to admirable rigors. We receive Hedda ripe for her catastrophe, and if we ask for antecedents and explanations we must simply find them in her character. Her motives are just her passions. What the four acts show us is these motives and that character—complicated, strange, irreconcilable, infernal—playing themselves out. We know too little why she married Tesman, we see too little why she ruins Lövborg; but we recognize that she is infinitely perverse, and Heaven knows that, as the drama mostly goes, the crevices we are called upon to stop are singularly few. That Mrs. Tesman is a perfectly ill-regulated person is a matter of course, and there are doubtless spectators who would fain ask whether it would not have been better to represent in her stead a person totally different. The answer to this sagacious question seems to me to be simply that no one can possibly tell. There are many things in the world that are past finding out, and one of them is whether the subject of a work had not better have been another subject. We shall always do well to leave that matter to the author (*he* may have some secret for solving the riddle); so terrible would his revenge easily become if we were to accept a responsibility for his theme.

The distinguished thing is the firm hand that weaves the web, the deep and ingenious use made of the material. What material, indeed, the dissentient spirit may exclaim, and what "use," worthy of the sacred name, is to be made of a wicked, diseased, disagreeable woman? That is just what Ibsen attempts to gauge, and from the moment such an attempt is resolute the case ceases to be so simple. The "use" of Hedda Gabler is that she acts on others and that even her most disagreeable qualities have the privilege, thoroughly undeserved doubtless, but equally irresistible, of becoming a part of the history of others. And then one isn't so sure she is wicked, and by no means sure (especially when she is represented by an actress who makes the point ambiguous) that she is disagreeable. She is various and sinuous and graceful, complicated and natural; she suffers, she struggles, she is human, and by that fact exposed to a dozen interpretations, to the importunity of our suspense. Wrought with admirable closeness is the whole tissue of relations between the five people whom the author sets in motion and on whose behalf he asks of us so few concessions. That is for the most part the accomplished thing in Ibsen, the thing that converts his provincialism into artistic urbanity. He puts *us* to no expense worth speaking of — he takes all the expense himself. I mean that he thinks out our entertainment for us and shapes it of thinkable things, the passions, the idiosyncrasies, the cupidities and jealousies, the strivings and struggles, the joys and sufferings of men. The spectator's situation is different enough when what is given him is the mere dead rattle of the surface of life, into which *he* has to inject the element of thought, the "human interest." Ibsen kneads the soul of man like a paste, and often with a rude and indelicate hand to which the soul of man objects. Such a production as *The Pillars of Society*, with its large, dense complexity of moral cross-references and its admirable definiteness as a picture of motive and temperament (the whole canvas charged, as it were, with moral color), such a production asks the average moral man to see too many things at once. It will never help Ibsen with the multitude that the multitude shall feel that the more it looks the more intentions it shall see, for of such seeing of many intentions the multitude is but scantily desirous. It keeps indeed a positively alarmed and jealous watch in that direction; it smugly insists that intentions shall be rigidly limited.

This sufficiently answers the artless question of

whether it may be hoped for the author of *The Pillars of Society* that he shall acquire popularity in this country. In what country under heaven might it have been hoped for him, or for the particular community, that he *should* acquire popularity? Is he, in point of fact, so established and cherished in the Norwegian theatre? Do his countrymen understand him and clamor for him and love him, or do they content themselves—a very different affair—with being proud of him when aliens abuse him? The rumor reaches us that *Hedda Gabler* has found no favor at Copenhagen, where we are compelled to infer that the play had not the happy interpretation it enjoys in London. It would doubtless have been in danger here if tact and sympathy had not interposed. We hear that it has had reverses in Germany, where of late years Ibsen has been the fashion; but, indeed, all these are matters of an order as to which we should have been grateful for more information from those who have lately had the care of introducing the formidable dramatist to the English and American public. He excites, for example, in each case, all sorts of curiosity and conjecture as to the quality and capacity of the theatre to which, originally, such a large order was addressed; we are full of unanswered questions about the audience and the school.

What, however, has most of all come out in our timid and desultory experiments is that the author of *The Pillars of Society* and of *The Doll's House*, of *Ghosts*, of *The Wild Duck*, of *Hedda Gabler*, is

destined to be adored by the "profession." Even
in his comfortless borrowed habit he will remain
intensely dear to the actor and the actress. He
cuts them out work to which the artistic nature in
them joyously responds — work difficult and interesting, full of stuff and opportunity. The opportunity
that he gives them is almost always to do the deep
and delicate thing—the sort of chance that, in proportion as they are intelligent, they are most on the
lookout for. He asks them to paint with a fine
brush; for the subject that he gives them is ever
our plastic humanity. This will surely preserve him
(leaving out the question of serious competition) after our little flurry is over. It was what made the
recent representation of *Hedda Gabler* so singularly
interesting and refreshing. It is what gives importance to the inquiry as to how his call for "subtlety" in his interpreters has been met in his own
country. It was impossible the other day not to be
conscious of a certain envy (as of a case of artistic
happiness) of the representatives of the mismated
Tesmans and their companions—so completely, as
the phrase is, were they "in" it and under the charm
of what they had to do. In fact, the series of Ibsen's
"social dramas" is a dazzling array of parts. Nora
Helmer will be undertaken again and again—of a
morning, no doubt, as supposedly, though oddly, the
more "earnest" hour—by young artists justly infatuated. The temptation is still greater to women than
to men, as we feel in thinking, further, of the Rebecca of *Rosmersholm* of Lona Hessel and Martha

Bernick, in the shapely *Pillars* of the passionate mother and the insolent maid, in the extraordinarily compact and vivid *Ghosts*—absurd and fascinating work; of Mrs. Linden, so quietly tragic, so tremulously real, in *The Doll's House* and of that irresistibly touching image, so untainted with cheap pathos, Hedvig Ekdal, the little girl with failing eyes, in *The Wild Duck* who pores over her story-book in the paltry photographic studio of her intensely humbugging father. Such a figure as this very Hialmar Ekdal, however, the seedy, selfish—subtly selfish and self-deceptive—photographer, in whom nothing is active but the tongue, testifies for the strong masculine side of the list. If *The League of Youth* is more nearly a complete comedy than any other of Ibsen's prose works, the comedian who should attempt to render Stensgard in that play would have a real portrait to reproduce. But the examples are numerous: Bernick and Rosmer, Oswald and Manders (Ibsen's compunctious "pastors" are admirable), Gregers Werle, the transcendent meddler in *The Wild Duck* Rörlund, the prudish rector in the *Pillars*, Stockmann and the Burgomaster in *The Enemy of the People*, all stand, humanly and pictorially, on their feet.

This it is that brings us back to the author's great quality, the quality that makes him so interesting in spite of his limitations, so rich in spite of his lapses—his habit of dealing essentially with the individual caught in the fact. Sometimes, no doubt, he leans too far on that side, loses sight too much of the type-quality, and gives his spectators free play to say that even caught in the fact his individuals are mad. We are not at all sure, for instance, of the type-quality in Hedda. Sometimes he makes so queer a mistake as to treat a pretty motive, like that of *The Lady from the Sea*, in a poor and prosaic way. He exposes himself with complacent, with irritating indifference to the objector as well as to the scoffer, he makes his "heredity" too short and his consequences too long, he deals with a homely and unæsthetic society, he harps on the string of conduct, and he actually talks of stockings and legs, in addition to other improprieties. He is not pleasant enough nor light enough nor casual enough; he is too far from Piccadilly and our glorious standards. Therefore his cause may be said to be lost; we shall never take him to our hearts. It was never to have been expected, indeed, that we should, for in literature religions usually grow their own gods, and *our* heaven—as every one can see—is already crowded. But for those who care in general for the form that he has practised he will always remain one of the talents that have understood it best and extracted most from it, have effected most neatly the ticklish transfusion of life. If we possessed the unattainable, an eclectic, artistic, disinterested theatre, to which we might look for alternation and variety, it would simply be a point of honor in such a temple to sacrifice sometimes to Henrik Ibsen.

II

ON THE OCCASION OF *THE MASTER-BUILDER*

In spite of its having been announced in many quarters that Ibsen would never do, we are still to have another chance, which may very well not be the last, of judging the question for ourselves. Not only has the battered Norseman had, in the evening of his career, the energy to fling yet again into the arena one of those bones of contention of which he has in an unequalled degree the secret of possessing himself, but practised London hands have been able to catch the mystic missile in its passage and are flourishing it, as they have flourished others, before our eyes. In addition to an opportunity of reading the play, I have had the pleasure of seeing a rehearsal of the performance—so that I already feel something of responsibility of that inward strife which is an inevitable heritage of all inquiring contact with the master. It is perhaps a consequence of this irremediable fever that one should recklessly court the further responsibility attached to uttering an impression into which the premature may partly enter. But it is impossible, in any encounter with Ibsen, to resist the influence of at least the one kind of interest that he exerts at the very outset, and to which at the present hour it may well be a point of honor promptly to confess one's subjection. This immediate kind is the general interest we owe to the refreshing circumstance that he at any rate gives us the sense of life, and the practical effect of which is ever to work a more or less irritating spell. The other kind is the interest of the particular production, a varying quantity and an agreeable source of suspense—a happy occasion, in short, for that play of intelligence, that acuteness of response, whether in assent or in protest, which it is the privilege of the clinging theatregoer to look forward to as a result of the ingenious dramatist's appeal, but his sad predicament, for the most part, to miss yet another and another chance to achieve. With Ibsen (and that is the exceptional joy, the bribe to rapid submission) we can always count upon the chance. Our languid pulses quicken as we begin to note the particular direction taken by the attack on a curiosity inhabiting, by way of a change, the neglected region of the brain.

In *The Master-Builder* this emotion is not only kindled very early in the piece—it avails itself to the full of the right that Ibsen always so liberally concedes it of being still lively after the piece is over. His independence, his perversity, his intensity, his vividness, the hard compulsion of his strangely inscrutable art, are present in full measure, together with that quality which comes almost uppermost when it is a question of seeing him on the stage, his peculiar blessedness to actors. *Their* reasons for liking him it would not be easy to overstate; and, surely, if the public should ever completely renounce him, players enamoured of their art will still be found ready to interpret him for that art's sake to empty benches. No dramatist of our time has had more the secret, and has kept it better, of making their work interesting to them. The subtlety with which he puts them into relation to it eludes analysis, but operates none the less strongly as an incitement. Does it reside mainly in the way he takes hold of their imagination, or in some special affinity with their technical sense; in what he gives them, or in what he leaves it to them to give; in the touches by which the moral nature of the character opens out a vista for them, or in the simple fact of connection with such a vivified whole? These are questions, at any rate, that Mr. Herbert Waring, Miss Robins, Miss Moodie, enviable with their several problems, doubtless freely ask themselves, or even each other, while the interest and the mystery of *The Master-Builder* fold them more and more closely in. What is incontestable is the excitement, the amusement, the inspiration of dealing with material so solid and so fresh. The very difficulty of it makes a common cause, as the growing ripeness of preparation makes a common enthusiasm.

I shall not attempt to express the subject of the play more largely than to say that its three acts deal again, as Ibsen is so apt to deal, with the supremely critical hour in the life of an individual, in the history of a soul. The individual is in this case not a Hedda nor a Nora nor a Mrs. Alving nor a Lady from the Sea, but a prosperous architect of Christiania, who, on reaching a robust maturity, encounters his fate all in the opening of a door. This fate —infinitely strange and terrible, as we know before the curtain falls—is foreshadowed in Miss Elizabeth Robins, who, however, in passing the threshold, lets in a great deal more than herself, represents a heroine conceived, as to her effect on the action, with that shameless originality which Ibsen's contemners call wanton and his admirers call fascinating. Hilde Wangel, a young woman whom the author may well be trusted to have made more mystifying than her curiously charmless name would suggest, is only the indirect form, the animated clock-face, as it were, of Halvard Solness's destiny; but the action, in spite of obscurities and ironies, takes its course by steps none the less irresistible. The mingled reality and symbolism of it all give us an Ibsen within an Ibsen. His subject is always, like the subjects of all first-rate men, primarily an idea; but in this case the idea is as difficult to catch as its presence is impossible to overlook. The whole thing throbs and flushes with it, and yet smiles and mocks at us through it as if in conscious supersubtlety. The action, at any rate, is superficially simple, more single and confined than that of most of Ibsen's other plays; practically, as it defines itself and rises to a height, it leaves the strange, doomed Solness, and the even stranger apparition of the joyous and importunate girl (the one all memories and hauntings and bondages, the other all health and curiosity and youthful insolence) face to face on unprecedented terms—terms, however, I hasten to add, that by no means prevent the play from being one to which a young lady, as they say in Paris, may properly take her mother. Of all Ibsen's heroines Hilde is, indeed, perhaps at once the most characteristic of the author and the most void of offence to the "general." If she has notes that recall Hedda, she is a Hedda dangerous precisely because she is *not* yet *blasée*—a Hedda stimulating, fully beneficent in intention; in short, "reversed," as I believe the author defined her to his interpreters. From her encounter with Halvard Solness many remarkable things arise, but most of all perhaps the spectator's sense of the opportunity offered by the two rare parts; and in particular of the fruitful occasion (for Solness from beginning to end holds the stage) seized by Mr. Herbert Waring, who has evidently recognized one of those hours that actors sometimes wait long years for—the hour that reveals a talent to itself as well as to its friends, and that makes a reputation take a bound. Whatever, besides refreshing them, *The Master-Builder* does for Ibsen with London playgoers, it will render the service that the curious little Norwegian repertory has almost always rendered the performers, even to the subsidiary figures, even to the touching Kaia, the touching Ragnar, the inevitable Dr. Herdal, and the wasted wife of Solness, so carefully composed by Miss Moodie.

1891–1893.

MRS. HUMPHRY WARD

An observer of manners, called upon to name today the two things that make it most completely different from yesterday (by which I mean a tolerably recent past), might easily be conceived to mention in the first place the immensely greater conspicuity of the novel, and in the second the immensely greater conspicuity of the attitude of women. He might perhaps be supposed even to go on to add that the attitude of women *is* the novel, in England and America, and that these signs of the times have therefore a practical unity. The union is represented, at any rate, in the high distinction of Mrs. Humphry Ward, who is at once the author of the work of fiction that has in our hour been most widely circulated and the most striking example of the unprecedented *kind* of attention which the feminine mind is now at liberty to excite. Her position is one which certainly ought to soothe a myriad discontents, to show the superfluity of innumerable agitations. No agitation, on the platform or in the newspaper, no demand for a political revolution, ever achieved anything like the publicity or roused anything like the emotion of the earnest attempt of this quiet English lady to tell an interesting story, to present an imaginary case. "Robert Elsmere," in the course of a few weeks, put her name in the mouths of the immeasurable English-reading multitude. The book was not merely an extraordinarily successful novel; it was, as reflected in contemporary conversation, a momentous public event.

No example could be more interesting of the way in which women, after prevailing for so many ages in our private history, have begun to be unchallenged contributors to our public. Very surely and not at all slowly the effective feminine voice makes its ingenious hum the very ground-tone of the uproar in which the conditions of its interference are discussed. So many presumptions against this interference have fallen to the ground that it is difficult to say which of them practically remain. In England to-day, and in the United States, no one thinks of asking whether or no a book be by a woman, so completely, to the Anglo-American sense, has the tradition of the difference of dignity between the sorts been lost. In France the tradition flourishes, but literature in France has a different perspective and another air. Among ourselves, I hasten to add, and without in the least undertaking to go into the question of the gain to literature of the change, the position achieved by the sex formerly overshadowed has been a well-fought battle, in which that sex has again and again returned to the charge. In other words, if women take up (in fiction for instance) an equal room in the public eye, it is because they have been remarkably clever. They have carried the defences line by line, and they may justly pretend that they have at last made the English novel speak their language. The history of this achievement will, of course, not be completely written unless a chapter be devoted to the resistance of the men. It would probably then come out that there was a possible form of resistance, of the value of which the men were unconscious—a fact that indeed only proves their predestined weakness.

This weakness finds itself confronted with the circumstance that the most serious, the most deliberate, and most comprehensive attempt made in England in this later time to hold the mirror of prose fiction up to life has not been made by one of the hitherto happier gentry. There may have been works, in this line, of greater genius, of a spirit more instinctive and inevitable, but I am at a loss to name one of an intenser intellectual energy. It is impossible to read " Robert Elsmere " without feeling it to be an exceedingly matured conception, and it is difficult to attach the idea of conception at all to most of the other novels of the hour; so almost invariably do they seem to have come into the world only at the hour's notice, with no pre-natal history to speak of. Remarkably interesting is the light that Mrs. Ward's celebrated study throws upon the expectations we are henceforth entitled to form of the critical faculty in women. The whole complicated picture is a slow, expansive evocation, bathed in the air of reflection, infinitely thought out and constructed, not a flash of perception nor an arrested impression. It suggests the image of a large, slow-moving, slightly old-fashioned ship, buoyant enough and well out of water, but with a close-packed cargo in every inch of stowage-room. One feels that the author has set afloat in it a complete treasure of intellectual and moral experience, the memory of all her contacts and phases, all her speculations and studies.

Of the ground covered by this broad-based story the largest part, I scarcely need mention, is the ground of religion, the ground on which it is reputed to be most easy to create a reverberation in the Anglo-Saxon world. "Easy" here is evidently easily said, and it must be noted that the greatest reverberation has been the product of the greatest talent. It is difficult to associate "Robert Elsmere" with any effect cheaply produced. The habit of theological inquiry (if indeed the term inquiry may be applied to that which partakes of the nature rather of answer than of question) has long been rooted in the English-speaking race; but Mrs. Ward's novel would not have had so great a fortune had she not wrought into it other bribes than this. She gave it indeed the general quality of charm, and she accomplished the feat, unique so far as I remember in the long and usually dreary annals of the novel with a purpose, of carrying out her purpose without spoiling her novel. The charm that was so much wind in the sails of her book was a combination of many things, but it was an element in which culture—using the term in its largest sense

—had perhaps most to say. Knowledge, curiosity, acuteness, a critical faculty remarkable in itself and very highly trained, the direct observation of life and the study of history, strike the reader of "Robert Elsmere"—rich and representative as it is—as so many strong savors in a fine moral ripeness, a genial, much-seeing wisdom. Life, for Mrs. Humphry Ward, as the subject of a large canvas, means predominantly the life of the thinking, the life of the sentient creature, whose chronicler at the present hour, so little is he in fashion, it has been almost an originality on her part to become. The novelist is often reminded that he must put before us an action; but it is, after all, a question of terms. There are actions and actions, and Mrs. Ward was capable of recognizing possibilities of palpitation without number in that of her hero's passionate conscience, that of his restless faith. Just so in her admirable appreciation of the strange and fascinating Amiel, she found in his throbbing stillness a quantity of life that she would not have found in the snapping of pistols.

This attitude is full of further assurance; it gives us a grateful faith in the independence of view of the new work which she is believed lately to have brought to completion and as to which the most absorbed of her former readers will wish her no diminution of the skill that excited, on behalf of adventures and situations essentially spiritual, the suspense and curiosity that they had supposed themselves to reserve for mysteries and solutions on quite another plane.

There are several considerations that make Mrs. Ward's next study of acute contemporary states as impatiently awaited as the birth of an heir to great possessions; but not the least of them is the supreme example its fortune, be it greater or smaller, will offer of the spell wrought to-day by the wonderful art of fiction. Could there be a greater proof at the same time of that silent conquest that I began by speaking of, the way in which, pen in hand, the accomplished sedentary woman has come to represent with an authority widely recognized the multitudinous, much-entangled human scene? I must in conscience add that it has not yet often been given to her to do so with the number of sorts of distinction, the educated insight, the comprehensive ardor of Mrs. Humphry Ward.

1891.

CRITICISM

IF literary criticism may be said to flourish among us at all, it certainly flourishes immensely, for it flows through the periodical press like a river that has burst its dikes. The quantity of it is prodigious, and it is a commodity of which, however the demand may be estimated, the supply will be sure to be in any supposable extremity the last thing to fail us. What strikes the observer above all, in such an affluence, is the unexpected proportion the discourse uttered bears to the objects discoursed of — the paucity of examples, of illustrations and productions, and the deluge of doctrine suspended in the void; the profusion of talk and the contraction of experiment, of what one may call literary conduct. This, indeed, ceases to be an anomaly as soon as we look at the conditions of contemporary journalism. Then we see that these conditions have engendered the practice of "reviewing" — a practice that in general has nothing in common with the art of criticism. Periodical literature is a huge, open mouth which has to be fed — a vessel of immense capacity which has to be filled. It is like a regular train which starts at an advertised hour, but which is free to start only if every seat be occupied. The seats are many, the train is ponderously long, and hence the manufacture of dummies for the seasons when there are not passengers enough. A stuffed mannikin is thrust into the empty seat, where it makes a creditable figure till the end of the journey. It looks sufficiently like a passenger, and you know it is not one only when you perceive that it neither says anything nor gets out. The guard attends to it when the train is shunted, blows the cinders from its wooden face and gives a different crook to its elbow, so that it may serve for another run. In this way, in a well-conducted periodical, the blocks of *remplissage* are the dummies of criticism—the recurrent, regulated breakers in the tide of talk. They have a reason for being, and the situation is simpler when we perceive it. It helps to explain the disproportion I just mentioned, as well, in many a case, as the quality of the particular discourse. It helps us to understand that the " organs of public opinion " must be no less copious than punctual, that publicity must maintain its high standard, that ladies and gentlemen may turn an honest penny by the free expenditure of ink. It gives us a glimpse of the high figure presumably reached by all the honest pennies accumulated in the cause, and throws us quite into a glow over the march of civilization and the way we have organized our conveniences. From this point of view it might indeed go far towards making us enthusiastic about our age. What is more calculated to inspire us with a just complacency than the sight of a new and flourishing industry, a fine economy of production? The great business of reviewing has, in its roaring routine, many of the signs of blooming health, many of the features which beguile one into rendering an involuntary homage to successful enterprise.

Yet it is not to be denied that certain captious persons are to be met who are not carried away by the spectacle, who look at it much askance, who see but dimly whither it tends, and who find no aid to vision even in the great light (about itself, its spirit, and its purposes, among other things) that it might have been expected to diffuse. "Is there any such great light at all?" we may imagine the most restless of the sceptics to inquire, "and isn't the effect rather one of a certain kind of pretentious and unprofitable gloom?" The vulgarity, the crudity, the stupidity which this cherished combination of the off-hand review and of our wonderful system of publicity have put into circulation on so vast a scale may be represented, in such a mood, as an unprecedented invention for darkening counsel. The bewildered spirit may ask itself, without speedy answer, What is the function in the life of man of such a periodicity of platitude and irrelevance? Such a spirit will wonder how the life of man survives it, and, above all, what is much more important, how literature resists it; whether, indeed, literature does resist it and is not speedily going down beneath it. The signs of this catastrophe will not in the case we suppose be found too subtle to be pointed out—the failure of distinction, the failure of style, the failure of knowledge, the failure of thought. The case is therefore one for recognizing with dismay that we are paying a tremendous price for the diffusion of penmanship and opportunity; that the multiplication of endowments for chatter may be as fatal as an infectious disease; that literature lives essentially, in the sacred depths of its being, upon example, upon perfection wrought; that, like other sensitive organisms, it is highly susceptible of demoralization, and that nothing is better calculated than irresponsible pedagogy to make it close its ears and lips. To be puerile and untutored about it is to deprive it of air and light, and the consequence of its keeping bad company is that it loses all heart. We may, of course, continue to talk about it long after it has bored itself to death, and there is every appearance that this is mainly the way in which our descendants will hear of it. They will, however, acquiesce in its extinction.

This, I am aware, is a dismal conviction, and I do not pretend to state the case gayly. The most I can say is that there are times and places in which it strikes one as less desperate than at others. One of the places is Paris, and one of the times is some comfortable occasion of being there. The custom of rough-and-ready reviewing is, among the French, much less rooted than with us, and the dignity of criticism is, to my perception, in consequence much higher. The art is felt to be one of the most difficult, the most delicate, the most occasional; and the material on which it is exercised is subject to selection, to restriction. That is, whether or no the French are always right as to what they do notice, they strike me as infallible as to what they don't. They publish hundreds of books which are never noticed at all, and yet they are much neater bookmakers than we. It is recognized that such volumes have nothing to say to the critical sense, that they do not belong to literature, and that the possession of the critical sense is exactly what makes it impossible to read them and dreary to discuss them—places them, as a part of critical experience, out of the question. The critical sense, in France, *ne se dérange pas*, as the phrase is, for so little. No one would deny, on the other hand, that when it does set itself in motion it goes further than with us. It handles the subject in general with finer finger-tips. The bluntness of ours, as tactile implements addressed to an exquisite process, is still sometimes surprising, even after frequent exhibition. We blunder in and out of the affair as if it were a railway station — the easiest and most public of the arts. It is in reality the most complicated and the most particular. The critical sense is so far from frequent that it is absolutely rare, and the possession of the cluster of qualities that minister to it is one of the highest distinctions. It is a gift inestimably precious and beautiful; therefore, so far from thinking that it passes overmuch from hand to hand, one knows that one has only to stand by the counter an hour to see that business is done with baser coin. We have too many small school-masters; yet not only do I not question in literature the high utility of criticism, but I should be tempted to say that the part it plays may be the supremely beneficent one when it proceeds from deep sources, from the efficient combination of experience and perception. In this light one sees the critic as the real helper of the artist, a torch-bearing outrider, the interpreter, the brother. The more the tune is noted and the direction observed the more we shall enjoy the convenience of a critical literature. When one thinks of the outfit required for free work in this spirit, one is ready to pay almost any homage to the intelligence that has put it on; and when one considers the noble figure completely equipped—armed *cap-à-pie* in curiosity and sympathy—one falls in love with the apparition. It certainly represents the knight who has knelt through his long vigil and who has the piety of his office. For there is something sacrificial in his function, inasmuch as he offers himself as a general touchstone. To lend himself, to project himself and steep himself, to feel and feel till he understands, and to understand so well that he can say, to have perception at the pitch of passion and expression as embracing as the air, to be infinitely curious and incorrigibly patient, and yet plastic and inflammable and determinable, stooping to conquer and serving to direct—these are fine chances for an active mind, chances to add the idea of independent beauty to the conception of success. Just in proportion as he is sentient and restless, just in proportion as he reacts and reciprocates and penetrates, is the critic a valuable instrument; for in literature assuredly criticism *is* the critic, just as art is the artist; it being assuredly the artist who invented art and the critic who invented criticism, and not the other way round.

And it is with the kinds of criticism exactly as it is with the kinds of art—the best kind, the only kind worth speaking of, is the kind that springs from the liveliest experience. There are a hundred labels and tickets, in all this matter, that have been pasted on from the outside and appear to exist for the convenience of passers-by; but the critic who lives *in* the house, ranging through its innumerable chambers, knows nothing about the bills on the front. He only knows that the more impressions he has the more he is able to record, and that the more he is saturated, poor fellow, the more he can give out. His life, at this rate, is heroic, for it is immensely vicarious. He has to understand for others, to answer for them; he is always under arms. He knows that the whole honor of the matter, for him, besides the success in his own eyes, depends upon his being indefatigably supple, and that is a formidable order. Let me not speak, however, as if his work were a conscious grind, for the sense of effort is easily lost in the enthusiasm of curiosity. Any vocation has its hours of intensity that is so closely connected with life. That of the critic, in literature, is connected doubly, for he deals with life at second-hand as well as at first; that is, he deals with the experience of others, which he resolves into his own, and not of those invented and selected others with whom the novelist makes comfortable terms, but with the uncompromising swarm of authors, the clamorous children of history. He has to make them as vivid and as free as the novelist makes *his* puppets, and yet he has, as the phrase is, to take them as they come. We must be easy with him if the picture, even when the aim has really been to penetrate, is sometimes confused, for there are baffling and there are thankless subjects; and we make everything up to him by the peculiar purity of our esteem when the portrait is really, like the happy portraits of the other art, a text preserved by translation.

1891.

AN ANIMATED CONVERSATION

It took place accidentally, after dinner at a hotel in London, and I can pretend to transcribe it only as the story was told me by one of the interlocutors, who was not a professional reporter. The general sense of it—but general sense was possibly just what it lacked. At any rate, by what I gather, it was a friendly, lively exchange of ideas (on a subject or two in which at this moment we all appear to be infinitely interested) among several persons who evidently considered that they were not destitute of matter. The reader will judge if they were justified in this arrogance. The occasion was perhaps less remarkable than my informant deemed it; still, the reunion of half a dozen people with ideas at a lodging-house in Sackville Street on a foggy November night cannot be accounted a perfectly trivial fact. The apartment was the brilliant Belinda's, and the day before she had asked Camilla and Oswald to dine with her. After this she had invited Clifford and Darcy to meet them. Lastly, that afternoon, encountering Belwood in a shop in Piccadilly, she had begged him to join the party. The "ideas" were not produced in striking abundance, as I surmise, till the company had passed back into the little sitting-room, and cigarettes, after the coffee, had been permitted by the ladies, and in the case of one of them (the reader must guess which) perhaps even more actively countenanced. The train was fired by a casual question from the artless Camilla: she asked Darcy if he could recommend her a nice book to read on the journey to Paris. Then immediately the colloquy took a turn which, little dramatic though it may appear, I can best present in the scenic form:

Darcy. My dear lady, what do you mean by a nice book? That's so vague.

Belinda. You could tell her definitely enough, if she asked for a n—for one that's not nice.

Darcy. How do you mean—I could tell her?

Belinda. There are so many; and in this cosmopolitan age they are in every one's hands.

Camilla. Really, Belinda, they are not in mine.

Oswald. My wife, though she lives in Paris, doesn't read French books; she reads nothing but Tauchnitz.

Belinda. She has to do that, to make up for *you*—with your French pictures.

Camilla. He doesn't paint the kind you mean; he paints only landscapes.

Belinda. That's the kind I mean.

Oswald. You may call me French if you like, but don't call me cosmopolitan. I'm sick of that word.

Belwood. You may call *me* so—I like it.

Belinda. Oh, you of course—you're an analyst.

Clifford. Bless me, how you're abusing us!

Belinda. Ah, not *you*—you certainly are not one.

Darcy. (*to Clifford*). You don't get off the better. But it's as you take it.

Clifford. A plague on analysis!

Darcy. Yes, that's one way. Only, you make me ashamed of my question to Camilla—it's so refined.

Camilla. What, then, do you call a book when you like it? I mean a nice, pretty, pleasant, interesting book; rather long, so as not to be over quickly.

Oswald. It never is with *you*, my dear. You read a page a day.

Belwood. I should like to write something for Camilla.

Belinda. To make her read faster?

Camilla. I shouldn't understand it.

Belinda. Precisely—you'd skip. But Darcy never likes anything—he's a critic.

Darcy. Only of books—not of people, as you are.

Belinda. Oh, I like people.

Belwood. They give it back!

Belinda. I mean I care for them even when I *don't* like them—it's all life.

Darcy (*smiling*). That's just what I often think about books.

Belwood. Ah, yes, life—life!

Clifford. Oh, bother life! Of course you mean a novel, Camilla.

Belinda. What else can a woman mean? The book to-day *is* the novel.

Oswald. And the woman is the public. I'm glad I don't write. It's bad enough to paint.

Belwood. I protest against that.

Belinda. Against what?

Belwood. Against everything. The woman being the public, to begin with.

Belinda. It's very ungrateful of you. Where would you be without them?

Darcy. Belwood is right, in this sense: that though they are very welcome as readers, it is fatal to write for them.

Belwood. Who writes for them? One writes for one's self.

Belinda. They write for themselves.

Darcy. And for each other.

Oswald. I didn't know women did anything for each other.

Darcy. It shows how little you read; for if they are, as you say, the great consumers to-day, they are still more the great producers. No one seems to notice it—but no one notices anything. Literature is simply undergoing a transformation — it's becoming feminine. That's a portentous fact.

Oswald. It's very dreadful.

Belinda. Take care—we shall paint yet.

Oswald. I've no doubt you will—it will be fine!

Belwood. It will contribute in its degree to the great evolution which as yet is only working vaguely and dumbly in the depths of things, but which is even now discernible, by partial, imperfect signs, to the intelligent, and which will certainly become the huge "issue" of the future, belittling and swallowing up all our paltry present strife, our armaments and wars, our international hatreds, and even our international utopias, our political muddles, and looming socialisms. It will make these things seem, in retrospect, a bed of roses.

Belinda. And pray what is it?

Belwood. The essential, latent antagonism of the sexes—the armed opposed array of men and women, founded on irreconcilable interests. Hitherto we have judged these interests reconcilable, and even practically identical. But all that is changing because women are changing, and their necessary hostility to men—or that of men to them, I don't care how you put it—is rising by an inexorable logic to the surface. It is deeper—ah, far deeper, than our need of each other, deep as we have always held that to be; and some day it will break out on a scale that will make us all turn pale.

Belinda. The Armageddon of the future, *quoi!*

Camilla. I turn pale already!

Belinda. I don't—I blush for his folly.

Darcy. Excuse the timidity of my imagination, but it seems to me that we *must* be united.

Belwood. That's where it is, as they say. We shall be united by hate.

Belinda. The Kilkenny cats, *quoi!*

Oswald. Well, *we* shall have the best of it—we can thrash them.

Belwood. I am not so sure; for if it's a question of the power of the parties to hurt each other, that of the sex to which these ladies belong is immense.

Camilla. Why, Belwood, I wouldn't hurt you for the world.

Belinda. I would, but I don't want to wait a thousand years.

Belwood. I'm sorry, but you'll have to. Meanwhile we shall be comfortable enough, with such women as Camilla.

Belinda. Thank you—for *her*.

Belwood. And as it won't be for a thousand years, I may say that Darcy's account of the actual transformation of literature is based on rather a partial, local view. It isn't at all true of France.

Darcy. Oh, France! France is sometimes tiresome; she contradicts all one's generalizations.

Belinda. Dame, she contradicts her own!

Belwood. They're so clever, the French; they've arranged everything, in their system, so much more comfortably than we. They haven't to bother about women's work; that sort of thing doesn't exist for them, and they are not flooded with the old maids' novels which (a cynic or a purist would say) make English literature ridiculous.

Darcy. No, they have no Miss Austen.

Belinda. And what do you do with George Sand?

Belwood. Do you call her an old maid?

Belinda. She was a woman; we are speaking of that.

Belwood. Not a bit—she was only a motherly man.

Clifford. For Heaven's sake, and with all respect to Belwood, don't let us be cosmopolitan! Our prejudices are our responsibilities, and I hate to see a fine, big, healthy one dying of neglect, when it might grow up to support a family.

Belwood. Ah, they don't support families now; it's as much as they can do to scrape along for themselves.

Clifford. If you weren't a pessimist I should nearly become one. Our literature is good enough for *us*, and I don't at all complain of the ladies. They write jolly good novels sometimes, and I don't see why they shouldn't.

Oswald. It's true they play lawn-tennis.

Belwood. So they do, and that's more difficult. I'm perfectly willing to be English.

Belinda. Or American.

Belwood. Take care—that's cosmopolitan.

Belinda. For you, yes, but not for me.

Belwood. Yes, see what a muddle—with Clifford's simplifications. That's another thing the French have been clever enough to keep out of: the great silly schism of language, of usage, of literature. They have none of those clumsy questions—American-English and English-American. French is French, and that's the end of it.

Clifford. And English is English.

Belinda. And American's American.

Belwood. Perhaps; but that's not the end of it, it's the very beginning. And the beginning of such a weariness!

Darcy. A weariness only if our frivolity makes it so. It is true our frivolity is capable of anything.

Clifford. Oh, I like our frivolity!

Darcy. So it would seem, if you fail to perceive that our insistence on international differences is stupid.

Clifford. I'm not bound to perceive anything so metaphysical. The American papers are awfully funny. Why shouldn't one say so? I don't insist—I never insisted on anything in my life.

Oswald. We are awfully different, say what you will.

Darcy. Rubbish—rubbish—rubbish!

Oswald. Go to Paris and you'll see.

Clifford. Oh, don't go to Paris again!

Darcy. What has Paris to do with it?

Belwood. We must be large—we must be rich.

Oswald. All the American painters are there. Go and see what they are doing, what they hold painting to be; and then come and look at the English idea.

Belinda. Do you call it an idea?

Darcy. You ought to be fined, and I think I shall propose the establishment of a system of fines, for the common benefit of the two peoples and the discouragement of aggravation.

Belinda. Dear friend, can't one breathe? Who does more for the two peoples than I, and for the practical solution of their little squabbles? Their squabbles are purely theoretic, and the solution is real, being simply that of personal intercourse. While we talk, and however we talk, association is cunningly, insidiously doing its indestructible work. It works while we're asleep—more than we can undo while we're awake. It is wiser than we—it has a deeper motive. And what could be a better proof of what I say than the present occasion? All our intercourse is a perpetual conference, and this is one of its sittings. They're informal, casual, humorous, but none the less useful, because they are full of an irrepressible give-and-take. What other nations are continually meeting to talk over the reasons why they shouldn't meet? What others are so sociably separate — so intertwinedly, cohesively alien? We talk each other to sleep; it's becoming insipid—that's the only drawback. Am I not always coming and going, so that I have lost all sense of where I "belong."? And aren't we, in this room, such a mixture that we scarcely, ourselves, know who is who and what is what? Clifford utters an inarticulate and ambiguous sound, but I rejoice in the confusion, for it makes for civilization.

Belwood. All honor to Belinda, mistress of hospitality and of irony!

Clifford. Your party is jolly, but I didn't know it was so improving. Don't let us at any rate be insipid.

Belinda. We shall not, while you're here — even though you *have* no general ideas.

Belwood. Belinda has an extraordinary number, for a woman.

Belinda. Perhaps I am only a motherly man.

Oswald. Sisterly, rather. Talk of the *fraternité* of the French! But I feel rather out of it, in Paris.

Belinda. You're not in Paris — you're just here.

Camilla. But we are going to-morrow, and no one has yet told me a book for the train.

Clifford. Get "The Rival Bridesmaids"; it's a tremendous lark. And I am large, I am rich, as Belwood says, in recommending it, because it's about New York — one of your "society-novels," full of "snap"! And by a woman, I guess; though it strikes me that with American novels you can't be very sure.

Camilla. The women write like men?

Clifford. Or the men write like women.

Camilla. Then I expect (if you like that better) that it's horrid, one of those American productions that are never heard of *là-bas* and yet find themselves circulating in England.

Clifford. I see — the confusion commended by Belinda. It's very dense.

Camilla. Besides, whoever it was that said a book is as a matter of course a novel, it wasn't I.

Belwood. As no one seems prepared to father that terrible proposition, I will just remark, in relation to the matter we are talking about—

Oswald. Lord, which? We are talking of so many!

Belwood. You will understand when I say that an acuteness of national sentiment on the part of my nation and yours (as against each other, of course, I mean) is more and more an artificial thing—a matter of perverted effort and deluded duty. It is kept up by the newspapers, which must make a noise at any price, and whose huge, clumsy machinery (it exists only for that) is essentially blundering. They are incapable of the notation of private delicacies, in spite of the droll assumption of so many sheets that private life is their domain; and they keep striking the wrong hour with a complacency which misleads the vulgar. Unfortunately the vulgar are many. All the more reason why the children of light should see clear.

Darcy. Ah, those things are an education which I think even the French might envy us.

Oswald. What things?

Darcy. The recriminations, the little digs, whatever you choose to call them, between America and England.

Oswald. I thought you just said they were rubbish.

Darcy. It's the perception that they are rubbish that constitutes the education.

Oswald. I see — you're educated. I'm afraid I'm not.

Clifford. And I, too, perceive how much I have to learn.

Belinda. You are both naughty little boys who won't go to school.

Darcy. An education of the intelligence, of the temper, of the manners.

Clifford. Do you think your manners to us show so much training?

Oswald (to Clifford). They are perhaps on the whole as finished as yours to *us!*

Belinda. A fine, a fine to each of you!

Darcy. Quite right, and Belinda shall impose them. I don't say we are all formed — the formation will have to be so large: I see it as majestic, as magnificent. But we are forming. The opportunity is grand, there has never been anything like it in the world.

Oswald. I'm not sure I follow you.

Darcy. Why, the opportunity for two great peoples to accept, or rather to cultivate with talent, a common destiny, to tackle the world together, to unite in the arts of peace—by which I mean of course in the arts of life. It will make life larger and the arts finer for each of them. It will be an immense and complicated problem of course — to see it through; but that's why I speak of it as an object of envy to other nations, in its discipline, its suggestiveness, the initiation, the revelation it will lead to. Their problems, in comparison, strike me as small and vulgar. It's not true that there is nothing new under the sun; the *donnée* of the drama that England and America may act out together is absolutely new. Essentially new is the position in which they stand towards each other. It rests with all of us to make it newer still.

Clifford. I hope there will be a scene in the comedy for international copyright.

Darcy. A-ah!

Belinda. O-oh!

Belwood. I *say!*

Darcy. That will come — very soon : to a positive certainty.

Clifford. What do you call very soon? You seem to be talking for the ages.

Belwood. It's time — yes, it's time now. I can understand that hitherto—

Clifford. I can't!

Darcy. I'm not sure whether I can or not. I'm trying what I can understand. But it's all in the day's work—we are learning.

Clifford. Learning at our expense! That's very nice. I observe that Oswald is silent; as an example of good manners he ought to defend the case.

Belinda. He's thinking of what he can say, and so am I.

Camilla. Let me assist my husband. How did Clifford come by "The Rival Bridesmaids"? Wasn't it a pirated copy?

Clifford. Do you call that assisting him? I don't know whether it was or not, and at all events it needn't have been. Very likely the author lives in England.

Camilla. In England?

Clifford. Round the corner, *quoi*, as Belinda says.

Oswald. We have had to have cheap books, we have always been hard-working, grinding, bread-earning readers.

Clifford. Bravo — at last! You might have had them as cheap as you liked. What you mean is you wanted them for nothing. Ah, yes, you're so poor!

Belwood. Well, it has made you, your half-century of books for nothing, a magnificent public for us now. We appreciate that.

Belinda. Magnanimous Belwood! Thank you for that.

Darcy. The better day is so surely coming that I was simply taking it for granted.

Clifford. Wait till it comes and then we'll start fair.

Belinda. Yes, we really can't talk till it does.

Darcy. On the contrary, talking will help it to come.

Belinda. If it doesn't come, and very soon — to-morrow, next week — our mouths will be shut forever.

Darcy. Ah, don't be horrible!

Clifford. Yes, you won't like that.

Oswald. You will; so it's perhaps your interest.

Darcy. I don't mean our shut mouths — I mean the reason for them.

Belinda (to Oswald). You remind me that you and Clifford are fined. But I think it must only be a farthing for Clifford.

Clifford. I won't pay even that. I speak but the truth, and under the circumstances I think I'm very civil.

Oswald. Don't give up your grievance — it will be worth everything to you.

Belinda. You're fined five dollars!

Darcy. If copyright doesn't come, I'll — (*hesitating*).

Clifford (*waiting*). What will you do?

Darcy. I'll get me to a nunnery.

Clifford. Much good will that do!

Darcy. My nunnery shall be in the United States, and I shall found there a library of English novels in the original three volumes.

Belinda. I shall do very differently. I shall come out of my cell like Peter the Hermit; I shall cry aloud for a crusade.

Clifford. Your comparison doesn't hold, for you are yourself an infidel.

Belinda. A fig for that! I shall fight under the cross.

Belwood. There's a great army over there now.

Clifford. I hope they'll win!

Belwood. If they don't, you Americans must make a great literature, such as we shall read with delight, pour it out on us unconditionally, and pay us back that way.

Clifford. I shall not object to that arrangement if we *do* read with delight!

Belwood. Ah, that will depend partly also on us.

Darcy. Delicate Belwood! If what we do becomes great, you will probably understand it—at least I hope so! But I like the way you talk about great literatures. Does it strike you that they are breaking out about the world that way?

Clifford. Send us over some good novels for nothing, and we'll call it square.

Belwood. I admit, our preoccupations, everywhere —those of the race in general—don't seem to make for literature.

Clifford. Then we English shall never be repaid.

Oswald. Are the works you give to America then so literary?

Clifford. We give everything—we have given all the great people.

Oswald. Ah, the great people—if you mean those of the past—were not yours to give. They were ours too; you pay no more for them than we.

Clifford. It depends upon what you mean by the past.

Darcy. I don't think it's particularly in our interest to go into the chronology of the matter. We pirated Byron—we pirated Scott. Nor does it profit to differ about which were the great ones. They were all great enough for us to take, and we took them. We take them to-day, however the superior may estimate them; and we should take them still, even if the superior were to make more reservations. It has been our misfortune (in the long run, I mean) that years and years ago, when the taking began, it was, intelligently viewed, quite inevitable. We were poor then, and we were hungry and lonely and far away, and we had to have something to read. We helped ourselves to the literature that was nearest, which was all the more attractive that it had about it, in its native form, such a fine glamour of expense, of the guinea volume and the wide margin. It was aristocratic, and a civilization can't make itself without that. If it isn't the bricks, it's the mortar. The first thing a society does after it has left the aristocratic out is to put it in again: of course, I use the word in a loose way. We couldn't pay a fancy price for that element, and we only paid what we could. The booksellers made money, and the public only asked if there wasn't more — it asked no other questions. You can treat books as a luxury, and authors with delicacy, only if you've already got a lot: you can't *start* on that basis.

Clifford. But I thought your claim is precisely that you *had* a lot—all our old writers.

Darcy. The old writers, yes. But the old writers, uncontemporary and more or less archaic, were a little grim. We were so new ourselves, and our very newness was in itself sufficiently grim. The English books of the day (their charm was that they were of the day) were our *society* — we had very little other. We were happy to pay the servant for opening the door—the bookseller for republishing; but I dare say that even if we had thought of it we should have had a certain hesitation in feeing the visitors. A money-question when they were so polite! It was too kind of them to come.

Clifford. I don't quite recognize the picture of your national humility, at any stage of your existence. Even if you had thought of it, you say? It didn't depend upon that. We began to remind you long ago—ever so long ago.

Darcy. Yes, you were fairly prompt. But our curse, in the disguise of a blessing, was that meanwhile we had begun to regard your company as a matter of course. Certainly, that should have been but a detail when reflection and responsibility had come. At what particular period was it to have been expected of our conscience to awake?

Clifford. If it was last year it's enough.

Darcy. Oh, it was long ago—very long ago, as you say. I assign an early date. But you can't put your finger on the place.

Clifford. On your conscience?

Darcy. On the period. Our conscience—to speak of that—has the defect of not being homogeneous. It's very big.

Clifford. You mean it's elastic?

Darcy. On the contrary, it's rigid, in places; it's

numb; it's not animated to the extremities. A conscience is a natural organ, but if it's to be of any use in the complications of life it must also be a cultivated one. Ours is cultivated, highly cultivated, in spots; but there are large, crude patches.

Clifford. I see—an occasional oasis in the desert.

Darcy. No — blooming farms in the prairie. The prairie is rich, but it's not all settled; there are promising barbarous tracts. Therefore the different parts of the organ to which I have likened it don't, just as yet, all act together. But when they do—

Clifford. When they do we shall all be dead of starvation.

Belinda. I'll divide my own pittance with you first.

Camilla. I'm glad we live in Paris. In Paris they don't mind.

Darcy. They mind something else.

Oswald (bracing himself). He means the invidious duty the American government has levied on foreign works of art. In intention it's prohibitive — they won't admit free any but American productions.

Belwood. That's a fine sort of thing for the culture of a people.

Clifford. It keeps out monarchical pictures.

Belinda (to Oswald). Why did you tell — before two Englishmen?

Camilla. I never even heard of it—in Paris.

Belwood. Ah, there they are too polite to reproach you with it.

Oswald. It doesn't keep out anything, for in fact

the duty, though high, isn't at all prohibitive. If it were effective it would be effective almost altogether against the French, whose pictures are not monarchical, but as republican as our own, so that Clifford's taunt is wasted. The people over there who buy foreign works of art are very rich, and they buy them just the same, duty and all.

Darcy. Doesn't what you say indicate that the tax restricts that ennobling pleasure to the very rich? Without it amateurs of moderate fortune might pick up some bits.

Oswald. Good pictures are rarely cheap. When they are dear only the rich can buy them. In the few cases where they *are* cheap the tax doesn't make them dear.

Belinda. Bravo—I'm reassured!

Darcy. It doesn't invalidate the fact that French artists have spoken of the matter to me with passion and scorn, and that I have hung my head and had nothing to say.

Belinda. Oh, Darcy—how *can* you? Wait till they go!

Clifford. Hadn't we better go now?

Belinda. Dear me, no—not on that note. Wait till we work round.

Clifford. What can you work round to?

Camilla. Why, to the novel. I *insist* on being told of a good one.

Oswald. The foreigners were frightened at first, but things have turned out much better than they feared.

Belinda. We're working round!

Oswald. Otherwise do you think I could bear to stay in Paris?

Darcy. That makes me wince, as I have the face to stay in London.

Oswald. Oh, English pictures—!

Darcy. I'm not thinking of English pictures; though I might, for some of them are charming.

Belwood. What will you have? It's all protection.

Darcy. We protect the industry and demolish the art.

Oswald. I thought you said you were not thinking of the art.

Darcy. Dear Oswald, there are more than one. The art of letters.

Oswald. Where do you find it to-day—the art of letters? It seems to me to be the industry, all round and everywhere.

Clifford (*to Belwood*). They squabble among themselves—that may be good for us!

Darcy. Don't say squabble, say discuss. Of course we discuss; but from the moment we do so *vous en êtes*, indefeasibly. There is no such thing as "themselves," on either side; it's all *our*selves. The fact of discussion welds us together, and we have properties in common that we can't get rid of.

Oswald. My dear Darcy, you're fantastic.

Clifford. You *do* squabble, you do!

Darcy. Call it so, then: don't you see how you're in it?

Belwood. I see very well—I feel it all.

Clifford. I don't then—hanged if I'm in it!

Camilla. Now *they* are squabbling!

Belwood. Our conversation certainly supports Belinda's contention that we are in indissoluble contact. Our interchange of remarks just now about copyright was a signal proof of union.

Clifford. It was humiliating for these dear Americans—if you call *that* union!

Belwood. Clifford, I'm ashamed of you.

Camilla. They *are* squabbling—they are!

Belinda. Yes, but *we* don't gain by it. I *am* humiliated, and Darcy was pulled up short.

Clifford. You're in a false position, *quoi!* You see how intolerable that is. You feel it in everything.

Belinda. Yes, it's a loss of freedom—the greatest form of suffering. A chill has descended upon me, and I'm not sure I can shake it off. I don't want this delightful party to break up, yet I feel as if *we*—I mean we four—had nothing more to say.

Oswald. We have all in fact chattered enough.

Camilla. Oh, be cheerful and talk about the novel.

Clifford. Innocent Camilla—as if the novel to-day were cheerful!

Belinda. I see Darcy has more assurance.

Belwood. You mean he has more ideas.

Darcy. It is because dear Belwood is here. If I were alone with Clifford I dare say I should be rather low. But I *have* more to say, inconsequent, and perhaps even indecent, as that may be. I have it at heart to say that the things that divide us appear to me, when they are enumerated by the people who profess to be acutely conscious of them, ineffably small.

Clifford. Small for you!

Belinda. Clifford, if you are impertinent I shall rise from my ashes. Darcy is so charming.

Oswald. He's so ingenious.

Belwood. Continue to be charming, Darcy. That's the spell!

Darcy. I'm not ingenious at all; I'm only a God-fearing, plain man, saying things as they strike him.

Camilla. You *are* charming.

Darcy. Well, it doesn't prevent me from having noticed the other day, in a magazine, in a recriminatory, a retaliatory (I don't know what to call it) article, a phrase to the effect that the author, an American, *would* frankly confess, and take his stand on it, that he liked rocking-chairs, Winchester rifles, and iced water. He seemed a very bristling gentleman, and they apparently were his ultimatum. It made me reflect on these symbols of our separateness, and I wanted to put the article into the fire before a Frenchman or a German should see it.

Clifford. Iced water, rocking-chairs, and copyright.

Darcy. Well, add copyright after all!

Belinda. Darcy *is* irrepressible.

Darcy. It wouldn't make the spectacle sensibly less puerile, or I may say less grotesque, for a Frenchman or a German. *They* are not quarrelling about copyright—or even about rocking-chairs.

Clifford. Or even about fisheries, or even about the public manners engendered by presidential elections.

Oswald (to Darcy). Don't you know your countrypeople well enough to know just how much they care, by which I mean how little, for what a Frenchman or a German may think of them?

Clifford. And don't you know *mine?*

Oswald. Or an Englishman?

Clifford. Or an American?

Darcy. Oh, every country cares, much more in practice than in theory. The form of national susceptibility differs with different peoples, but the substance is very much the same.

Belwood. I am appalled, when I look at the principal nations of the globe, at the vivacity of their mutual hatreds, as revealed by the bright light of the latter end of the nineteenth century. We are very proud of that light, but that's what it principally shows us. Look at the European family—it's a perfect menagerie of pet aversions. And some countries resemble fat old ladies — they have so many pets. It is certainly worse than it used to be; of old we didn't exchange compliments *every* day.

Darcy. It is only worse in this sense, that we see more of each other now, we touch each other infinitely more.

Belwood. Our acrimonies are a pleasant result of that.

Darcy. They are not a final one. We must get used to each other. It's a rough process, if you like, but there are worse discomforts. Our modern intimacy is a very new thing, it has brought us face to face, and in this way the question comes up for each party of whether it likes, whether it can live with the other. The question is practical, it's social now; before it was academic and official. Newspapers, telegraphs, trains, fast steamers, all the electricities and publicities that are playing over us like a perpetual thunder-storm, have made us live in a common medium, which is far from being a non-conductor. The world has become a big hotel, the Grand Hotel of the Nations, and we meet—I mean the nations meet —on the stairs and at the *table d'hôte*. You know the faces at the *table d'hôte*, one is never enthusiastic about them; they give on one's nerves. All the same, their wearers fall into conversation, and often find each other quite nice. We are in the first stage, looking at each other, glaring at each other, if you will, while the *entrée* goes round. We play the piano, we smoke, we chatter in our rooms, and the sound and the fumes go through. But we won't pull down the house, because by to-morrow we shall have found our big polyglot inn, with its German waiters, rather amusing.

Belinda. Call them Jews as well as Germans. The landlord is German, too.

Oswald. What a horrible picture! I don't accept it for America and England; I think those parties have each a very good house of their own.

Darcy. From the moment you resent, on our behalf, the vulgarity of the idea of hotel-life, see what a superior situation, apart in our duality and distinguished, you by that very fact conceive for us. Belwood's image is, to my sense, graceful enough, even though it may halt a little. The fisheries, and all the rest, are simply the piano in the next room. It may be played at the wrong hour, but that isn't a *casus belli;* we can thump on the wall, we can rattle the door, we can arrange. And for that matter, surely it is not to be desired that *all* questions between us should cease. There must be enough to be amusing, *que diable!* As Belinda said, it's already becoming insipid.

Clifford. Perhaps we had better keep the copyright matter open for the fun of it. It's remarkable fun for *us.*

Oswald. It's fun for you that our tongues are tied, as Belinda and Darcy declare.

Clifford. Are they indeed? I haven't perceived it.

Belinda. Every one on our side, I admit, has not Darcy's delicacy.

Darcy. Nor Belinda's.

Oswald. Yet I think of innumerable things we *don't* say—that we might!

Clifford. You mean that you yourself might. If you think of them, pray say them.

Oswald. Oh, no, my tongue is tied.

Clifford. Come, I'll let you off.

Oswald. It's very good of you, but there are others who wouldn't.

Clifford. How would "others" know? Would your remarks have such a reverberation?

Belinda. I won't let him off, and please remember that this is my house.

Clifford. It's doubtless a great escape for me.

Oswald. You are all escaping all the while, under cover of your grievance. There would be a great deal to be said for the policy of your not letting it go. The advantage of it may be greater than the injury. If we pay you we can criticise you.

Clifford. Why, on the contrary, it's *that* that will be an advantage for us. Fancy, immense!

Oswald. Oh, you won't like it!

Clifford. Will it be droller than it is already? We shall delight in it.

Belwood. Oh, there are many things to say!

Darcy. Detached Belwood!

Belwood. Attached, on the contrary. Attached to everything we have in common.

Darcy. Delightful Belwood!

Belwood. Delightful Darcy!

Belinda (to Clifford). That's the way you and Oswald should be.

Clifford. It makes me rather sick, and I think, from the expression of Oswald's face, that it has the same effect upon him.

Oswald. I hate a fool's paradise; it's the thing in the world I most pray to keep clear of.

Darcy. There is no question of paradise—that's the last thing. Your folly as well as your ecstasy is, on the contrary, in your rigid national consciousness; it's the extravagance of a perpetual spasm. What I go in for is a great reality, and our making it comprehensive and fruitful. Of course we shall never do anything without imagination—by remaining dull and dense and literal.

Oswald. *Attrappe!*

Clifford. What does Oswald mean? I don't understand French.

Oswald. I have heard you speak it to-night.

Clifford. Then I don't understand your pronunciation.

Oswald. It's not that of Stratford-at-Bow. The difference between your ideas about yourselves and the way your performances strike the rest of the world is one of the points that might be touched upon if it were not, as I am advised, absolutely impossible. The emanation of talent and intelligence from your conversation, your journals, your books—

Clifford. I give you up our conversation, and even our journals. As for our books, they are clever enough for you to steal.

Belinda. See what an immense advantage Clifford has!

Oswald. I acknowledge it in advance.

Camilla. I like their books better than ours. I love a good English novel.

Oswald. If you were not so *naïve*, you wouldn't dare to say so in Paris. Darcy was talking about what a German, what a Frenchman thinks. *Parlons-en,* of what a Frenchman thinks!

Belinda. I thought you didn't care.

Belwood. He means thinks of *us.*

Darcy. An intelligent foreigner might easily think

it is open to us to have the biggest international life in the world.

Oswald. Darcy has formed the foolish habit of living in England, and it has settled upon him so that he has become quite provincialized. I believe he really supposes that that's the centre of ideas.

Clifford. Oh, hang ideas!

Oswald. Thank you, Clifford. He has lost all sense of proportion and perspective, of the way things strike people on the continent—on the continents—in the clear air of the world. He has forfeited his birthright.

Darcy. On the contrary, I have taken it up, and my eye for perspective has grown so that I see an immensity where you seem to me to see a dusky little *cul-de-sac*.

Clifford. Is Paris the centre of ideas?

Belinda. I thought it was Berlin.

Camilla. Oh, dear, must we go and live in Berlin?

Darcy. Why will no one have the courage to say frankly that it's New York?

Belwood. Wouldn't it be Boston, rather?

Oswald. I am not obliged to say where it is, and I am not at all sure that there *is* such a place. But I know very well where it's not. There are places where there are more ideas—places where there are fewer—and places where there are none at all. In Paris there are many, in constant circulation; you meet them in periodicals, in books, and in the conversation of the people. The people are not afraid of them—they quite like them.

Belinda. Some of them are charming, and one must congratulate the people who like them on their taste.

Oswald. They are not all for women, and, *mon Dieu*, you must take one with another. You must have all sorts to have many, and you must have many to have a few good ones.

Clifford. You express yourself like a preliminary remark in a French *étude*.

Belinda. Clifford, I shall have to double that farthing!

Belwood. If the book at present is the novel, the French book is the French novel. And if the ideas are in the book, we must go to the French novel for our ideas.

Clifford. Another preliminary remark — does any one follow?

Darcy. We must go everywhere for them, and we may form altogether, you and we—that this our common mind may form — the biggest net in the world for catching them.

Oswald. I should like to analyze that queer mixture—our common mind—and refer the different ingredients to their respective contributors. However, it doesn't strike me as true of France, and it is not of France that one would mean it, that the book is the novel. Across the Channel there are other living forms. Criticism, for instance, is alive: I notice that in what is written about the art I endeavor to practise. Journalism is alive.

Belwood. And isn't the novel alive?

Oswald. Oh, yes, there are ideas in it—there are ideas about it.

Darcy. In England, too, there are ideas about it; there seems to be nothing else just now.

Oswald. I haven't come across one.

Belwood. You might pass it without noticing it — they are not so salient.

Belinda. But I thought we agreed that it was in England that it is *the* form?

Oswald. We didn't agree; but that would be my impression. In England, however, even "*the* form" — !

Belwood. I see what you mean. Even "*the* form" doesn't carry you very far. That's a pretty picture of our literature!

Oswald. I should like Darcy to think so.

Darcy. My dear fellow, Darcy thinks a great many things, whereas you appear to him to be able to think but one or two.

Belinda. Do wait till Belwood and Clifford go.

Belwood. We must, or at least I must, in fact, be going.

Clifford. So must I, though there is a question I should have liked still to ask Darcy.

Camilla. Oh, I'm so disappointed — I hoped we should have talked about novels. There seemed a moment when we were near it.

Belinda. We must do that yet — we must all meet again.

Camilla. But, my dear, Oswald and I are going to Paris.

Belinda. That needn't prevent; the rest of us will go over and see you. We'll talk of novels in your salon.

Camilla. That will be lovely—but will Clifford and Belwood come?

Clifford. Oh, I go to Paris sometimes; but not for "*the* form." Nor even for *the* substance!

Oswald. What do you go for?

Clifford. Oh, just for *the* lark!

Belwood (*to Camilla*). I shall go to see *you.*

Camilla. You're the nicest Englishman I ever saw. And, in spite of my husband, I delight in your novels.

Oswald. I said nothing against Belwood's. And, in general, they are proper enough for women — especially for little girls like you.

Clifford (*to Camilla*). Have you read "Mrs. Jenks of Philadelphia"?

Camilla. Of Philadelphia? *Jamais de la vie!*

Darcy (*to Oswald*). You think me so benighted to have a fancy for London; but is it your idea that one ought to live in Paris?

Belwood. Paris is very well, but why should you people give yourself away at such a rate to the French? Much they thank you for it! They don't even know that you do it!

Oswald. Darcy is a man of letters, and it's in Paris that letters flourish.

Belinda. *Tiens*, does Darcy write?

Belwood. He writes, but before he writes he observes. Why should he observe in a French medium?

Oswald. For the same reason that I do. *C'est plus clair.*

Darcy. Oswald has no feeling of race.

Belwood. On the contrary, he feels it as a Frenchman. But why should you Americans keep pottering over French life and observing that? They themselves do nothing else, and surely they suffice to the task. Stick to *our* race — saturate yourself with that.

Oswald. Do you mean the English?

Darcy. I know what he means!

Oswald. You are mighty mysterious if you do.

Darcy. I am of Camilla's opinion — I think Belwood's the nicest Englishman I ever saw.

Belinda. I am amused at the way it seems not to occur to any of us that the proper place to observe our own people is in our own country.

Darcy. Oh, London's the place; it swarms with our own people!

Oswald. Do you mean with English people? You have mixed things up so that it's hard to know what you *do* mean.

Darcy. I mean with English people and with Americans—I mean with all. Enough is as good as a feast, and there are more Americans there than even the most rapacious observer can tackle.

Belinda. This hotel is full of them.

Darcy. You have only to stand quiet and every type passes by. And over here they have a relief— it's magnificent!

Belinda. They have a relief, but sometimes *I* have none! You must remember, however, that life isn't *all* observation. It's also action; it's also sympathy.

Darcy. To observe for a purpose is action. But there are more even than one can sympathize with; I am willing to put it that way.

Oswald. Rubbish—rubbish—rubbish!

Belinda. You're rough, Oswald.

Oswald. He used the same words a while ago.

Darcy. And then there are all the English, too—thrown in. Think what that makes of London, think of the collection, the compendium. And Oswald talks of Paris!

Oswald. The Americans go to Paris in hordes—they are famous for it.

Darcy. They used to be, but it's not so now. They flock to London.

Oswald. Only the stupid ones.

Darcy. Those are so many, then, that they are typical; they must be watched.

Belinda. Go away, you two Englishmen; we are washing our dirty linen.

Belwood. I go. But we have washed *ours* before you.

Clifford. I also take leave, but I *should* like to put in my question to Darcy first.

Belinda. He's so exalted — he doesn't hear you.

Oswald. He sophisticates scandalously, in the interest of a fantastic theory. I might even say in that of a personal preference.

Darcy. Oh, don't speak of my personal preferences —you'll never get to the bottom of them!

Oswald (*to Camilla*). *Ain't* he mysterious?

Belinda. I have an idea he hasn't any personal preferences. Those are primitive things.

Camilla. Well, *we* have them—over there in the Avenue Marceau. So we can't cast the first stone. I *am* rather ashamed, before these gentlemen. We're a bad lot, we four.

Clifford. Yes, you're a bad lot. That's why I prefer "Mrs. Jenks." Can't *any* of you stand it, over there?

Belinda. I am going home next year, to remain forever.

Belwood. Then Clifford and I will come over—so it will amount to the same thing.

Darcy. Those are details, and whatever we do or don't do, it will amount to the same thing. For we are weaving our work together, and it goes on forever, and it's all one mighty loom. And we are all the shuttles—Belinda and Camilla, Belwood, Clifford, Oswald, and Darcy—directed by the master-hand. We fly to and fro, in our complicated, predestined activity, and it matters very little where we are at a particular moment. We are all of us here, there, and everywhere, wherever the threads are crossed. And the tissue grows and grows, and we weave into it all our lights and our darkness, all our quarrels and reconciliations, all our stupidities and our strivings, all the friction of our intercourse, and all the elements of our fate. The tangle may seem great at times, but it is all an immeasurable pattern, a spreading, many-colored figure. And the figure, when it is finished, will be a magnificent harmony.

Oswald. He *is* exalted!

Camilla. C'est très-joli.

Belinda. If I'm only an unconscious, irresponsible shuttle, and it doesn't matter where I am, I think I won't, after all, go home.

Darcy. I don't care where you go. The world is ours!

Clifford. Yes, our common mind is to swallow it up. But what about our common language?

Belinda. This is Clifford's great question.

Darcy. How do you mean, what about it?

Clifford. Do you expect Belwood and me to learn American?

Belwood. It *is* a great question.

Darcy. Yes, if you like.

Clifford. Will it be obligatory?

Darcy. Oh, no, quite optional.

Oswald. What do you mean by American?

Clifford. I mean your language. (*To Darcy.*) You consider that you will continue to understand *ours?*

Belinda. The upper classes, yes.

Camilla. My dear, there will be no upper classes when we are all little drudging bobbins!

Belinda. Oh, yes, there'll be the bobbins for silk and the bobbins for wool.

Camilla. And I suppose the silk will be English.

Oswald (*to Clifford*). What do you mean by my language?

Clifford. I mean American.

Oswald. Haven't we a right to have a language of our own?

Darcy. It was inevitable.

Clifford (to Oswald). I don't understand you.

Belinda. Already?

Clifford. I mean that Oswald seems at once to resent the imputation that you have a national tongue and to wish to insist on the fact that you have it. His position is not clear.

Darcy. That is partly because our tongue itself is not clear as yet. We must hope that it will be clearer. Oswald needn't resent anything, for the evolution was inevitable. A body of English people crossed the Atlantic and sat down in a new climate on a new soil, amid new circumstances. It was a new heaven and a new earth. They invented new institutions, they encountered different needs. They developed a particular physique, as people do in a particular medium, and they began to speak in a new voice. They went in for democracy, and that alone would affect—it *has* affected—the tone immensely. *C'est bien le moins* (do you follow?) that that tone should have had its range and that the language they brought over with them should have become different to express different things. A language is a very sensitive organism. It must be convenient—it must be handy. It serves, it obeys, it accommodates itself.

Clifford. Ours, on your side of the water, has certainly been very accommodating.

Darcy. It has struck out different notes.

Clifford. He talks as if it were music!

Belinda. I like that idea of our voice being new; do you mean it creaks? I listen to Darcy with a certain surprise, however, for I am bound to say I have heard him criticise the American idiom.

Darcy. You have heard me criticise it as neglected, as unstudied: you have never heard me criticise it as American. The fault I find with it is that it's irresponsible—it isn't American enough.

Clifford. C'est trop fort!

Darcy. It's the candid truth. I repeat, its divergence was inevitable. But it has grown up roughly, and we haven't had time to cultivate it. That is all I complain of, and it's awkward for us, for surely the language of such a country ought to be magnificent. That is one of the reasons why I say that it won't be obligatory upon you English to learn it. We haven't quite learned it ourselves. When we shall at last have mastered it we'll talk the matter over with you. We'll agree upon our signs.

Camilla. Do you mean we must study it in books?

Darcy. I don't care how — or from the lips of the pretty ladies.

Belinda. I must bravely concede that often the lips of the pretty ladies—

Darcy (interrupting). At any rate, it's always American.

Camilla. But American improved — that's simply English.

Clifford. Your husband will tell you it's simply French.

Darcy. If it's simply English, that perhaps is what was to be demonstrated. Extremes meet!

Belwood. You have the drawback (and I think it a

great disadvantage) that you come so late, that you have not fallen on a language-making age. The people who first started our vocabularies were very *naïfs*.

Darcy. Oh, *we* are very *naïfs*.

Belwood. When I listen to Darcy I find it hard to believe it.

Oswald. Don't listen to him.

Belwood. The first words must have been rather vulgar.

Belinda. Or perhaps pathetic.

Belwood. New signs are crude, and you, in this matter, are in the crude, the vulgar stage.

Darcy. That no doubt is our misfortune.

Belinda. That's what I mean by the pathos!

Darcy. But we have always the resource of English. We have lots of opportunity to practise it.

Clifford. As a foreign tongue, yes.

Darcy. To speak it as the Russians speak French.

Belwood. Oh, you'll grow very fond of it.

Clifford. The Russians are giving up French.

Darcy. Yes, but *they've* got the language of Tolstoï.

Clifford (groaning). Oh, heavens, Tolstoï!

Darcy. Our great writers have written in English. That's what I mean by American having been neglected.

Clifford. If you mean *ours*, of course.

Darcy. I mean—yours—ours—yes!

Oswald. It isn't a harmony. It's a labyrinth.

Clifford. It plays an odd part in Darcy's harmony, this duality of tongues.

Darcy. It plays the part of amusement. What could be more useful?
Clifford. Ah, then, we may laugh at you?
Darcy. It will make against tameness.
Oswald. Camilla, come away!
Clifford. Especially if you get angry.
Belinda. No, you and Belwood go first. We Americans must stay to pray.
Camilla (to Clifford). Well, mind you come to Paris.
Clifford. Will your husband receive me?
Oswald. Oh, in Paris I'm all right.
Belinda. I'll bring every one.
Clifford (to Camilla). Try "Mrs. Gibbs of Nebraska," the companion-piece to "Mrs. Jenks."
Oswald. That's another one *you* stole!
Belwood. Ah, the French and Germans!
Belinda (pushing him out with Clifford). Go, go. *(To the others.)* Let us pray.

1889.

THE END

www.ingramcontent.com/pod-product-compliance
Lightning Source LLC
Chambersburg PA
CBHW022056230426
43672CB00008B/1190